Praise for *In Search of the Perfect Loaf*

Named a Best Book of 2014 by
The Atlantic and *National Geographic*

"Terrific . . . This is the book for beginning and would-be bread bakers."
—*The Atlantic* ("The Best Food Books of 2014")

"A memoir, recipe book, and ultimately, a meditation on reviving diversity and flavor in a food too many take for granted."
—*National Geographic* (*The Plate*, "Best Books of 2014")

"[Fromartz] mixes practical advice and age-old wisdom and leavens the combination with interesting characters and irresistible writing. What arises is an absolute must-have book for the bread baker on your list . . . but it is also a page-turning read for anyone with a vicarious curiosity about how this miracle food is made."
—Barry Estabrook, *Civil Eats* ("10 Book Recommendations for Conscientious Eaters")

"[Samuel] Fromartz is much more than an obsessive cook. He's also a fine reporter and writer. And *Perfect Loaf* is much more than a book about baking bread. . . . What Fromartz is really writing about is how a deeper understanding of something leads to a deeper appreciation of it. He is showing us the world through a slice of bread."
—*Los Angeles Times*

"A flavorful delight . . . Fromartz's 'Odyssey' is just that; he has stoked every coal when it comes to bread. Though this isn't a cookbook by any means, he does include nine recipes . . . all graded by difficulty and annotated so that it's like having an expert at your side. Does he find the perfect loaf? He finds a lot more than that."
—*The Kansas City Star*

"*In Search of the Perfect Loaf* asks and answers some essential questions. . . . I hope his book leads other people to go on their own search for the perfect loaf."
—Jim Lahey, *The Wall Street Journal*

"[Fromartz] educates readers through a journeyman narrative. . . . If you don't know much about how or why handcrafted bread is vastly different from what's sold in bakeries and grocery stores, start with this book."
—*Pittsburgh Post-Gazette*

Samuel Fromartz writes about food and environmental topics and is the author of *Organic, Inc.: Natural Foods and How They Grew*. Fromartz is the editor in chief of the Food & Environment Reporting Network and his work has appeared in *The New York Times*, *The Washington Post*, *The Atlantic*, *Salon*, *Inc.*, *Fortune*, *BusinessWeek*, *The Nation*, and other publications, and has been selected for *The Best Business Stories of the Year*. A native of Brooklyn, he lives with his wife and daughter in Washington, D.C., where he bakes all his family's bread.

IN SEARCH

of the

PERFECT LOAF

A
Home Baker's
Odyssey

Samuel Fromartz

PENGUIN BOOKS

PENGUIN BOOKS
An imprint of Penguin Random House LLC
375 Hudson Street
New York, New York 10014
penguin.com

First published in the United States of America by Viking Penguin,
an imprint of Penguin Random House LLC, 2014
Published in Penguin Books 2015

THE LIBRARY OF CONGRESS HAS CATALOGED THE HARDCOVER EDITION AS FOLLOWS:
Fromartz, Samuel.
In search of the perfect loaf: a home baker's odyssey / Samuel Fromartz
pages cm
Includes bibliographical references and index.
ISBN 978-0-670-02561-9 (hc.)
ISBN 978-0-14-312762-8 (pbk.)
1. Bread.   I. Title.
TX769.F76 2014
641.81'5—dc23 2014004522

Set in Bembo Book MT Std
Designed by Francesa Belanger
Decorative ornaments by Nick Misani

147028622

For Nina

In memory of two bread lovers:
Bernard Fromartz (1917–2004)
and
Sol Yurick (1925–2013)

Oh, they took something beautiful
Straightened the curves and they filled in the cracks
'Til it was unrecognizable
They shined it, refined it
Until they could see their own reflection
It could only be death by perfection

—"Death by Perfection,"
by Maia Sharp and Georgia Middleman

Contents

Contents

In Search of the Perfect Loaf

Introduction

I t was December 2008, two months after Lehman Brothers imploded and a week before Christmas, when I got the call. One of my editors at a university magazine wouldn't be needing my services anymore. Budget cuts were under way. Even he didn't know how long his job would last. I hung up. Forty percent of my freelance income had just evaporated. I went out for a walk on that chilly morning in Washington, thinking how typical this was—the news coming just before Christmas. When I worked years earlier as a business reporter, I had *covered* these announcements of thousands of people cut, usually on Fridays, just before the holidays. After walking around the manicured lawns of the U.S. Capitol, I came back to my desk only to get more bad news. In disbelief, I listened as another editor, a good friend of mine, told me how he was being forced to end contract work. He hoped to keep me on but things didn't look good. Sit tight for two or three months, he said. So in one day, I'd lost perhaps three fourths of my income. I looked at the picture of my young daughter staring back at me from my desk.

Freelancing is often filled with ups and downs, but that's okay. It comes with the territory. The goal is to mix and match different projects, scraping by through lulls and working late or on weekends when things are really busy. But this was no lull. In a decade of freelance journalism, I had never experienced anything like this.

Since much of this contract work comes from people I know, I got busy, really busy. I started to send out e-mails to every friend, colleague, and former colleague who might know of work. I got a couple of responses pretty quickly, including one from an editor I had known for years, who was now heading a travel magazine start-up called *Afar*. A travel magazine in a near depression, the worst since the 1930s, when airline seats were going begging? I didn't ask. This was a lead. A few days later I talked with her and you could hardly tell how bad things were. She described jaunts by writers to Madagascar, Venezuela, and Morocco. It was all about "experiential travel"—diving into the culture of a place rather than following the guidebook. Naturally, food was a big focus. Apparently this kind of immersion travel was a passion of the founders, who were committed to the magazine, recession or not. So did I have any ideas?

"Sure," I stammered, trying to think of something fast. "You know, I've always wanted to visit Paris and work in a *boulangerie*, because I've never been able to make a true baguette." Then I launched into the backstory: How I'd been baking at home for more than a decade, and how I always thought I could benefit from doing a stint at a real bakery. Though it was true that I'd fantasized about this, the destination I'd had in mind was Portland, San Francisco, Vermont, or New York. But on the spur of the moment, with the travel editor on the line, my destination had suddenly become Paris. After all, I spit out, a new wave of French artisan bakers had rescued bread—that national cultural symbol—from years of neglect, bringing back truly great loaves. So yes, maybe ten days in Paris would do it. Could I line this up in a couple of weeks and go soon after that? Maybe get the article in on time for their premier issue? "Sure," I replied, knowing not one baker in Paris. Three weeks later, early in 2009, I was on a jet to Charles De Gaulle airport, surrounded by rows and rows of empty seats.

I felt like I had scored the ideal gig, but it also felt odd because I had rarely conflated my bread-baking hobby with work. Making bread was that special moment of the day when I could take my hands off the keyboard, stand up from my chair, and go downstairs to the kitchen and play with flour, water, sourdough, and salt. Instead of wasting time surfing the Internet on breaks, I would rummage through a cabinet filled with wheat, rye, and spelt flours; gathering sesame seeds and flaxseeds and tending to my sourdough starter. In this way, baking was the antithesis of writing, my version of chopping wood, crucial to maintaining my sanity amid the daily pressures of work. And that's the way I wanted it. Cordoned off from writing, baking offered a brief reprieve, and for many years I sought to keep it that way.

But now, faced with a crisis and the need to generate work, any work, I had become pragmatic. This baguette excursion was the rationale to go deeper into bread and get paid at the same time, but I also knew that for a home baker the exercise wouldn't be easy. Even if I did learn to master a baguette in a *boulangerie*, I would need to translate the technique to my home kitchen. I wouldn't achieve a great baguette in a day or even a week. I knew, because I had tried many times and finally given up, convinced that a decent baguette couldn't be made at home. But standing next to a baker, and one in Paris no less, maybe I could learn that one tip or technique that would fundamentally alter what I did. If so, if I really got that kind of "aha!" moment, the entire trip would be worth it. So the baguette became many things: a story, an unexpected source of income, and a challenge, for this bread had defeated me. But it also became something else—a template that I would later repeat with professional bakers in the United States and Europe, applying the same hands-on approach to bread-making problems I so often encountered at home. I thought this work would bring me much closer to the perfect loaf, but what I didn't appreciate was how this quest would fundamentally alter the way I viewed bakers, grains, and this basic sustenance, bread.

B read was always a part of my life, even if I didn't get interested in bread making until well into adult life. I never recall a time growing up in Brooklyn when we didn't have bread on the table. To be honest, there was usually bread *and* rice, representing the two cultural poles of my upbringing. My father, who came from a family of Russian Jewish immigrants, liked bread with every meal. My mother, who is Japanese American, usually had a pot of rice on the stove. This rich personal relationship with starches, from Japanese short-grain rice to Russian black bread, has become part of my identity.

My dad's family had emigrated from Kiev in Ukraine at the turn of the twentieth century. But the links to our Russian heritage were indirect, for I don't remember eating anything in particular with my grandparents. There was no quintessential "Nana" food, no memorable dishes, no homemade loaves. Instead, the Jewish foods associated with New York—knishes, blintzes, pastrami, matzo ball soup, smoked fish, pickles, and, yes, bread—figured as prominently for me as they did for many New Yorkers, whether you were Jewish, Chinese, or Puerto Rican. Sometimes we got pumpernickel or a seeded rye at a Jewish bakery on Church Avenue in Brooklyn, or Levy's Jewish rye, which I liked toasted. "Where's the *broyt?*" my dad would ask at dinner, using the Yiddish word for bread. On Sundays, we often had fist-size bagels with cream cheese and Nova Scotia lox or smoked whitefish, which we picked up on Flatbush Avenue after ice skating at the Wollman Rink in Prospect Park. I still recall the bakery, with the white-haired guys in aprons and hats, turning the steaming bagels off wet wooden boards and popping them back into the oven for their final bake. In the evenings, we had rice with dinner. No one had even heard of a low-carb diet.

Later, after my parents split, my dad moved into an apartment on Bedford Street in Greenwich Village, which broadened my culinary horizons simply because of the neighborhood. A. Zito & Sons Bakery was around the corner on Bleecker Street, with a marble counter stacked with Italian American loaves. It had just enough room for a half-dozen customers to buy the bread. Many of the customers were elderly Italians who lived nearby and had been buying Zito's bread for years. The bakers dragged up the hot loaves in big plastic bins from the coal-fired oven in the basement through the steel trapdoor in the sidewalk. The bakery had its badge of honor prominently displayed: a picture of Sinatra holding one of its loaves.

My job, as a somewhat morose, long-haired teenager visiting my newly divorced dad and his younger girlfriend, was to run around the corner and buy the bread for dinner, a job I always relished because I could get out of the house. I would first visit Murray's cheese shop—not the current store on Bleecker Street, which is an emporium of artisan cheeses, cured meats, and other delights, but the small, cramped place on Cornelia Street—where it often took twenty minutes just to get to the counter. Cheese in hand, I would walk around the corner to Zito's, which had three types of bread: a torpedo-shaped white loaf, a whole wheat that I'd now guess was probably two-thirds white flour, and a round crown loaf studded with small bits of prosciutto from the leftover heels. When that prosciutto loaf came up from the basement, it filled the store with an incomparable smell—you had to rip into it as soon as you left the bakery. I'd bring the bread and cheese back to my dad's place, and if the loaf wasn't still warm by dinner, he would throw it in the oven for a few minutes.

Like Jewish rye and Russian black bread, these loaves were part of an era in New York, one that has now largely vanished. One by one, the old men retired and those bakeries shut down: the bagel place on Flatbush, the Jewish bakery on Church Avenue, and Vesuvio Bakery in SoHo, with the iconic storefront window. Then Zito's shut down in 2003, ending an eighty-year run. The bakery stood empty for a long time, and whenever I passed by it I would wonder about its brick oven in the basement—whether it was still there, sitting dark and cold, maybe waiting for another baker to fire it up one day.

Zito's didn't make "artisan" bread or the Italian loaves currently in fashion, like *pane pugliese*, *ciabatta*, or *filone*. At the counter, the clerks would simply ask, "White or wheat?" The bread wouldn't win any contests, for the crumb had an even and spongy texture that felt like a concession to squishy American bread. But the crust crackled and the entire package was perfect for mopping up spaghetti sauce. So why wax on about it, when its memory would unlikely make any top-ten great bread lists? Like many foods that sustained generations of immigrants, these neighborhood bakeries defined bread for me when I was growing up. This wasn't plastic packaged supermarket bread, nor was it the denser whole wheat bricks from health food stores. It was the bread of immigrants: Italian breads with sesame seeds, chewy bagels, flavorful ryes, even steaming hot pita coming right out of the brick ovens run by Arabs in Brooklyn. It was all just good, fresh bread from the oven. It wasn't artisanal and it wasn't a movement.

When I moved to Washington, D.C., in the mid-1990s, artisan bread was starting to become popular. I knew little of the topography of the capital's culinary scene, though I began to think about bread in a way I hadn't before. That is, I actually began to think about it. When bread's available, a part of a daily or weekly habit, you don't really bother. But when it's absent, the mind begins to work: Where is it? Who makes it? Where can I get it? Such musings, in times of intense shortages, have led to events like the French Revolution or the Arab Spring. Yet, as far as I could tell, amid the surfeit of steak houses in the capital, there was little great bread to be had and there hadn't been so much as a protest, never mind a revolt. Bread, it seemed, lacked a constituency.

The bagel chains had arrived and left their mark on the town in the form of soft, doughy concoctions filled with sweeteners and blueberries. Aside from Uptown Bakers, a notable wholesale operation, with few stores, there was little to remark upon. Mark Furstenberg, a rare local baker of renown, known for his crusty and critical mien, was between ventures. He hadn't yet opened what later became a favorite haunt of mine, Breadline, a bustling luncheon joint near the White House that featured house-made bread. In the meantime, I was stuck with other passable loaves that took a lot of effort to buy. When I finally met up with Furstenberg years later, he had an explanation for D.C.'s lackluster loaves. The city, he told me, didn't have a great tradition of bread because it didn't have a strong base of immigrants, like New York, Chicago, San Francisco, even Baltimore. What Washington had instead were lobbyists, the federal government, and big wholesale bakeries that fed the restaurants, grocery stores, and numerous hotels. A popular sandwich joint, Taylor, which opened a decade after I arrived, even trucked its trademark sesame loaves all the way from Philadelphia, though, facing one too many breakdowns of its van on I-95, it finally prevailed on a local bakery to make the bread instead. Aside from Breadline, which Furstenberg owned and ran for several years, there wasn't a single notable bakery in town where the bread was baked in the back and sold in the front.

Now, for most people, this isn't an issue; an absence not even worth remarking upon, if it is noticed at all. For many, bread is an afterthought, even though globally it provides one fifth of humanity's calories and is the highest source of protein—yes, we get more protein from wheat than meat. Half of the world's poor depend on wheat as their main source of nutrition. But in the part of the world where we live, the gluten-intolerant and the carb-phobic seem to be far more aware of wheat than the rest of us who blindly consume the stuff. For me, though, probably because of my upbringing, bread never was simply an afterthought. I was always on the prowl for a good loaf, the best pizza, or the freshest handmade pita, but I had never even thought about making bread myself—that is, until I was confronted with its absence. I decided to give it a go.

I started out with two bread books, Joe Ortiz's classic *The Village Baker* and Daniel Leader's *Bread Alone*. Both were professional bakers who had traveled to Europe and then recounted stories in their books about the bakers they had met and the recipes they had learned. It was the stories that really hooked me. Leader had an especially infectious tale about his friend Basil Kamir, who had opened a world music record store in an old abandoned *boulangerie* in Paris. When the building was slated for demolition in an urban renewal project, he decided to save the place by firing up the long-neglected brick oven in the basement, thus making it a cultural artifact worthy of preservation. The protest saved the place—which still exists and sits across the street from a row of drab apartment buildings. But in order to preserve the building, Kamir had to make good on his word and become a baker. So he did, putting away his records and helping renew France's bread tradition. Stories like this were so compelling that I recall fantasizing I might want to meet these bakers one day. I hadn't an inkling that I was going to bake in any serious way, or pursue such travels, or eventually even visit Kamir's bakery, but I began, prodded by the simple quest for a decent loaf of bread in a city largely devoid of it.

Introduction

It took a lot of practice, but I eventually fell into a rhythm. On days when I wasn't facing a deadline, I'd walk downstairs from my office on the second floor, turn the dough out on the island counter, knead it for a minute or two to strengthen the gluten, then cover it, wash up, and return to the keyboard. On busy days when the phone was ringing I couldn't bake. Or worse, I'd be in the middle of a crucial phone interview just as the bread was due to come out of the oven. (Talking on a portable headset, I would slide the loaf out of the oven, trying not to miss a beat.) Usually, I could find two days a week in which I could bake fresh loaves, which was more than enough for our household. And when I was on a roll, I'd bake every day, often mixing my dough late in the afternoon or evening, letting it rise through the night in the refrigerator, and then baking the next morning or afternoon. This really worked for my schedule, but for something else as well—the quality of the bread. Though making good bread takes time, the work itself wasn't time consuming. It amounted to five to ten minutes here or there to take the bread to the next stage, whether feeding my sourdough starter bubbling away in a kitchen cabinet, hand-mixing the dough, or shaping and baking a loaf in the oven. Each was a distinct step that had to be carried out at the right moment, but it didn't mean slogging away in the kitchen for hours at a time. It involved a lot of waiting while the bread fermented or baked, which meant I could do something else, like write. Once I figured that out, I began baking a lot and the craft began to feel more natural.

This came home to me one day as I slid a loaf of sourdough onto the baking stone in the oven, then set the digital timer on my oven (a KitchenAid electric oven, which I point out only because everyone asks). I had made this bread dozens of times, so each stage was familiar. But that day, as I was working in my office, I forgot about the bread and went about my work until a kind of toasty hazelnut aroma brought me to attention. I stopped, jogged downstairs, and arrived in front of the oven with just a minute left on the timer. I peered inside. The crust was dark, toasted. I grabbed the flat wooden peel, opened the oven door, and slid the loaf off the baking stone. I tapped the bottom and heard a rich, hollow knock—not a deadened thud. That loaf was done. My sense of smell had, in effect, woken me up and told me the loaf was ready. This wasn't chance. Not then, not now. No matter how long a loaf takes, smell guides me. Like so much else about baking, your senses—sight, smell, and especially touch—are your most valuable tools.

Over the years, I realized I had much to learn, not only about the science of making bread but about the vagaries of this craft, because the recipes were at best a faint map of the process. There are many bread books out there, but books geared to home bakers often tell you just enough to get going and then focus on the recipe. The more I baked, the more I realized that the recipe was the least of my concerns. Far more important were the techniques, which were difficult to explain in a step-by-step format precisely because they depend on touch and feel. So let's just say I made a lot of bad bread by following very good recipes. I expect if you follow the few recipes I offer in this book you will at first make poor loaves, too (what cookbook author admits that!). But if you keep at it, you will no doubt improve, because your technique and understanding will grow. It was only after baking for some time that I realized: when you get good enough to follow a bread recipe and actually succeed, you're at the point where you no longer need a recipe. To reach that point, I read a lot, cornered professionals for advice, scoured the Internet for tips, and focused on that key phrase or paragraph in a book that would change my entire understanding of bread, even if the author mentioned it only in passing. And I baked. I baked a lot.

Baking bread depended on recognizing the moist sheen on a well-mixed loaf, the subtle spring of relaxed gluten, or the hollow knock of a loaf removed from the oven. It's what home bakers knew long ago. How much water did you use in a loaf? Just enough. How long did you bake it? Until it was done. Giant communal ovens in villages had no temperature gauges or timers. Flour was far more inconsistent than it is today, so each batch of dough had to be fine-tuned. Old varieties of wheat were highly diverse and wheat wasn't even widely available in many parts of Europe until the eighteenth century, so loaves were more often made from barley, spelt, or rye (a weed that grew between wheat). Each of these grains required a slightly different method and opened up endless variation. In Germany and Poland, dense ryes were far more common because it was the primary grain in the cold north. Loaves made with brewer's yeast were common in England because it was a by-product of a nation of beer drinkers. In Scandinavia, rye crackers were favored because they kept well through the long winter months. And barley was for millennia the common man's flour, because it grows from Ethiopia nearly to the Arctic Circle and has a thick enough hull to thwart insects. It was hardy, nutritious, and filling, feeding the slaves who built the pyramids and the gladiators of Rome. When sprouted and dried, it became malt for beer.

Bread making is something humanity has done for thousands of years. The impregnation of dough, its slow rise, and the spring upward of the loaf in the heat of the oven, before the yeast died, was a metaphor for life. The ancient Romans held an annual festival of the ovens on February 17 called Fornicalia, which shares the same Latin root as fornication. Even in prehistoric times, baking was associated with procreation. Baking was a metaphor for life because bread is life giving.

The story of why I began to make bread might end there, but another ingredient played a crucial role. I remember, at age eight or so, chiseling a piece of marble in my father's basement woodworking shop after I had seen Michelangelo's *David*. All I managed was the rough outline of a snake, but I worked at it for days. I remember, too, spending hours after school watching a team of carpenters who were building out the interior of a small store in Brooklyn. Eventually they put me to work. After college, I worked in an art framing shop in a second-story loft on the Bowery, just below Houston Street in New York. It was there that I really dove into this enduring interest in hand work.

The area where the shop was located was still seedy then—a mix of vagrants, artists in loft buildings, restaurant supply stores, and junkies who frequented the nearby park over on Chrystie Street. It wasn't yet home to the trendy eateries and clubs—and the Whole Foods supermarket—that you find there today. Arlan, a painter, and Karl, who had trained as an architect, owned the shop and both were true craftsmen. But the place also had the feel of a private social club, which was part of the appeal. Arlan would often work all day, then return at night to paint in a cramped studio in the back of the loft. Sometimes I'd arrive in the morning to find Karl crashed out on a lawn chair next to the kitchenette after a night of fishing on Long Island. We'd ramp up when things were busy, and drink coffee and chat when things were slow. At the end of the day, after the sanders and table saws were shut down, the frames piled on the tables ready for artwork, we'd pull out the pieces—by Sol LeWitt or Richard Diebenkorn—destined for a SoHo gallery, collector, or museum and just look at them. There were a lot of moments like that in the shop.

If there was an ethos at Squid Frames, it came from the elevation of craft. When a piece of wood was stained and finished particularly well, eyebrows were raised but little was said. The type of things that would score the most admiration were precisely the things that others would not recognize at all, because when the frames were well made, the eye would simply travel to the art.

I also remember the shock of first coming to work and spending hours sanding wood, or trying to sand wood, because I couldn't manage to do this simple task correctly. The work was dusty, noisy, and monotonous but it was a good lesson, for it forced me to be attentive to the most tedious of tasks. And that was necessary before I could accomplish anything else—not just at the frame shop but really in any endeavor. Thinking back on this two-year experience, the lesson I learned was to pay attention. I also learned that by virtue of constant repetition, the body, or senses, eventually took over in this craft work so that it felt as if my hands were "thinking." But that didn't happen quickly. It took a long time to develop, and you can easily lose those sensory skills once you stop. Decades later, I know enough to be cautious near power tools. They aren't second nature to me any longer, so usually, I leave that kind of work to others. Roger Gural, who once worked as a baker at the French Laundry Kitchen and now teaches bread baking in New York, mentioned something like this to me when we were baking together one evening. He told me that when he went away on vacation for a couple of weeks he could lose the feel of the dough. It took a day or two to get it back. "I usually measure how good I am by how quickly 'it' returns," he said.

And what precisely is the "it" that "returns"? Recognizing the sound of the dough in the mixer, knowing its feel as you pinch it, or the sheen of the dough's skin during fermentation; these visual, tactile, and auditory cues become the signals for what you should or should not do. It takes time to learn. Repetition keeps those senses honed. But if you stop baking, making frames, or whatever it is that you do, you can lose that sensory edge, just like that.

So when beginning bakers try a "recipe" and get frustrated when it doesn't work out, they are kind of missing the point. The real recipe is to make bread time and again, until one day it becomes second nature. Beginners can make good, even extraordinary bread. But until they understand the craft, under- and overfermented loaves and misshapen and dense breads will be the rule. That's what happened to me, but perhaps I saw enough of a promise to keep going. Maybe, too, I knew enough about craft work from my time at Squid to understand the nature of these failures: that they are not ultimately failures. If you take one lesson away from the attempt, then it's worth it. Maybe, too, I just valued the meditative nature of the work, and the respite it offered.

My own progression as a home baker also mirrored what happened in food culture, as heirloom, handcrafted, and local foods became much more valued. As much as I liked all the bakeries I grew up with—whose breads hold a special place in my memory—I did not try to reproduce their loaves. I've moved on, continually trying to find new ways of making bread at home. It was an approach that became clear when I tried, almost in desperation, to make a decent baguette in Paris in the darkest days of the recession.

A Note on the Recipes

While this is not a recipe book, I do provide recipes. Many are quite simple, such as flatbread, but others require more commitment and I've tried to illuminate this by labeling each recipe *Easy, Moderate,* or *Difficult.* While they were influenced by many bakers I encountered, and the recipes I read, they reflect methods that became part of my baking regime. I continue to make all of these breads today, and I find them endlessly fascinating and flexible. That said, if you're starting out and really want to learn the craft of baking, I would point you to books highlighted in my bibliography.

In these recipes, I use a scale to weigh ingredients and I measure weights in grams, which can be unfamiliar, especially for someone used to measuring flour in cups or even ounces. While volume measurements are more common, weighing is more accurate. Many baking books also include metric measurements—now the de facto standard at least among artisan bakers. While weighing ingredients might be a foreign concept, it's not difficult. Nor is it a big investment. The first scale I bought was a small plastic version from a grocery store that cost $9.99. I used it for several years and learned how to bake with it. It broke, and I've since graduated to digital scales which can be found for about $25.

I sometimes use the phrase "natural leaven" to refer to the substance commonly known in the United States as "sourdough" or "sourdough starter." French bakers refer to this substance as *levain*. Rather than pick one term, I use all three depending on the context. But they refer to the same thing: natural leaven, sourdough, and *levain* contain populations of wild yeast and bacteria, which when added to dough cause it to ferment—a process I explain in depth in chapter 2.

Although I provide rising times, they depend on a dough temperature of around 75°F (24°C). If your kitchen is 80°F (27°C) or higher in the summer, the dough will ferment more quickly. If the rise is moving too quickly, you can add cooler water of around 65°F (18°C) when you mix the dough. If the rise is sluggish in the winter, because your kitchen is a cool 65°F (18°C), then mix the dough with 85°F (29°C) water and ferment the dough in a closed space, such as an oven, with just the light on. The bottom line: you will need to adjust based on your experience.

A word on flours: I use unbleached "all purpose" flour, although all-purpose can mean many things. Ideally, the flour should be milled from hard red winter wheat with a protein level of about 11 to 11.7 percent. Some all-purpose flours aim for protein levels of around 10 percent, which might be challenging for bread making. (You should be able to find this information at a company's Web site or through a call to its customer service line.) I find "bread flour," which has a protein level of around 13 percent, too strong for handmade breads, though it is well suited for bagels, pretzels, and pizza. If you do use bread flour, you will need to adjust the hydration by adding a bit more water.

Generally, I bake with Whole Foods' 365 Unbleached Organic All Purpose Flour (10.5 to 11 percent protein), but I've found many other flour brands perform just as well, including King Arthur and Gold Medal flours. I've also found that whole wheat flour is more variable than white flour, in the amount of water it requires and the way it performs, because the milling can vary. So once you settle on a brand, you might want to stick with it. I've had good success with stone ground whole wheat flour from Bob's Red Mill, though I've used many others as well, including those from smaller, specialty mills as I discuss in the pages ahead.

CHAPTER 1

Boulangerie Delmontel's Baguette

At three A.M., Rue des Martyrs, a narrow artery in the ninth arrondissement of Paris, was empty and the stores dark except for a narrow ray of light coming out of the side bakery entrance of Boulangerie Delmontel, nestled in the corner of a rococo building. The day before, the street had been crowded with couples out for a Sunday stroll, taking in the wine shops, bistros, and small food stores. It reminded me of Greenwich Village in the 1970s, before it gentrified. The ninth was popular—hip, even—but still had the close-knit feel of a residential neighborhood, the kind of place where a restaurant maître d' would banter with the regulars when they arrived. But now in the predawn hours the streets were quiet.

I had woken up a half hour before, weary from the jet lag and the early hour, and gotten dressed in my white cotton baking jacket and pants. I didn't need a lot of time to get ready for there wasn't a lot to do—not even a cup of coffee to be had. I drank a glass of water and went down to the hotel lobby, surprising the night clerk. You're leaving? he asked, perhaps wondering if I were headed to the Pigalle, the red light district nearby. No, I'm going to bake bread, I replied. He looked puzzled as I headed out into the cool February night air.

How many bakers over the centuries had walked these same dark streets, heading to the *fournils*—the baking rooms—to give Paris its daily bread? Marx had called them the white miners. They began well before midnight, sweating over hundreds of pounds of dough that they kneaded by hand in basements and baked in wood-fired ovens. The boys were known as *les geindres*, "the groaners." The poorest slept by the hearth, inhaling flour, often suffering from tuberculosis. "There is no species more repugnant than that of the *geindre*," a French physician remarked, "naked to the waist, pouring out sweat, gasping in the last throes, spilling and mixing into the dough that you will eat several hours later all the secretions of his overheated body and all the excretions of his lungs, congested by the impure air of the asphyxiating bakeroom." But if they did their job well in this sweltering basement dungeon, faithful to the demanding and time-consuming task of coaxing bread out of natural leaven, flour, water, and salt, the resulting loaves might well have surpassed many sold today, excretions notwithstanding. As I walked down the cobblestone streets that early morning, I felt as if I was following in the footsteps of these ghosts.

I was closing in on the final chapter of what had been a long quest—one that actually began many years ago when I first began baking. At that time, the baguette defined bread for me and I saw no reason why I shouldn't try to bake it, even as a beginner. This isn't unusual. Many novices start out with this iconic loaf. And that's where the trouble begins, because it's the equivalent of wanting to knock out a Beethoven sonata when you sit down at the piano for the first time. So what is it about this loaf that nearly guarantees failure? First, there is the flavor, which must be coaxed out of the flour—it doesn't come by simply mixing the ingredients together. Second, the crumb: It must be light and open, full of holes so prized by bakers that they have their own technical name, alveoli. Third comes the crust. The baker slashes the loaf with a razor blade, right before sliding it into the hot oven. Properly formed, the loaf bursts open through the slashes. But if the surface of the dough is at all flaccid, the slash, or *grigne*, becomes a diminutive wiggly line.

Fourth, the crust must crackle when you bite into it, adding depth to the taste and aroma of the bread. To achieve a crust like this requires a method of creating steam in your home oven, which might result in second-degree burns if you're not careful. All of this, of course, depends on yet a fifth factor—your ability to shape sticky, loose dough by hand into a long cylindrical form that must have a taut skin and yet be open and pliable within. Sprinkle too much flour on the counter and you will fail because the dough will slide around and you won't be able to create surface tension in the dough. But sprinkle too little flour and the dough will stick to the counter and you might rip the skin open. (You want just a dusting, which you achieve, I learned, by taking a pinch of flour in your thumb and two fingers and flicking it across the surface by snapping your wrist.) None of this is easy, but it's further compounded by the fact that the baker needs to have a solid understanding of what is perhaps the most difficult aspect of bread making—fermentation. If you misjudge this—and fermentation is truly a judgment call— then the defects will be magnified in every other step of the process. The result is that you'll often end up saying, This isn't a baguette, it's shit.

I became convinced that it was impossible to make the loaf at home despite all the recipes and lessons that baking books contained. (This was compounded by a not infrequent ruse in baking books: the authors often use specialized bread-baking ovens that easily run into the tens of thousands of dollars to bake the breads pictured in their books, putting them out of reach for the home baker.) So, I moved on to other breads. Though I learned quite a bit over the years, I kept the baguette at bay, feeling defeated. I really didn't return to it until that fateful call with the travel editor, who was willing to commission a story on precisely what I wanted to do.

After we'd spoken, I had no idea how to proceed. I didn't speak much French—I could order a meal, but not much more. The only

French bakers I'd met were in the United States. But then I remembered: I had a friend in Paris who might be able to help out, Denise Young, a former colleague now living in Paris with her French husband and daughter. When I e-mailed her, she graciously offered to help. Within a few days, we had gathered a list of around eight *boulangeries* that looked promising and then she began calling. Now, Denise is well schooled in French manners, but has a kind of full-throttle reporter's approach that gets results quickly. Her assessments were brief, opinionated: "He was kind of gruff, not what you would want," or "Sounds like she just got out of bed, and doesn't speak a word of English, but wants to know the dates," and so on. Within a few days, she had gotten three positive responses, including one from Arnaud Delmontel, who had recently won the annual prize for the best baguette in Paris. He had also worked in the States for a time and spoke English. "Very charming, typically French, here's his mobile number," she said. I e-mailed him pictures of my bread and then gave him a call. I explained the nature of the project. He listened politely. But he was busy, and really, there wasn't much to discuss: when would I be there, he wanted to know. When I suggested a date, he said it would be best to arrive before four A.M. on a Monday. His head baker would meet me. His name was Thomas Chardon. And that was it.

When I arrived that first day in the predawn hours, Chardon let me in. A wiry energetic man in his mid-twenties, he said "*Salut!*," then slid across the flour-specked floor to go back to his dough. He was placing baguette loaves onto a *couche*, a linen cloth that supports the shape of baguettes as they undergo a final rise before baking. He was covered in flour, his blue fleece a snowy white. Pop music blared from a portable radio. I could smell the unmistakable toasty, faintly nutty aroma of freshly baking bread from the oven that filled about a third of the room. Thomas had to rearrange everything just to let me in the cramped space: he slid aside bins filled with just-baked baguettes, rolled cabinets that held the rising loaves, and pushed aside the steel frame loader which is used to slip the loaves into the oven. There wasn't much time for pleasantries. He pointed me toward a narrow circular staircase to a small dressing room where I could keep my things. Then I returned to the baking room, where he motioned me to join in.

Delmontel was one of the new artisans in France, uncompromising when it came to ingredients and technique. But as I soon found out, Delmontel mostly spent his time running the business—three dozen workers more or less, two bakeries (now three, as I write this), making breads, pastries, cakes, and macarons—so it fell to Thomas to be my teacher. Although he spoke no English, the language barrier hardly mattered as he guided me through the entire bread-making cycle, prompting me with hand gestures and a few words. The techniques weren't unique—it wasn't as if Thomas were sharing Delmontel's "secret recipe"—but they did reflect methods that serious bakers were now applying to bread. Time was their most important tool: the time to let the dough come together gently, the time to let fermentation work its magic, and the fortitude not to be pushed by anything but the demands of the bread itself.

This approach was evident when Thomas first dumped flour, a small bit of yeast, salt, and water into a massive mixing bowl and let the mixing arm run for a few minutes at a slow speed. Once the shaggy dough came together, he turned off the machine and then let the dough sit for twenty minutes as the flour slowly absorbed the water. This crucial moment of rest is known in French as *autolyse* (autolysis, which means self-digestion, and which is often accomplished without yeast or salt). What happens in this time of do-nothingness is that the water slowly hydrates the proteins and starches in the flour, beginning the process of dough formation. The mixer can develop the dough, too, but it also incor-

Boulangerie Arnaud Delmontel in Paris

porates oxygen, which can bleach out the flour, tighten the loaf, and alter the inherent flavor of the grain, especially if overdone, as mixing often is. It's better just to let the dough sit in this initial stage and let time do the work.

We mixed again briefly, with two more twenty-minute rest periods. After this one-hour period of mixing and sitting, we scooped chunks of this heavy dough and put them in plastic bins that went into a refrigerated cabinet for a full day. Again, time came into play. While the dough rested at 40°F (5°C) during this first rise (known as the *pointage*), it also slowly fermented, meaning that the flavor, texture, crumb, and crust would all improve. Without this languid first rise, the bread would be bland, lacking character.

Chardon's sense of craft was also apparent. Sure, there were scales to measure flour and water, since bakers measure by weight, and a timer above the mixer, but the main gauge he used to tell if the dough was ready was observation. He looked at the dough, then pinched it between his thumb and fingers. As the mixer turned slowly, he poured in more water at one point because the dough looked slightly stiff. You can't teach that in a cookbook. Delmontel later told me he had been flown to South Korea to consult on a new bakery operation; the company timed his every move with a stopwatch, trying to re-create what he was doing as a measured series of steps. "They kept asking me, 'How long do you do that?' and I just shrugged." He laughed. "I do it until it's done!"

I saw this approach with Chardon after we had shaped a series of baguettes. The loaves finished their second rise—the *apprêt*—resting on a linen *couche* for about thirty minutes. The timing of this final rise depends on the temperature of the bakery, for bread rises more quickly when it's warm. The key question I always have at this point is, "Are they ready for the oven?" The moment, which can't really be measured, is a point of tension when the dough is both relaxed and elastic. If the baker gets the timing just right, the loaves will spring up in the oven. But if he doesn't, the crumb will be tight, and at worst, gummy. The thing is, this inferior crumb can result from either under- or overfermenting the loaf. But how do you know when it's ready? Ultimately, it's a judgment call. This takes time to learn. It took me many awful loaves to know when the dough had fermented properly. When I asked Thomas how he knew when the rise was finished he pointed to his eyes. I studied the loaves closely, poked the skin to feel the tension, which is a common method, and said, "*Finis?*" I thought they were. He peered close without touching a thing and replied, "*Cinq minutes.*" So we waited five minutes for the dough to relax a bit more, then carefully transferred the thin, long *pâtons* onto a canvas mechanical oven loader. I had the honor of making the five swift signature slashes on the top of the baguettes with a *lame* (a curved razor), which create the bulging *grigne* when baked, and then we quickly slid them into the 500-degree oven.

This work slashing the bread was really my first significant lesson—and if I left the bakery at that moment, never to return, it would have been enough, because I slashed maybe twenty-five loaves at a time, and then did so repeatedly through the morning as we loaded more and more baguettes into the oven. At home, I never really got to practice this technique because I'd slash maybe two or three loaves at a time with a razor. At that rate, you tend to obsess over each cut. It's difficult to figure out the speed and pressure of the blade, or the depth or length. So home bakers tend to slash too slowly and then go back, correcting what they perceive as defects. This is far too fastidious. Watch a professional and they simply slash down the loaf quickly, in a rhythmic series of cuts (and actually if you count the beats while you do it, this helps, for each beat corresponds to the time the blade is touching the dough). Slash dozens of baguettes in the course of a morning or two and pretty soon the action becomes so natural that your wrist, fingers, and arm will never forget it—even when you return to just two or three loaves a day. It's technique, craft, and rhythm wrapped up in a loaf.

Thomas, a machine, never stopped moving. There was never a wasted moment, never a break, and this wasn't even Sunday when he knocked out two thousand loaves (so much for the notion of the languorous French worker in the socialized state). After three hours, it was now seven A.M. and there was a lull as we waited for the loaves to finish baking. So Chardon dashed across the street to grab a couple of *cafés*, which we sipped with hot croissants that the pastry chefs had just taken out of the convection oven downstairs. They crackled and blasted open when you bit into them. The only drawback was the coffee, which for some reason the French have not elevated to anything near the croissants. Then the baguettes were ready, darkly spotted, crisp, and caramelized in sections. As we removed them, the crust crackled as it met the cooler air outside the oven. "*Ils chantent*," he said—they're singing.

The baguette wasn't always so melodic. Despite the worldwide appreciation of the loaf as a symbol of France, its quality had declined so precipitously by the 1960s it was an open secret in the trade. Two decades later, truly great French bread was in danger of becoming an artisanal artifact. Neighborhood bakeries were failing. By 1987, a cultural critic writing in *Le Nouvel Observateur* proclaimed that the baguette had become "horribly disgusting . . . Bloated, hollow, dead white. Soggy or else stiff. Its crusts come off in sheets like diseased skin." Renowned French baking professor Raymond Calvel, who had come up with the *autolyse* method—the resting period for dough so crucial to a superior loaf—wondered whether the best baguette would soon be made in Tokyo. What had brought this on?

One chilly morning, after I unloaded the last batch of crackling hot baguettes from the oven at Delmontel, I took the Métro across the Seine to a café in the Montparnasse. There, I met Steven Kaplan, the world's preeminent historian of French bread, who has spent his adult life considering such questions. A Brooklyn-born bread lover who grew up with dense Jewish "corn" rye, Kaplan went on to become a historian of French society at Cornell University. Through bread, he believes, one could understand French culture, social and economic organization, the rise of early capitalism, and the political fabric of society, since keeping people fed and bakers and grain traders honest was an enduring concern. Now, as a professor emeritus, Kaplan resides in Paris, critiquing baguettes in the city's annual competition, writing scholarly tomes, and appearing in French media, where he can frequently be seen thrusting his nose into a freshly cut loaf, which plays particularly well on TV. Back in the States, he's gotten some media attention as well. On an appearance on *Late Night with Conan O'Brien*, he flew off on a tan-

Professor Steven Kaplan inhaling the aromas of a baguette

gent, as he discussed bakers' "impregnating" flour with a fermenting agent, "mounting the dough" as they kneaded it, then tearing into the freshly baked loaf and encountering a "surging geyser of aromas." Conan leaned over to the professor and confided, "I'll be surprised if this actually airs." He has won accolades for championing French bread and has pissed off numerous bakers for dismissing their products as "insipid." His harsh critique about the quality of American artisan bread at one time caused such a schism with the Bread Bakers Guild of America that the trade group has never sought out his knowledge on numerous Guild-arranged trips to Paris. French bakers are not so thin-skinned. Behind the scenes in France, he has worked closely with millers and bakers, promoting the resurgence of artisanal breads; he has been named a Chevalier of the Legion of Honor—twice—by the government, recognizing his critical work in this arcane field. For me, Kaplan was instrumental in understanding French bread. So over coffee in a two-and-a-half-hour discussion—and several follow-up conversations—I got a full dose of history and professorial digressions.

For Kaplan, bread is the most democratic of foods, because it feeds everyone. Yet, when the imperatives of sustenance are propelled by mass production and efficiency, the results can be disastrous culturally. In his book *Good Bread Is Back*, Kaplan tells the story of how French bakers nearly lost their way, as fabrication speeded up and loaves became more airy and light, devoid of taste. He had seen it himself, as a graduate student in Paris in the late 1960s, when bread was losing its place at the dinner table. "For years I had watched the sensorial quality of French bread palpably deteriorate," he told me. "And for too long, it remained a professional secret. Bakers refused to talk about it and the specialized press approached it obliquely or in a highly technical way."

If the decline could be pinned on one thing, he said, focusing his narrow eyes on me, it would be the loss of patience. Bakers compromised when they shifted away from *levain* (sourdough) and increased the pace of fermentation by using baker's yeast instead. This proved popular because yeast—first obtained from brewers and then commercialized in the late nineteenth century—worked more quickly and didn't have the acidic overtones of a *levain*-fermented loaf. Plus, *levain* took skill: a fist-sized piece of sourdough would be refreshed repeatedly with flour and water, providing food for the wild cultures of yeast and bacteria that live in the substance and cause a loaf to rise. These species of organisms are many in number and incredibly diverse, whereas commercial yeast consists of one specialized strain that does its job quickly and effectively. *Levain* loaves might weigh as much as four kilos (nine pounds) and last for a week or more because their acidity retards spoilage. They were often made with whole wheat and rye flours, sustaining French workers and peasants well into the twentieth century.

In Paris, where a preference for white flour had reigned at least since the eighteenth century, the switch to commercial yeast was natural, for it made a lighter loaf. It also coincided with a new method of bread making known as *fabrication en direct*—a process of mixing flour, water, salt, and yeast together all at once rather than building the dough through successive additions of water and flour, as with *levain*. "There was no danger of a badly maintained *levain* ruining a whole day's production," the Montreal baker and writer James MacGuire has pointed out.

Yeast, by itself, wasn't a disaster. Nor was the so-called direct method of mixing everything together at once, which can make a fabulous loaf, so long as a couple of basic tenets are followed—ones I saw at Boulangerie Delmontel. First, mixing should be kept to a minimum, which Chardon accomplished by running the mixer briefly and then letting the dough rest for the three twenty-minute periods. During these rests, the gluten in the dough develops on its own. (Hand kneading with three or four successive rest periods, which is my chosen method, accomplishes the same thing.) Second, only a small bit of yeast is added so that the dough takes time to rise, allowing the acidity to increase slightly and improving the flavor. Home bakers experienced this approach en masse with the "no knead" bread technique developed by New York baker Jim Lahey and then championed by Mark Bittman in *The New York Times*. Just one-quarter teaspoon of yeast is used; all the ingredients of the dough are mixed together and then fermented for up to twenty hours. The dough is then shaped minimally and baked in a Dutch oven. It's a foolproof method for beginning bakers.

If you are seeking expediency, however, you start adding more yeast and mix the dough at a high speed to develop the gluten. In a warm kitchen, fermentation speeds up dramatically and you can make a loaf in two hours or less. The results of this approach are frankly disastrous. Without the benefit of a proper fermentation, the crumb will be tight and the crust a pale color; the bread will taste "yeasty." Such compromises might be rationalized as "efficient"—and this is exactly what occurred in France as baker's yeast became a crutch. Mixing everything together in a *fabrication en direct* and then cutting the fermentation time became a way to make bread quickly. "What that did was suppress the first fermentation that is the source of all aroma, all taste," Kaplan said.

The baguette appeared after World War I, with many factors contributing to its ascendance. Aside from yeast, the steam-injected oven, which crisps up the crust, had arrived from Austria in the mid-nineteenth century. Highly refined flour made by Hungarian roller mills—an invention of the industrial age—also had become available. Add in the variable of the First World War, which reduced the availability of white flour, and the rise of this loaf seems to make sense. Customers revolted against whole grain breads of the war years by choosing the long white loaf with the thin crust, just as they did in the years following World War II. The baguette was a kind of highly refined Parisienne loaf made in a matter of hours and then consumed in one sitting while the crust was still crispy. Nothing about it was long-lasting. Before the 1920s, you might find similarly shaped long loaves but there was no reference to a "baguette," food writer Jim Chevallier notes. Then the loaf appears suddenly, spreading out from Paris, though in some regions it took decades to supplant regional breads.

If made slowly, with a judicious amount of yeast, this would be a loaf to savor. But the shift toward quickly made bread solidified with the semi-industrialization of baking in the 1950s, when another development came along that further improved the efficiency of the bakery. This was the highly intensive kneading machine that whipped the dough around like a roller coaster. Where older mixers turned at about forty revolutions per minute, the new electric-driven motors doubled the speed and kept running for twenty minutes. In doing so, they drove oxygen into the dough, bleaching out the yellowish carotenoids in the flour and compromising the nutritional content of the bread. This satisfied consumer desires for an ever-whiter crumb at the expense of flavor. (If you've ever tasted a bland white bread that has the texture of cotton candy, you've eaten oxidized dough.) Ever more salt was added to make up for the lack of taste, and additives, such as fava bean flour, were used to propel the oxidation process and bleach out pigments. Ascorbic acid (vitamin C) was sprinkled in to tighten the gluten and increase the volume of the loaf. The result would be an enormous open cut (or *grigne*), masking the lack of flavor inside.

Pressing forward with these "innovations," bakers added dividers to cut the dough into properly sized loaves, and then mechanical shapers to form the baguette. This standardized production but also hemmed the baker in to a mechanized and highly predictable world that was the antithesis of craft. He could do little to offer anything distinctive, because the machines determined the direction. Fast forward to the 1980s and even industrially produced frozen dough became acceptable, with trucks delivering "par-baked" bread that would be finished in supermarkets or even *boulangeries*. What was even more ironic was that this frozen bread was, at times, better than the inferior "handmade" loaves coming out of neighborhood bakeries. I saw the latest coup in this evolution—or devolution—at EuroPain, the continent's largest trade show devoted to bread, held outside Paris every few years. A vast, complex, stainless steel machine much larger than most bakeries I've visited had flour going in one end, and hundreds of baguettes coming out the other. The only job of the "baker," or rather technician, was to make sure the damn thing was running correctly. These industrialized versions of the bread were indistinguishable from the quick, mechanized, oxidized breads that had become popular with bakers themselves. So, naturally, consumers began to vote with their feet, by reducing their consumption of this debased product, or buying it at the supermarket, which was cheaper. In pursuit of modernity, French bakers had lost their most crucial ingredients—time and craft. The quest for efficiency and speed all argued against it.

Not surprisingly, bread consumption declined from about 260 grams per person in 1960 to 160 grams in 1980. Some customers never returned. Today in France, one quarter of the nation doesn't bother to patronize their local *boulangerie*. Even Kaplan told me that when traveling, he has found better bread at supermarkets than at *boulangeries*. Though it's taboo to criticize a "national treasure," Kaplan did so starting in the 1980s in opinion pieces and eventually in meetings with bakers and millers. "For me, bread was a crucial dimension of what the French proudly call their 'cultural exception,' and they did not seem to be aware that they were putting it at risk, in grave peril," Kaplan said. He was among a coterie of like-minded critics who championed revisionists, such as Lionel

Poilâne, who baked bread in one of the few wood-fired ovens left in Paris and became a world-renowned baker. Poilâne described his signature *miche* as a "retro-innovation" because he was taking age-old techniques of sourdough fermentation into the modern era and winning over a new generation of bread eaters with his denser, darker loaves. He was bypassing the baguette altogether to bring back bread from an earlier era.

Prominent bakers, professors such as Calvel, and critics spoke out about the decline. Small and medium-scale millers, cut out of the industrial baking trade, were especially worried about these trends, because if people no longer bought bread from their local bakeries, the millers who supplied the flour would vanish. Only the biggest would survive. So the millers tried a new tactic, forming associations and reinvigorating the trade with breads they hoped would entice back supermarket customers. The millers weren't just selling flour. They offered bakers expertise in management, logistics, and store design, even bread-baking technique. Then they sold this bread under a single recognizable brand. Banette was the first. Others soon followed, including a family-owned enterprise in Beauce, the breadbasket of France. This was the Viron mill, which supplied flour to Boulangerie Delmontel.

Kaplan had spent time with the patriarch of this enterprise, Philippe Viron, who was a fifth-generation miller worried about this national decline in bread. "Viron associated the deepest values of Frenchness, even of humanity, with the best bread in the world," Kaplan writes. In the late 1980s, Viron was approached by a baker in the nineteenth arrondissement, a working-class neighborhood far from central Paris. The *boulanger*, Gérard Meunier, told Viron he wanted flour without any of the additives millers typically sprinkled in to help fermentation and correct inconsistencies. Avoiding these ameliorants was virtually unheard of at the time, at

PHOTOGRAPH BY BRIAN DOBEN

A bin filled with Delmontel's long-fermentation baguettes

least for the rapidly made breads designed for the intensive mixing machines. But Meunier had in mind an entirely different method. Viron was at first skeptical. He told Meunier that an additive-free baguette wouldn't rise—it would end up like a galette, as flat as a pancake. But he sold him the flour nonetheless and when he returned to the bakery to see what the baker had done, he was amazed. Meunier's baguette was a revelation.

The story is mythic in the annals of Viron Mill, and Philippe's son, Alexandre, who now runs the company, recounted it for me, when I met up with him at the company's exhibit at EuroPain. As we talked, assistants brought flutes of champagne, delicate ham and cheese sandwiches, and of course a variety of breads from the massive oven that Viron, like every other miller, had installed on the trade show floor. Below our second-floor perch, bakers strolled about, snacking on the sandwiches, chatting and drinking champagne; most of them were associated with Viron in one way or another.

"It was very hard to produce flour for only one customer and that's why we developed this," he said, holding up a baguette. "We thought if we showed it to others, they would want to do it, too." In other words, Meunier's baguette was so intriguing that the elder Viron thought the loaf might secure the mill's future, or at least offer a strategic response to the rise of industrial breads. The mill's chief baker visited Meunier to observe his technique, which involved minimal mixing time, slightly more water than was usual, half the yeast, and an extended first rise. Meunier himself was a student of Professor Calvel, who had championed these methods and even showed Julia Child how to make a baguette. Calvel pointed out that such practices had been used in the 1920s, when bakers had one-speed mixers and couldn't ramp up the speed. They had to rely on time to do the work instead.

When this slower method was applied, flavor dramatically improved, with a sweetness that arose from the wheat itself. The minimal mixing allowed the flour to retain its color, rather than losing it to oxidation. The crumb opened up with those uneven holes connected by razor-thin membranes which create an airy but chewy quality. The crust was often well done (*bien cuit*) and richly caramelized, the result of sugars, starches, and proteins combining in the so-called Maillard reaction, which occurs when the loaf is properly baked. This is so rarely the case with supermarket baguettes.

"This forced us to do our job, which is to select and blend wheat," Viron continued, "because before this time, we were buying wheat and using additives to standardize the flour." The mill sourced wheat varieties from farms around Chartres, a premier wheat-growing region of northern France, about sixty miles from Paris. In the past, they occasionally blended in U.S. and Canadian wheats to raise the protein level and correct for annual variations in the flour. Now, Viron's entire grain supply would originate from the region around the mill, which meant that the bread sold in Paris under their umbrella was locally grown, though this isn't trumpeted by the mill or its retinue of *boulangeries*.

The flour—and the technique—became the basis for Viron's Rétrodor baguette and, slowly, it took off. Alexandre Viron told me he thought their timing was good. Consumers were growing more concerned about what was actually going into their food in the aftermath of the mad cow scares in Europe in the mid-1990s. "People wanted natural things," Viron said. "And we said, 'This is one hundred percent natural, it's just wheat and knowledge.'"

Viron and its Rétrodor baguette were by no means alone. Many others were also trying to undo a few decades of highly compromising baking practices and rescue the small *boulangeries* that were now competing with supermarket chains. In the midst of this ardent movement, the state entered the baking trade once again, aiding the besieged bakers in their battle. The turning point came in 1993, when the French government regulated the term *baguette tradition*, which was precisely the baguette Thomas Chardon taught me how to make (and which Delmontel branded *"La Renaissance"*). Regulations deemed that this loaf could be made only with flour, water, salt, and yeast—no chemical ameliorants—and it had to be made on the premises where it was sold. The state also cordoned off supermarkets and those selling loaves made out of frozen dough from even using the term *boulangerie*. In one act, both the *boulangerie* and its premier product—the baguette—could stand apart from its industrial competitors. The state had intervened to help save the small bakers and millers.

After I began baking in the 1990s, I read about these remarkable breads in Paris—not only the hearty *miche* at Poilâne, which probably got the most attention, but also Philippe Gosselin's *baguette à l'ancienne*, Éric Kayser's baguette on Rue Monge, and many others. The renaissance was in full swing.

D elmontel began his career in the midst of this fervor. Trained as a cook and pastry chef, he initially looked down upon bread making. Bakers had the reputation of being the screw-ups in school; it was assumed they'd had few prospects aside from vocational trades. "I thought all they were doing was mixing flour and water, and what's so hard about that?" he told me, over a dish of Catalonian beef cheeks at a restaurant down the street from the *boulangerie*. With his ponytail, cravat, and smart blazer, he had the air of a well-to-do businessman or successful chef.

This attitude wasn't unusual, since French kids who aren't suited for school are quickly pigeonholed into the trades—carpentry, baking, cooking—and that class stigma tends to follow them through life. Kaplan told me the psychological scars associated with flunking out of school and entering the working class of French society might have had something to do with its bread, since these young bakers were not particularly invested in the craft. The job chose them, not the other way around. That made sense considering that several notable bakers I met in France had switched careers in midlife, coming from sales or software and seeking something new. They were less prone to just follow a rote system because they had never learned it in trade school. There are prominent bakers who came from families where baking was a generational tradition and highly respected. Others did the usual flunk-out-and-go-to-trade-school route but distinguished themselves in the trade.

In this stratified society, the pastry chef was a cut above the *boulanger*. It wasn't until the mid-1990s, when he came to the States to run the pastry department at Whole Foods Market in Madison,

Wisconsin, that Delmontel's view of bread baking changed. That he landed in Madison was fortuitous, for it had a burgeoning network of local farms and notable bakers. "They were doing all these wonderful loaves, with sourdough and whole grains, and I realized there was more to it than just flour and water," he said. Upon his return to France eighteen months later, he worked in a friend's *boulangerie*, then visited the test kitchen run by Viron, where he went through basic training. He learned how to make his signature baguette—one made to this day with Viron's flour.

The height of recognition for Delmontel came in 2007, during the blind tasting for the Prix de la Meilleure Baguette de Paris (Best Baguette in Paris). Delmontel submitted two loaves that were among the hundreds that the judges, Kaplan among them, tasted. He took home first prize for the loaf with the best crumb, flavor, crust, and appearance. "When they called me with the news, I said, 'If this is a joke it is not a very nice one!'" Delmontel recounted. It was no joke. As part of the prize, Delmontel delivered his baguettes to the Élysée Palace for the president's dinner table for a year. Sales shot up 30 percent. Delmontel was the fourth bakery associated with the Viron mill to win the prize.

After several days at Boulangerie Delmontel, I became familiar with the process. So, I began to think about how I might try their technique at home. Noticing the recipe for several hundred baguettes taped to the wall, I calculated the ratio of water, salt, flour, and yeast. Then, I figured out the amount I'd need for just three baguettes and showed it to Thomas. "*Oui?*" he said. "*Un test,*" I replied.

During a rare lull, we weighed out the small quantity of ingredients. Then, to his surprise, I began mixing the flour, water, and yeast by hand, until it was just combined, and then added the salt after the *autolyse*, or rest period. "I haven't done that since baking school," he said. The flour absorbed less water than American flours, because the protein level was lower (protein soaks up water). It also had a different aroma, more grassy perhaps than my flours at home. I then began kneading the dough, lifting it with both hands, slapping it down on the counter, and then folding it over on itself, a technique that I picked up from a video by the UK-based French baking teacher Richard Bertinet. When the dough looked fully developed, springing back when I pulled on it, I showed it to Thomas. He looked and signaled me to work it a bit more. So I slapped and folded the dough a couple of more minutes. Then I let the dough sit, so that the gluten strands could rearrange themselves and strengthen on their own. I kneaded in short bursts every twenty minutes, just as Thomas had done with the mixer. Then we put the dough in the refrigerator for an overnight rise, a modest

PHOTOGRAPH BY BRIAN DOBEN

Mixing my "test" dough at Boulangerie Delmontel

round of dough amid the bins that filled each shelf. I revealed the experiment to Delmontel when he walked into the *fournil*. He merely smiled and went on his way.

Returning the next morning, I waited for another lull in the routine and then pulled out the dough. It had risen nicely and domed up slightly in the plastic bin. It was also creamy colored as opposed to the whitish hue of oxidized dough; it was a good sign that it would have a complex taste.

We shaped the baguettes by hand, let them rise once more, for about thirty minutes, then baked them off in the huge oven. They sprang up and opened at the *grignes*, and when we removed them with the long baker's peel—a flat wooden spatula with a long handle—I saw they had a deep golden brown color. The slashes were nicely extenuated. Once they cooled, I picked out one and took it upstairs to the chef.

"*Le test*," I announced, entering Delmontel's office.

He looked amused as I gave him the loaf.

"Nice slashes," he said. "Good color. May I cut it open?"

Of course, I nodded.

So he took out a serrated knife and cut the full length of the loaf, like a sandwich, then thrust his nose inside, squeezing the bread to release the bouquet—just as Kaplan had done so often. "Ah, good smell," he said, and looking at the uneven air pockets in the crumb, he smiled and showed the loaf to his wife, Valérie. "I didn't know that my formula could be done on such a small scale," he said.

Then he took a bite.

"Ah, *c'est bien!*" he said, smiling.

A French baker had told me I made good bread. What else did I need? I flew out of the office and went downstairs to tell Chardon the good news.

. . . . .

Boulangerie Delmontel's Baguette

M y days in Paris fell into a routine: up at three in the morning, over to the bakery until noon, then a nice leisurely lunch at a choice restaurant as my main meal of the day. This is a nice way to eat in Paris, because lunch is as good as dinner, it's a third cheaper, and you bypass the crowds. Then I'd do a bit of sightseeing, or visit *boulangeries* throughout the city. Sometimes I hopped on the Métro, though I also relied on the ubiquitous Vélib' public bicycles, picking up one at a stand, then riding to the next *boulangerie*, where I could usually find another kiosk to drop it off. It was an amazing way to see Paris, even in chilly, wet February. When evening came around, I had a light repast—a sandwich, salad, or charcuterie with a glass of wine—then was in bed by eight.

There may be 1,200 bakers in Paris, but the same names often arise when it comes to spectacular bread. So I ate many good loaves, but honestly, not one stood out above all others. Techniques, for the most noble or selfish reasons, spread like wildfire. And luckily, these days, the best techniques were on the rebound, at least among committed *boulangers*.

You could see it at a gorgeous little bakery in the tenth arrondissement, Du Pain et Des Idées, which was open only weekdays. The baker, Christophe Vasseur, had a marvelous selection of loaves, including a *levain*-scented baguette with just a bit of chew in the crust. Or for a really novel take on French bread, there was Véronique Mauclerc, whose bakery is tucked into a working-class neighborhood in the nineteenth arrondissement. Her organic and whole grain loaves, made entirely with *levain*, had won critical notice from Paris to Tokyo. All the breads were shaped by hand and baked in a century-old wood-fired oven. Then there was Kayser, where I stood on a line that snaked down the Rue Monge in the evening, one of many seeking the crackling baguettes coming out of the oven. And, of course, Poilâne, whose bakery was now run by his daughter, Apollonia, and where a pilgrimage was a foregone conclusion. These were just a few of the bakers I visited in Paris whose methods kept the flavor vibrant and the bread alive.

I had tried so much bread in so many bakeries around Paris, I was approaching my limit, if such a thing is possible, and my enthusiasm began to flag. But one day, Kaplan told me that if I wanted to try a really superlative baguette, I should take the Métro down to Vaugirard in the fifteenth and meet Frédéric Pichard. "He might make the best baguette in Paris," Kaplan said provocatively. By this point I had eaten so many wonderful baguettes I had no idea what "best" meant, but after a few phone calls through my friend Denise, we arranged a meeting at the *boulangerie*.

By the time I arrived at La Maison Pichard that rainy afternoon, I was dripping wet. Denise and I entered the shop, which was quite small, almost utilitarian, without the elaborate displays of bread and pastries that might fill more flamboyant establishments. The place was crowded, bustling with the late afternoon trade. Denise said a few words to the woman behind the counter and we were immediately ushered into the back, past a giant wood-fired brick oven, where a baker stood loading baguettes onto the hearth with a long wooden peel. Pichard, a stocky man dressed in bakers' whites, said hello and motioned us to follow him downstairs to the basement. Unlike the warm and homey feel of the shop upstairs, the basement appeared almost antiseptic, with stainless steel counters, giant steel mixing troughs, and spotless floor tile. That Pichard had devoted this much attention to designing the bowels of the operation was telling. Many bakeries I visited—including Delmontel's—were tightly stacked with equipment, the workers squeezing by each other. By comparison, this basement was almost luxurious, with a lot of floor space. It was also a marked contrast to the small store out front.

Before I had even removed my dripping jacket or asked my first question, Pichard launched into a colloquy of his principles of baking, the ideal baguette, the problems with millers, the drawbacks of contemporary flour, the failures of the baking trade, the imbecilic journalists who came to interview him who knew nothing about bread, the poverty of skills among his fellow *boulangers*, a few of them media darlings whom he declared "*imposteurs!*"

"He's really on a roll," Denise said, trying to keep up with the translation.

Following him around the bakery for two and a half hours, it became clear he was really trying to make two related points. First, that the baguette stood as the pinnacle of the nation's culinary culture—"I fight for it because it's the quintessential French product!" he said. Second, bakers often fell short on reaching the heights of excellence because they were just following rote techniques and didn't fully understand fermentation. By then, I knew the argument he was making—that proper fermentation had been lost in the headlong plunge toward expediency and efficiency, even if a minority were fighting to bring it back. For Pichard, the stakes were much higher than simply good bread, because the essence of wheat itself had been sacrificed along the way.

In fact, when he began talking with us, he did not even mention bread. Instead, he began describing champagne, which undergoes a two-step fermentation. The grape is first crushed and the wine bottled, so that it ferments with whatever wild yeast is on the grape itself. "This is the first fermentation," he said, "the 'endogenous' fermentation. After that period which can last a few weeks, yeast is added and a second fermentation begins. This is the 'exogenous' fermentation." This process was crucial to bringing out the intrinsic taste of the grape, which in turn expressed its *terroir*—the soil, climate, and place where the fruit was grown. There was no reason that wheat itself couldn't achieve the same exalted heights.

Pichard motioned us over to a giant stainless steel mixing trough, perhaps three feet in diameter and eighteen inches high, filled with a cream-colored and extremely moist dough. He explained that it had been sitting undisturbed for twenty-four hours. "That's for the baguette?" I asked. I was incredulous, because if dough sat for that long at room temperature, it could easily overferment and lose the glutinous strength needed to form a loaf. To avoid this, bakers such as Delmontel put the dough in the refrigerator for a full day, developing flavor but not at the expense of the dough's plasticity. But Pichard explained that it wasn't the final dough, just a mixture of flour, water, and salt—no yeast. This was akin to that first fermentation in champagne, the "endogenous" fermentation, which allowed the inherent flavors of the wheat to develop, before baker's yeast was added.

"Look closely," he said. On the surface of the dough I could see bubbles, the telltale sign of a fermenting dough, because yeast digests sugar in the flour and then expels carbon dioxide gas. This gas causes the dough to rise. I suggested that the dough wasn't fermenting on its own, but was inoculated by microscopic amounts of yeast left in the mixer from previous batches. Pichard smiled. "We wash these mixers after each batch, and then clean them out with a bleach solution because we don't want to infect the dough," he said. He was sanitizing the mixers the same way beer makers cleaned out fermentation tanks, so maybe they were undergoing an "endogenous" fermentation after all. Then, after the long rest period and the addition of baker's yeast, the dough was minimally mixed and then left to ferment for four to seven hours. Finally, it was divided into baguette-sized pieces of dough, shaped into loaves, and loaded straight into the brick oven. It was highly unorthodox—in fact, I had never encountered anything like it in the United States or France. "This work is what produces the aromatic bouquet," he said.

His flour, an ancient variety whose name he didn't care to reveal, came from a single farmer in Picardy, in the north of France, and it was milled for his bakery. Because the origin was so limited, there wasn't an opportunity to blend it with other flours to create a uniform product. The baker got what the farmer produced. As a result, he had to keep adjusting his methods to suit the variations in the flour. "That's why I can show what I do, because no one can reproduce this," he said, sweeping his arm around the bakery. "You can only learn this by doing the work." Sometimes the dough fermented for twenty hours, sometimes thirty. At times, he ran the mixer for five minutes to develop the dough after this initial fermentation, but at other times, it ran far longer. It all came down to the flour, which varied by season and by year.

When I asked him where he got the idea for this method, he said that as a younger man, "I was very passionate about wine." Plus, he came from a family of bakers; he had apprenticed with his father just as his son was now apprenticing with him. "My father always believed there should be dough in the mixer. So when he finished for the day, he mixed one final dough and let it sit overnight. That was a bit like mine, but it did not rest as long," he said.

There were other differences in this baguette, too. He dramatically reduced the amount of salt in his dough, which is typically twenty grams per kilo of flour, or 2 percent of the flour weight. But I've seen recipes that go up to 2.5 or even 3.5 percent, which would verge toward "salty." Pichard's view: "Anyone who is adding 2.5 percent salt is trying to mask the lack of flavor, because salt exhausts the taste buds."

I tend to agree with him. I've found that with more flavor in the dough—from a long fermentation, or sourdough, or a higher percentage of whole grain flour—you can reduce salt without ill effect. In fact, on a sandwich with salty cold cuts, cheese, or olive tapenade you can even use a nearly unsalted bread and hardly notice the difference. You get the salt from the fixings. I usually benchmark salt at 1.8 percent, or eighteen grams per kilo of flour, which is an effective 10 percent reduction from the usual amount recommended in baking books. But Pichard cut the sodium in his dough by one fifth, to sixteen grams per kilo. This would be noticeable, and for many the bread might well taste bland, at least on the first bite.

"You didn't have any customers revolt when you did that?" I asked.

"No. I did it gradually, over time, and no one mentioned a thing," he replied.

That conformed with what I've found as well, which is that no one has ever remarked on the seasoning in my bread. But here is the other thing about salt: Pichard, like many French bakers I met, uses coarse sea salt, such as *gros sel de Guerande*, from the marshlands of Brittany. Compared with table salt or kosher salt, this sea salt already has roughly 12 percent less sodium because of the minerals and moisture it also contains. When combined with the already reduced amount of salt in the dough, the bread has perhaps a third less sodium than the norm—at least the norm in the United States. But Pichard's not cutting down on salt because of health concerns; he doesn't want salt to mask the intrinsic taste of wheat. He's not alone in that regard, at least in France. I met other French bakers who maintain salt at levels that would probably be unacceptable in the United States. In fact, the food in general tasted less salty, and while some American chefs might say it was improperly seasoned, perhaps we've just gotten used to more salt in our food.

Upstairs, a baker was loading baguettes into the brick oven on a peel, not the canvas mechanical loader that is a common piece of equipment in most other bakeries. The oven's circular hearth rotated with the turn of a mechanical wheel on the wall. This way, the baker could load baguettes on one portion of the hearth and then turn the wheel so another segment of the floor was exposed to the oven door. Between each baking session, wood was added to a fire box next to the hearth, which blew the hot air into the oven.

Frédéric Pichard in front of his wood-fired oven

This way the oven remained free of ash. Pichard clearly loved the wood oven, but when I asked him whether he thought it made better bread than a modern deck oven, he said, "*Non,*" and then paused. The oven was beautiful, folkloric, and related to the heritage of bread. If it altered the flavor at all, it was only because the oven's heat gradually receded during baking. This, of course, is a hot debate among bakers, because some swear by the flavors a wood-fired oven infuses into the bread. Of course, bread is not baked in an oven filled with burning wood. Even in cases where the wood is burned directly on the oven floor, the remaining ashes are swept out and then the hearth mopped before the bread goes in. In Pichard's case, the wood never even touched the oven because the firebox was located alongside it. All that's left is the heat radiating from the floor, ceiling, and thick stone walls, and maybe some residual flavor—or maybe not. Still, the wood fire suited Pichard's approach: he thought of it as working with the most essential elements—*fire* from the oven, *earth* in which the wheat grew, *water* to make the dough, and *air,* which fueled fermentation.

When we finally ate the bread—a light loaf with one long slash running the length of the bread instead of the usual series of cuts—it was extremely airy, almost floating in my hand as I held it, with a very mild and almost sweet, milky flavor to the crumb. The crust was crisp and chewy, and well done. On the first bite, though, I did notice the reduced salt. As we kept eating, it was no longer apparent.

A lot of work and thought went into this loaf, and the process was quite challenging. Was it worth it? The answer was in the work itself, for Pichard told me he wanted to keep baking intellectually exciting for himself and his bakers. "You have to be engaged and interested in what you're doing and learn the way dough ferments," he said. "That takes ten years. Those who say they can teach baking in six months, it's a big lie."

In one of his parting comments, he said he wanted to champion the baguette because that was what kept people coming to *boulangeries* each day. He made two to three thousand baguettes daily for his customers. He didn't knock Poilâne, and the dark *levain miche* the bakery sold, but that bread could last for a week, meaning customers would not have to return to the bakery very often. If you wanted a Pichard baguette, you had to buy it and eat it on the same day. It was the main staple of those who lived in the apartments overlooking the streets around him. "They are the most demanding clientele," he said, "but also the most loyal." He only charged one euro per loaf, which was much less than other *boulangeries* in Paris. If he offered the best bread possible to his neighbors, they in turn would support him, and he had no interest in doing anything else. There would be no Pichard chain, no international brand. Just one neighborhood bakery with its unrelenting focus on coaxing good bread from the wheat of one farmer in France. "It's a good living," he said. "It's enough."

When I returned from Paris, I took all that I had learned and went to work. I made baguette dough nearly every day, following the process I learned at the Boulangerie Delmontel of minimal mixing time, a long rise in the refrigerator, and then shaping what was an extremely wet dough. I also kept the final rise quite short, so that the loaf would get a nice upward burst in the oven. Gradually, I started to get good results, with an open crumb, crisp crust, and wide *grigne*. Still, I was disappointed. The flour was not quite the same, the flavor less sweet and grassy than I recalled. I couldn't figure out what was wrong, because the flour I used was well suited to artisan loaves, milled from hard red winter wheat with an ideal protein level of about 10.5 to 11.7 percent. Scour the Web and there are all sorts of comparisons between French and American flours, but the main point is that French flours have a lower protein level, requiring less hydration than American flours. So I increased the amount of water in the recipe to account for the higher protein in U.S. wheat, but still I wasn't happy. The bread smelled and tasted different.

I then returned to Kaplan's book *Good Bread Is Back*, and read through descriptions of the baguettes made by two influential bakers in France, Éric Kayser and Dominique Saibron. Both bakers added *levain* to their baguette dough in minor amounts along with baker's yeast. Although a contemporary narrative account of French bread, Kaplan's book gives just enough information about the technique to craft a recipe. And more important, he talks about why bakers apply certain techniques, which can be more valuable than any recipe. When I spoke to Dan Leader, whose book had started me down this path many years earlier, he mentioned that he, too, added a small amount of natural leaven to his baguettes. It wasn't as overpowering as a loaf made entirely with sourdough, but instead provided a hint of acidity. In fact, the more I read, the more I realized that many artisan bakers were using the technique, including the American bakers who had competed with French baking teams in the World Cup of Baking. And the Americans began winning these baking Olympics in 1996.

So I tweaked the recipe by adding a bit of sourdough and a minute amount of whole wheat flour to stimulate the fermentation. Soon, I began to get results I was pleased with. On the phone with Delmontel one day, I told him I was getting closer to the baguette I wanted. But I also expressed frustration with the flour I was using, which was not the same as the Viron flour he had in the bakery. But he was dismissive. "Look, it's not reasonable to import flour so you can make the same exact baguette as mine," he said. "It's like strawberries—you don't eat them in winter. The most important thing is to make people happy, to love what you have done! Whether it's the same flour, it's not important."

I knew he was right. I had to adapt the process to the flour I had. I would create my own baguette—which is what any serious baker would do.

Within a month or two, I felt I had nailed the recipe, finally achieving a slightly more complex flavor. It still wasn't the same as Delmontel's baguette but it was a good one just the same, with an open crumb, crisp crust, slight chew, and the slightest hint of acidity. It felt like the end of a very long journey, and a triumph, given that I had concluded so long ago that baguettes couldn't be made at home. I had just handed in my travel piece on the baking adventure when I got an e-mail from Tim Carman, a food writer then working for the

Washington City Paper. He asked how things were going, as he knew of my attempt to tackle the baguette. I invited him over and gave him a brief lesson in making the loaf. He had trouble handling the extremely moist dough, which is a challenge for any beginner. From another batch of dough which I had sitting in the refrigerator overnight, I shaped three loaves, let them rise at room temperature for thirty minutes, and baked them in the oven, pouring boiling water into a sheet pan on the bottom shelf to approximate the effect of a steam-injected oven. They came out nicely, golden brown in color, the bread bursting through the cuts. Once they had cooled a bit, we ripped into one.

"These are pretty good," Carman said.

"Yeah, not bad, for homemade," I replied.

"No, I mean really good," he added. "These might be the best I've had in Washington."

I told him the reason I started baking was precisely because I couldn't find good bread in the city, or at least anywhere near my house. Then, thinking of the Paris competition, I added, "If you really like the bread, why don't you have a competition and put my loaves against the professionals here in D.C.?"

Tim immediately liked the idea and a few weeks later had gathered the judges in a drab conference room of the paper for a blind tasting: Joan Nathan, a cookbook author; Eric Ziebold, chef at CityZen, a top-ranked restaurant in Washington; Mark Furstenberg, the local baker and an outspoken perfectionist about bread; and Jule Banville, a home baker and staffer at the paper. I had mixed my doughs the day before, sweating at the prospect of going up against professionals. Trying to gain whatever edge I could, I made sure the bread came out of the oven by around nine A.M., which meant that the crust would still be crisp when the loaves were eaten at eleven. Tim had asked several local bakeries to deliver bread, but only two complied—evidence perhaps of how highly they regarded this exercise. So he went around town fetching loaves that morning, and I helped out as well with a couple of samples, seeking out the best specimens I could find. But nearly all of them, it appeared, had been baked long in advance, which is a major drawback of the wholesale bakery business. My loaves were probably the freshest.

I submitted two loaves—one with a slightly higher proportion of sourdough than the other. While I had some trouble shaping the loaves, because the dough was more relaxed than usual after the overnight rise, they still came out fine: dark brown, a generous opening at the *grigne*, a decent shape, and, I hoped, a winning taste.

All the loaves were marked with numbered flags and each judged according to crust, crumb, appearance, flavor, and several other categories cribbed from the Paris competition. Some loaves were, to use Kaplan's words, "insipid," since they had obviously been made quickly, then languished on store shelves. (The shelf life of a baguette is about six hours, max.) When Tim cut them lengthwise, it was clear that only a few had the open, uneven interior crumb that I was striving for—a basic requirement of well-made loaves in France. Many had the kind of white uniform center that probably resulted from intensive mixing, ample yeast, and high-protein flour. In short, many were replicas of precisely the kind of loaves that had brought down bread in France in the preceding decades. I wasn't alone in these assessments. Sitting around the conference table and discussing each loaf as they tasted it, the judges were unsparing.

When it came time to taste my loaves, though, I was nearly shaking with nerves but tried hard to mask the fact that this was my bread. Tim sliced into my first loaf, then passed around the pieces. The judges smelled and then nibbled at the bread. I tasted it as well—it had the soft, open crumb I was seeking, a mild hint of *levain,* and, yes!, the crust was still crisp. Joan Nathan said simply,

"This is the best one so far." Even Furstenberg, who was unstinting in his critique of the other loaves, said: "This is a good baguette." Ziebold agreed. Now, this wasn't the Paris competition, or anything even remotely close. But when Carman later tallied up the results, my two loaves earned the highest scores. I had topped the professionals!

In the postgame interview, Furstenberg wasn't pleased. He thought the fact that I was only making a few baguettes at a time gave me an unfair advantage. But as I pointed out, I also lacked what the pros had on hand: commercial deck ovens, loaders, and the experience that comes from pounding out a few hundred loaves a day. For me, perhaps the most telling comment came from Loic Feillet, the owner of Panorama—a wholesale bakery in nearby Alexandria, Virginia. He mentioned that he had tried to sell a baguette similar to the one I was making, but his customers, restaurants and stores around D.C., revolted. He could not convince them that his loaf, made with a hint of sourdough, was superior. So he dumbed it down to their idea of what a baguette should be.

This isn't unusual. Even in Paris, bakeries routinely undercook their baguettes to meet their customers' expectations for an extremely pale loaf. By reinforcing this choice, the customer never experiences the taste of a crust infused with the flavor components of the Maillard reaction. It's like eating chicken with rubbery skin. Somehow customers learn to prefer it. Playing to the lowest common denominator might do wonders for a business, but it has never been a path to greatness. Working in my kitchen, I never had to worry about that. My only customer was the ideal loaf that I had tasted on occasion and had in my head. I didn't have to compromise. All I had to worry about was to do better next time.

I have made baguettes many times since the competition and the recipe has continued to evolve, less because I am seeking out new flavors than because I'm curious about how different methods alter the taste and appearance of the loaf. I have even done away with the natural leaven on occasion, trying to moderate the slight tug or chew when you bite into the loaf. I cut the yeast in half from the levels I used in the winning recipe. I'm experimenting with "poolish," in which up to half the flour in the loaf is pre-fermented twelve to fifteen hours before mixing, with just a pinch of yeast, so it's a bubbling mass by the time you mix it with the remaining flour, water, and salt. This tends to open up the crumb even more because poolish helps break down proteins in that long prefermentation. I'm also playing with the salt levels, so that the sodium doesn't overpower the natural flavor. The baguette tastes cleaner, more pure, but I imagine that in another few months, I'll go back to using *levain* again, or raise the amount of whole grains in the loaf for a more rustic feel. In the end, my goal is the same: flavor, an open crumb, a dark crust—in short, a dynamite loaf.

This quest of mine—and the resulting travel piece—got me through the darkest three months of the recession. Work started flowing again. But more than that, this one project—and the obsessive focus it required—grounded me at a tenuous moment. I wasn't making as much money as before, but I was making a helluva baguette. And that was certainly better than no bread at all.

Stirato

(MODERATE)

Makes 4 loaves

When I first started baking, I stumbled on *stirato,* which is like an easy-to-make baguette. I found it in Joe Ortiz's *The Village Baker.* Although I didn't know it at the time, this bread was actually a good one to begin with because it introduced me to the benefits of highly hydrated (that is, very wet) doughs, which create an incredibly airy crumb if handled with a light touch. Ortiz made the dough in a food processor, which you might want to try, but I use a method that combines minimal hand kneading, or more precisely folding, and periodic rests.

With Ortiz's recipe, the difficulty came in shaping the loaves. I mangled many, with dough stuck on my hands, apron, and counter. Here, I offer a much simpler technique I learned from Roland Feuillas (chapter 7): you simply form a rectangle and cut off the loaves. Then there's the fun part: hold the end of each one and stretch it out (hence the name, *stirato*), forming a long, thin, irregular baguette-like loaf.

This recipe can be made in one day but requires a long first rise to build flavor and crust color and help ensure you'll get those holes everyone tends to want in homemade bread. If you bake with sourdough, try adding a tablespoon or two to this dough, simply to build more flavor, though it comes out fine without it. If you mix it around nine A.M., it will be ready by dinner.

Tools

    Bowl or container

    Spatula

    Plastic dough scraper

    Rectangular baking stone

Rimmed baking sheet, for the oven
Dowel or wooden spoon with a long handle or a chopstick
Parchment paper, cut to the size of the baking stone
Cutting board or second baking sheet, to move the loaves to
    the oven
Cooling rack

Ingredients
    500 grams unbleached all-purpose flour
    375 grams water 80°F (27°C)
    ½ teaspoon instant yeast
    1 tablespoon sourdough (optional)
    10 grams sea salt
    Semolina flour, for dusting the loaves

Morning

Combine the flour, water, yeast, and sourdough, if using, in a bowl, mixing together with a spatula or your hand moistened with water for about 1 minute. After the ingredients are combined, make a small indentation on the top of the dough. Add the salt to the small well you've just made in the dough, and about 1 tablespoon of water to cover it, but don't mix it in yet. Cover the bowl and let the dough sit for 20 minutes.

Moisten your hands slightly and use the dough scraper to loosen the dough from the bowl. Rather than knead the dough, you're going to stretch and fold it in the bowl—a technique I use in nearly all the recipes in the book. Working from the edges of the dough, pull the dough out to stretch it and then fold it over toward the center. You can also squeeze the dough with your fingers to help incorporate the salt. If your hands begin to stick to the dough, moisten them again with water. Work around the dough and stretch and fold it 12 times. This action should take about 1 minute in total. Flip the dough over so the folds are underneath and the smooth side is on top. Cover the bowl and let the dough sit for another 20 minutes.

Do the stretch-and-fold action for one more round. By now you'll notice that the salt is incorporated and the gluten offers noticeable tension. After folding about 12 times, turn the dough over again, cover the bowl, and let the dough rest for 20 minutes.

Do the stretch-and-fold action 2 more times, at 20-minute intervals. In the final round, the dough should feel very elastic and should be glistening. If it isn't, add a few more stretch-and-fold actions but be careful not to rip the dough. Turn the dough over so the smooth side is face up.

Cover the bowl and let it sit for 6 to 7 hours. The goal here is for the dough to rise until it has at least tripled in size, but has not collapsed in on itself. By the end of the rise, you might see big air bubbles on the top of the dough.

Afternoon

Preheat the oven to 470°F (245°C), with your baking stone on the middle rack, 60 minutes before baking. In the lower part of the oven, or on the bottom, place a rimmed baking sheet that can hold half a cup of water.

Place a piece of parchment paper roughly the size of your baking stone on an overturned and lightly floured or a cutting board baking sheet. Dust the parchment lightly with a 50/50 mixture of white flour and semolina flour or just white flour and set it aside.

Flour a two-foot-square area of your counter generously with the flour/semolina mix or white flour. Dust the top of the dough lightly with flour. Using a plastic dough scraper, gently loosen the dough from the bowl and pour it out onto the counter, being careful to keep it in one piece. The outer, smooth surface will have landed on the floured surface, becoming the bottom of the dough. The top of the dough will be sticky. Dust it lightly with flour. Flour your hands and gently make a rectangle that's about ¾ to 1 inch thick and about 10 by 16 inches, with the long side on the east-west axis, or parallel to the edge of the counter. Don't fuss over it to make it perfect or you'll compress the dough, losing the open structure of the air holes.

Sprinkle a thick line of flour across the middle of the dough, moving east–west, marking where you will divide the rectangle in half lengthwise. Then sprinkle another two lines of flour through each of those portions, again moving east–west. You will cut the dough along the three lines, making four long loaves. Using a dowel, the wooden handle of a kitchen spoon, or a chopstick, press on the floured line so the pieces separate. A thick, dull tool works well because it joins the dough together at the seam. If the tool does not fully cut through the dough, use your dough scraper to finish cutting the pieces. Separate the pieces so they are not touching each other and cover them with a light towel.

This second fermentation will take about 20 minutes. When the loaves are ready, they will be very light and spring back within one second when you press your finger very lightly into the dough.

Baking

Pour ½ cup water into a measuring cup.

Sprinkle the loaves lightly with semolina/flour. Loosen two loaves gently with the dough scraper. If you put enough flour on the counter it won't take much effort. Place your hands under the dough at either end of one loaf, then turn it upside down onto the floured parchment paper. To prevent the dough from sagging in the middle while you move the loaf, you can move your two hands closer together, slightly crimping the loaf lengthwise. The floured underside is now facing up. Do this with the second loaf, too. (If your baking stone is big enough, you might be able to place all four loaves on the parchment paper and bake them at once.) Now, here's the fun part. Lightly grab either end of the dough and gently stretch out the loaf to just under the size of your baking stone. If it resists, don't pull it—the dough will rip. Do the same with the second loaf. You can straighten out the edges by gently repositioning the loaf with your dough scraper, but don't fuss too much. Open the oven and slide the parchment paper off the cutting board or baking sheet and onto the baking stone. The loaves will bake on the parchment paper the entire time. Close the oven. Take the ½ cup water and pour it onto the baking sheet, being careful not to get burned by the steam. Shut the oven door.

Bake for 18 to 22 minutes. Do not open the oven until at least 18 minutes into the bake. Bake until dark brown. Using a peel, or oven mitts, remove the loaves to a cooling rack, and let them stand for at least 20 minutes before eating. Repeat the baking method with the second two loaves.

These loaves are best eaten within four hours. If you do not eat all the bread, the loaves can be frozen in a plastic bag. When you're ready to eat a loaf, remove it from the freezer until it defrosts and bake it for 5 minutes in a 400°F (205°C) oven to crisp up the crust. Once reheated, it will go stale relatively quickly.

Levain Baguette

(DIFFICULT)

Makes 4 loaves

This recipe closely follows the one I used to make the winning baguettes in the contest. It might be intimidating, but experienced home bakers will likely recognize the steps. Beginners will need to be patient—to start baking bread with this recipe is like jumping into calculus after third-grade math, so try the *stirato* first. If you don't yet have any *levain,* you'll need to make it first.

The *levain* baguette is a wet, slack dough that is challenging to shape. If you end up with something that looks like a twisted branch, don't despair. Scarf it up—the rich flavor, bubbly internal crumb, and crisp crust will likely surprise you, even if it does not approach the ideal of a Parisian baguette. For additional tips and links to videos showing techniques, visit my Web site at ChewsWise.com.

Levain Baguette

Tools
  Bowl
  Spatula
  Plastic dough scraper
  Rectangular baking stone
  Rimmed baking sheet
  3 kitchen towels or a *couche* (linen baking fabric that holds the
      shape of the baguettes as they rise)
  Parchment paper, cut to the size of the baking stone
  Single-edged razor blade, *lame,* or knife
  Cutting board or second baking sheet, to move the loaves to
      the oven
  Cooling rack

Levain Ingredients
  25 grams ripe sourdough
  50 grams unbleached organic all-purpose flour
  50 grams water

Final Dough Ingredients
  90 grams *levain*
  2 teaspoons instant dry yeast (reduced to 1 teaspoon in the
      summer)
  420 grams water
  590 grams unbleached organic all-purpose flour
  10 grams organic whole wheat flour
  12 grams sea salt
  Olive oil, to grease the bowl
  Flour, to dust cutting the board

Morning, First Day

Mix the ingredients for the *levain* and let it ferment for 7 to 8 hours, until it has risen but not yet collapsed.

Evening, First Day

Pour the starter and the yeast into the bowl. Add the water and mix together with a spatula or your hand until the starter breaks up a bit. Add the white and whole wheat flours and mix with a spatula or your moistened hand for a couple of minutes until barely incorporated. The dough will be heavy and shaggy. Make a slight indentation on top of the dough, then add the salt and 1 tablespoon of water in this small well so the salt can hydrate. Cover the bowl and let it rest for 20 minutes.

Moisten your hands and use the dough scraper to loosen the dough from the bowl. Stretch out one side of the dough, then fold it into the center, moving around in a circle as you do so. Using a pinching action, squeeze the dough between your thumb and fingers to help incorporate the salt. Fold the dough into the center again, moving around in a circle 10 to 12 times, and then turn it over in the bowl, so that the smooth side of the dough is facing upward. Cover and let the dough rest 20 minutes.

Do the stretch-and-fold action 2 more times, with a 20-minute rest between each round, making sure to turn the dough over, so that the smooth side is face up and the bowl is covered when completed. By the third round, the dough should be elastic and have a satiny shine. Cover and let rest for 20 minutes.

Remove the dough from the bowl so that you can clean it out, oiling the bowl lightly. (Alternatively, you can simply move the dough into a lightly oiled plastic container that might fit better in your refrigerator. Make sure the container will allow enough room for the dough to double in size.) Let the dough rest for a half hour, then place it in the refrigerator for 12 to 24 hours.

Ideally, you want to bake your baguettes in the afternoon of the second day, so that you might have them ready for dinner.

Second Day

Put the baking stone on the middle rack of the oven. Place a rimmed baking sheet on the oven floor or lower shelf. Preheat the oven to 470°F (245°C) for at least 60 minutes. Lightly dust the counter with flour, so that it's barely present. Too much flour will impede the shaping of the baguettes.

Remove the dough from the refrigerated bowl or container. It should have at least doubled in size and contain noticeable gas bubbles. Cut the dough in half. Put the remaining half back into the bowl or container and into the refrigerator. Cut the dough into two pieces (weighing about 275 grams each) and gently stretch them into rectangles 5 by 7 inches with the long edge facing you, or along an east–west axis. The dough should be slightly stiff, because it's cool, but it will get noticeably more relaxed as it warms up.

Preshape the dough by stretching and gently folding the top (north) edge of the dough to the middle, then folding it again to the bottom (south) edge. Place the seam side down. Do this with the second loaf and then cover with a light towel and let rest for 5 to 10 minutes.

While the dough is resting, dust the parchment paper with flour. Roll up three kitchen towels tightly. Set aside. (If you have a *couche*, dust it lightly with flour.)

To shape the baguette, turn the preshaped loaf seam side up. Press and pull on the dough gently, so it's a thick rectangular shape, with the long edge again going east–west. Fold the top (north) side of the rectangle toward the middle. Then, using the thumb of your left hand to hold the dough in place, use your right hand to fold the dough again nearly all the way to the bottom edge of the dough, so that the north edge meets the south edge. Seal the seam with your thumb or the heel of your hand. You should have a log about 1.5 to 2 inches thick and about 8 to 9 inches long. Repeat with the remaining loaf.

Very lightly dust the counter. With both hands facing palm down on the loaf, gently roll it back and forth, moving each hand out to the ends of the loaf as you go, stretching it into a 14-inch loaf or just under the size of your baking stone. Don't worry if it's uneven. It won't be perfect the first time. Repeat with the second loaf.

Place each loaf on the perpared parchment paper about 5 inches apart, with the seam side down. Place one rolled-up towel underneath the paper between the loaves and one under each other edge, supporting their shape. (If using a *couche*, place the loaves *seam side up*.) Cover with a light kitchen towel and let rise for about 20 to 30 minutes. You want the dough to still spring up when you press into it, so be careful not to let the second rise go too long. If your kitchen is very warm (80°F), the second rise can be complete in 20 minutes.

Baking

Put ½ cup water in a measuring cup. (I boil the water to generate a maximum amount of steam, but if you do this be careful!)

Remove the towels from under the parchment paper and carefully slide the paper with the loaves onto a cutting board or flour-dusted overturned baking sheet. Dust the top of the loaves very lightly with flour. (If you used a *couche*, carefully lift the loaves and turn them over, so the seam is down. Place them on parchment paper on the cutting board.) Use a dough scraper to gently adjust the loaves and straighten them out.

Make four or five cuts on the top of the loaf with a razor blade,

¼ inch deep, running lengthwise with just a slight bias over the midline of the dough. A swift slash at a sharp 20-degree angle works best.

Lift the cutting board and slide the parchment paper with the baguettes onto the hot baking stone. Shut the oven door. Open the door, and carefully pour the water onto the baking sheet. Be very cautious if using boiling water. Shut the door. Do not open the oven again while baking.

Check the baguettes after 20 minutes. They should be dark brown and crusty. If pale, continue baking for another 1 to 2 minutes. Remove the loaves and let them cool on a rack for 20 minutes before eating. They are best eaten within 4 hours. If eating dinner at seven P.M., I aim to have the baguettes come out of the oven between five and six P.M., as long as it doesn't interfere with cooking dinner.

While the baguettes are baking, form the remaining dough into loaves or leave the dough in the refrigerator for up to 24 hours and make fresh loaves the following day. They will be slightly more sour and chewy. If you are not going to eat the baguettes on the day you make them, wrap them in a plastic bag and freeze them. Let them defrost at room temperature, then crisp up the loaves in a 400°F (205°C) oven for about 5 minutes. Eat immediately.

CHAPTER 2

Culturing Wild Leaven in My Kitchen

n a fluorescent-lit kitchen, a baker takes a small, golf-ball-size piece of dough from a plastic container. Maybe he calls it "mother," "starter," "sourdough," or "*levain*." He plops it into another larger container sitting on a scale, dumps in white or whole wheat or rye flour, pours in tepid water, and mixes it vigorously with his hands. Then he covers the container and puts this mixture on a shelf. When he returns several hours later, the substance is bubbling, and has risen to two to three times its original size. When he removes the cover, a pungent alcoholic smell hits his nostrils. This lively mixture, made with the flour, water, and the invisible organisms residing in the small doughy inoculator, is a wild leaven, more commonly known as sourdough starter. When this now bubbly ferment is added to dough, it causes the loaf to rise, but it's also responsible for the tang of a bread, its milky soft taste, the chewiness of the crumb, even the caramel-like richness of the crust. Wild yeast and bacteria—the organisms fermenting in sourdough—make this possible.

When I started baking, sourdough caught my fascination almost immediately. I wanted to grab these organisms that seemed to be present in the very air I breathed and conjure up a loaf of bread. But "grabbing" these organisms in the air turned out to be one of the many myths associated with the substance. Sourdough is a bit like magic, because you keep this living substance active with regular feedings of flour and water, yet because the microscopic-level work can't be seen by the eye, it's also subject to a lot of rumor and tall kitchen tales. The simplicity of the substance, brought alive on a kitchen counter by a plethora of wild organisms, feels so unlike packages of commercial baker's yeast, which contain just one strain of industrially manufactured fungi. When I began baking many years ago, sourdough felt raw and elemental, and actually it still does, many years later.

Once you start down this path of baking with natural leaven, a fascination takes hold. But it was a challenge to get it right in the early stages. I was attempting among the oldest of grain fermentation methods, one that dated back at least to Egyptian antiquity, if not the Babylonians before them. Because commercial baker's yeast was not invented until the mid-nineteenth century, sourdough, along with beer and wine yeasts, was the main fermentation agent in bread for thousands of years. But the difficulty I encountered wasn't unusual, considering sourdough had even escaped the talents of James Beard, a towering figure for my parents' generation. In his 1973 bestseller *Beard on Bread*, he called the method "overrated" and "fickle," and gave instructions for making a sourdough starter that wouldn't be recognized today. Bakers had relied on commercial yeast for so long that they had nearly forgotten sourdough. It took another decade for a generation to rediscover traditional methods.

By the time I mixed my first sourdough starter in the late 1990s, the artisan bread movement was well under way. Bakers had traveled to Europe, tasted Poilâne's famous *miche*, and studied the sourdough method with less prejudice than Beard. It was these bakers who began writing books read by people like me. Gradually the method of making sourdough bread—which is highly reliable, if you stick with it—spread. Now Google "sourdough recipe" and you get more than 4.5 million hits. Still, many baking books ignore sourdough at the outset and start off with simple bread recipes with store-bought baker's yeast. It's easier, after all. But this advice usually goes unheeded, especially for a generation obsessed with full sour pickles, kimchi, home brew, and kombucha. This is how it went with me. If I couldn't make a baguette, then at least I was going to make a proper sourdough, whether I knew how or not.

What I eventually realized was that sourdough is actually more forgiving than commercial yeast, precisely because it ferments at a more leisurely pace. There's less opportunity to screw up. But that's not really true for the beginner, who faces a series of tough judgment calls. He can under- or overferment the sourdough, bake the loaf too soon, when it hasn't risen enough, or bake it too late, when it has lost its internal stretchiness and just kind of lies dormant in the oven, with none of the "oven spring" you should expect in the first several minutes of baking. All of these were rookie mistakes, but I lived through them content that one day I would actually create a decent bread with the four elements: flour, water, salt, and a "starter" culture. Well, that and the most important ingredient: time.

When I mixed my first batch of sourdough, I kept it in a plastic pint container on top of the refrigerator, where it was warm, but occasionally it would burst through the lid and spill out. It was the price of a loaf in our household.

I was following a recipe from Daniel Leader's *Bread Alone*. Leader relies on a minute amount of packaged yeast to begin his sourdough starter, fermenting it with flour and water. You discard part of the mixture each day, then add fresh flour and water to the remainder—literally "feeding" the organisms that live in the slurry. Eventually, over many feedings, wild yeast and bacteria take up residence, multiply, and turn this once hospitable environment into such a tangy acidic soup that the industrial yeast can no longer tolerate it, so they die off. It's natural selection at work on your kitchen counter. Now, many bakers might think it would border on sacrilege to launch a natural starter with commercial yeast, because it's unnecessary. All you need to really start a culture is flour and water. Eventually, it ferments. True, but I've tried many methods and for a novice, Leader's was the easiest. Of course, I, too, had a nagging sense that I was somehow "cheating" by propagating my starter with packaged yeast, which wasn't available to any pre-nineteenth-century baker.

From there, I moved on to a method by Nancy Silverton, the Los Angeles pastry chef who started La Brea Bakery. I had a special fondness for Silverton's book *Breads from the La Brea Bakery*, which explored many facets of sourdough. But I was also attracted by her story. Silverton had opened La Brea Bakery in a small store right next to Campanile, the celebrated Los Angeles restaurant she cofounded. The place proved so popular that Silverton and her team—led by a savvy businessman, Manfred Krankl—grew tiny La Brea Bakery into a large outfit, first by hiring a team of bakers and delivering wholesale bread around the city. Then later, seeking to enter more distant markets, La Brea opened a largely automated bread factory. By the time I profiled the company, for a business magazine no less, La Brea Bakery had adapted a Japanese industrial machine to shape loaves in the giant facility out in the Sacramento Valley. The bread dough would pour from voluminous mixers into the stainless steel forming machine. From here, the loaves traveled down a production line onto an Italian-made spiral conveyor belt, almost a story tall. After an eight-hour fermentation, while slowly circling around, the loaves entered a long German tunnel oven where they were partially baked. One of the few workers on hand slashed every loaf with a razor before it went into the oven to keep the artisanal look. At the end of the process, the semibaked bread was flash frozen, then packaged for delivery so that it could be "baked fresh" in its final location. Sales had topped $50 million.

And the surprising thing was that the bread was actually quite good, underscoring how sourdough and a long fermentation can lead to surprising results even for frozen, industrialized, "artisan" loaves. La Brea Bakery was a success and eventually sold for tens of millions of dollars—a classic American entrepreneurial story built on the sourdough loaves Silverton had perfected in her tiny bakery.

When I visited Los Angeles to profile the bakery in 2001, I recall sitting at the bar at Campanile one night during its weekly sandwich night, as Silverton held court, creating and dispatching inventive sandwiches from a panini press. I was partial to the grilled tuna, with braised leeks and aioli on a thick slice of sourdough country bread. It suited the bar brilliantly, since the crowded area was more like a casual party than a restaurant meal. But Silverton admitted to me that bread lost its meaning when it was out of her hands, which it clearly was at the La Brea factory. At Campanile, the bread was made by actual bakers in the local, wholesale bakery operation, where there were no robotic shaping lines, no tunnel ovens or frozen bread. Just bakers crafting great bread that eventually ended up in my panini sandwich. Bread could go in any number of directions, but I knew which I wanted, and I assumed she did, too.

In a television segment on *Baking with Julia*—Julia Child's late-1990s show that featured many renowned bakers—Silverton explained how she made the starter that launched the company. She wrapped a pound of purple grapes in cheesecloth, bashing them to release the juices, then submerged the grapes into a flour-and-water mixture and left it alone for a week. "It smelled awful, looked awful, and I'd throw it away. I did this a couple of times until I had the patience to let the starter run the course of the week," she said. After two days, the substance looked just as it did when she mixed it. After four days it had a "cheese-like smell, not too pleasant." After six days, she discarded most of the grape, flour, and water concoction, then fed it with fresh flour and water. Eight hours later the leaven had doubled in size.

Was the initial fermentation sparked by the flour? The grapes? Or a combination of both? I didn't know, but when I tried the version she laid out in her book, it worked. The only quibble: Silverton called for copious amounts of flour to feed the starter, which was unnecessary. More than one billion bacteria cells and 10 million wild yeast cells can be found in a pea-size gram of sourdough, so you don't need much to fuel a new batch.

I always kept a starter on hand, but unlike others who like to nurture the original creation for years and then brag about its longevity, I made new ones just for fun. Over the years, I've fermented raisins, then mixed the raisin-wine water with flour. I've mixed honey with rye flour, an especially robust medium for fermentation,

A container of freshly made sourdough, with feeding notes

as recommended by Jeffrey Hamelman in his seminal work *Bread*. Many starter recipes call for honey, which shouldn't be surprising, because yeast feeds on sugar. But honey has other attributes that can jump-start a sourdough starter, including a minute amount of wild yeast adept at fermenting carbohydrates. Bees also harbor beneficial bacteria in their abdomens, where floral nectar is stored before bees return to the hive. This bacteria acts as an antibiotic on undesirable organisms, helping a young sourdough starter. Honey is also acidic, which encourages the growth of wild yeast. That's all a longwinded way of saying that honey seems to work when you want to launch a starter—but use raw honey, not the pasteurized stuff.

I've soaked figs and fermented them with flour, simply because I like figs. I've poured hot water over wheat bran, then used this bran tea to make sourdough starter. This works because arabinoxylan—the sugars that reside in bran cellulose—pump up the acidity in the medium and increase the metabolism of sourdough microbes. Minerals in bran also promote fermentation. I've sprouted barley in a three-day process in which you keep the grains damp until a little sprout appears, then dry them in a very low oven and grind them into barley malt; add a pinch to flour to energize a fermentation or darken a loaf. I've pounded whole wheat grains, then used this coarse flour to begin a starter, because the minerals and enzymes in freshly ground whole wheat flour make an especially active fermentation medium. I've also added sourdough to wort—the liquid that eventually is fermented into beer—and then made bread with this high-octane starter. I would recommend trying any and all of these methods. I found I've ended up with powerful leavens after each of these ferments matures—and also achieved subtle differences in the flavor profile.

. . . . .

This multitude of methods shouldn't be too surprising, considering how many foods are actually fermented—from soy sauce to sauerkraut. When someone asks me what's the best way to make a sourdough starter, I think of Pliny the Elder, who wrote about various methods in his encyclopedic *Natural History* in the first century A.D. What he recorded aren't "recipes" but descriptions of a multitude of ways to ferment grains common in the baking rooms of Rome at the dawn of recorded history. When it comes to sourdough, Pliny shows we have nothing on the Romans.

Pliny, for example, said that millet made the best sourdough when mixed with the three-day-old juice of freshly crushed grapes—known as "grape must." This doesn't seem too far off from Silverton's approach, though she used wheat instead of millet. Millet is also promising since it has a rich history of fermentation: millet wine has been found in Chinese tombs of the Xia and Shang dynasties, predating Pliny by at least a millennium. Pliny also says to soak wheat bran with white wine must for three days, then dry it in the sun and shape it into small cakes. To use it as a leavening agent, soak the cakes in water, heat the mixture with spelt flour, then knead them into the dough. "It is generally thought that this is the best method of making bread," he says. He also called for grapes "at the time of vintage," a telling piece of advice, as we shall see.

He describes yet another leaven made with barley and water, formed into cakes and then baked "till they turn reddish brown. When this is done, the cakes are shut close in vessels, until they turn quite sour." To use them as a leavening agent, they are steeped in water. But the most common method, he tells us, was to boil flour, water, and salt until it formed a porridge; it was then left to sit until it turned into sourdough. As a final aside, he notes that bakers "make use of a little of the dough that has been kept from the day before"—a common method still used today and known as *pâte fermentée*, or fermented dough. Bakers save a bit of dough for the next day's mix to enhance the flavor of the bread.

When I discussed these methods with Andrew Ross, a cereal scientist and avid baker at Oregon State University, he mentioned boiling was advantageous because it breaks open the starch in the grain, freeing sugars for yeast and bacteria to feast upon. Pliny's instructions "should make a particularly active starter," he said.

But Pliny's description raises another question, too, about the presence of grapes in so many of these recipes. As it turns out, *Saccharomyces cerevisiae*, the ubiquitous species of yeast used in baking, brewing, and wine making, is naturally found on grapes. But not just any grapes. Pristine grapes tend to have very little wild yeast on them, yet on about a quarter of grapes with ruptured skins the yeast shows up. One recently investigated vector for this yeast was wasps, especially queens, which harbor yeast in their intestines during the dormant winter and then spread them to their progeny the following year. The wasps peck at the ripe fruit in the summer, transferring yeast to the grapes when they pierce the fruit's skin. One study, which investigated wasps in Tuscany, found that their intestinal yeast varied seasonally, but *Saccharomyces cerevisiae* was most prevalent right at the time of the grape harvest. This gives a new meaning to seasonality, for not only was the fruit ripe for wine making, but so, too, were the populations of wasp gut yeast that could infect the grapes. The yeast found in the wasps' innards also matched the strains found in Tuscan wine and in baker's yeast. So, the wasps, grapes, bread, and wine of Tuscany were part of a singular yeast ecology that varied seasonally. No wonder Pliny specified "grapes at the time of harvest." The key, though, is to seek out ripe grapes with punctured or split skins, because each fruit can add between 10 million and 100 million organisms to a starter.

. . . . .

A t its most basic level, what baking does—what all grain fermentation does—is to rely on single-cell organisms to hack the seed's built-in process of germination and growth. By doing so, the seed is transformed and becomes food for us, rather than a plant.

Here's how it works. The seed has three components: the starchy endosperm; the oil- and vitamin-rich germ, which is where the embryo of the plant springs to life; and the nutritious and fibrous bran coating, which protects the seed. When the kernel becomes wet, hormones awaken and trigger the process of growth. Amylase enzymes located in the outermost layer of the endosperm, called the aleurone, come alive. They flow through the endosperm and begin to break down starch, a polysaccharide, made of long chains of sugar molecules, into shorter chains that can feed the plant embryo. Protease enzymes do the same thing to proteins, creating smaller chains of amino acids, so they, too, can feed the germinating plant. In this way, the seed offers a complete life-giving package. It contains its own protective casing (the bran), a backpack of high-energy food (the endosperm), an enzyme-rich food processing facility (the aleurone), and the plant embryo which springs to life (the germ). All this processing facility needs to get going is water and warmth. If the seed has all of these things, you get a wheat plant.

Bread baking subverts, or hijacks, this entire life process. Because when bakers make dough, they trigger the same chain of events: water activates amylase enzymes in the flour, which then flow through the viscous substance to reach the starch, breaking it into smaller chains of sugars. These sugars then feed the yeast or sourdough that the baker also adds to the mix. Malted barley, which is rich in amylase, helps this process along, which is why flours are often spiked with a judicious amount of the substance. Saliva, which contains ptyalin, an amylase enzyme, does the same thing, which is why native peoples from Asia to Africa to the Americas masticated grains and spit them into a bowl to spur fermentation.

These days, however, malted barley is a sufficient source of amylase, so there's no need to chew and spit unless you're so inclined.

With sugar levels rising in the dough, yeast release their own suite of enzymes to help convert the starch to sugar. The yeast initially consume oxygen in the dough, which is why a dough whipped up in a high-speed mixer will ferment so quickly. After taking in oxygen, the yeast cells will exhale carbon dioxide gas and sweat out water in a process of aerobic respiration, not unlike what you do when you go for a jog. But when the oxygen runs out, as it soon does, the yeast do not die as you would on your oxygen-deprived run. Instead, the yeast begin a process of anaerobic fermentation, continuing to process sugar without the fuel of oxygen. This fermentation process causes the yeast to burp carbon dioxide gas and emit ethanol alcohol, which not only allows the dough to rise but creates unique flavor compounds in the bread. Ethanol is also toxic to many species of bacteria that might compete with the yeast for these sugars.

Saccharomyces cerevisiae—the same yeast species found in the guts of Tuscan wasps—is particularly adept at this sugar-eating-carbon-dioxide-belching activity, which is why it has been employed as a fermenting agent for so long. Chinese wine making dates back more than nine thousand years; evidence of fermented beverages appears in Iran about six thousand years ago. Over many millennia, this yeast species was selected by humans and domesticated for fermentation. Recently, 651 variants of *Saccharomyces cerevisiae* were genetically mapped, revealing their relationship on a vast family tree (the parentage of French champagne yeast wasn't too distant from Sicilian bread yeast). Aside from these domesticated strains, *Saccharomyces cerevisiae* also live in the wild, found in everything from rotting grapes to the bark of oak trees. Yeasts—a fungi—are actually ubiquitous, with more than 1,500 species identified thus far with more genetic diversity than all the vertebrate species in the world. At least 23 yeast species have been found in various sourdough starters. *Saccharomyces cerevisiae* is the most common, though usually one or two others, such as *Candida humilis*, take up residence as well.

The reliance on these yeasts to ferment foods dates back to prehistoric—even to prehuman—times, since animals ranging from birds to elephants have been spotted eating fermented fruit and then getting drunk. Hence, the "drunken monkey hypothesis," which posits that we got our taste for alcohol from ancestral chimps who have been observed imbibing the fermented-fruit equivalent of two bottles of wine in twenty minutes and then staggering around. With this deep biological bias for drink, it's a short jump from chimps and rotten fruit to wine making, and from there to beer, which has the advantage of using a dried store of grains rather than ripe seasonal fruit. A long-lasting stash of dried barley berries meant our ancestors living in the Middle East could make an alcoholic beverage any time of the year, not just when grapes were ripe. Beer as opposed to wine, though, has a number of disadvantages: grains, specifically barley, must be sprouted and malted, or at least masticated and spit to stimulate enzymes that will turn carbohydrates into simple sugars. And that's much harder than picking ripe fruit, dropping it in an earthen vessel, mashing it with honey (which also contains wild yeast), and waiting, which is why many archeologists think that wine came first.

But if wine came before beer, the anthropologist Sol Katz, professor emeritus at the University of Pennsylvania, told me he thought beer came before bread. "A sprouted grain is easy to discover," Katz told me. "The grains get wet, they sprout, you eat them, and they taste sweet. The moment you detect sweetness, you connect it with the fermentation of fruit." Making the leap to beer would probably have been easier than taking the additional steps of grinding the grain, fermenting it, and then cooking it over fire, in

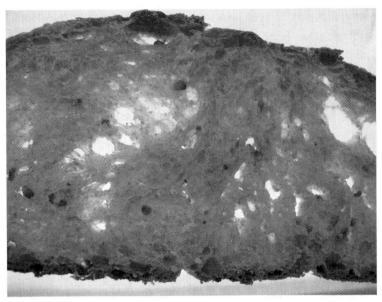

~ Bread made with a beer starter and "spent grains"
from the beer-making process

a form of bread. Plus the grain in question was barley, which was among the earliest wild cereals gathered at the dawn of agriculture. Although much of the evidence has been lost to time, archeologists have found chemical traces of barley beer in a jug from a site in western Iran dating from six thousand years ago. Another religious site in southwestern Turkey where wild grain was consumed might push the beer-making date back to more than eleven thousand years ago. But while the Middle East is often thought of as the birthplace of viniculture, it wasn't likely the first. Rice and honey mead, along with wild grapes and hawthorn fruit, were fermented in China around nine thousand years ago in the Yellow River valley.

Beer versus bread does become something of a chicken-and-egg problem, but whatever the progression, fermentation was one of the oldest food-processing technologies. As the archeologist Patrick

McGovern tells us in *Uncorking the Past*, yeast was employed for making wine since before the dawn of agriculture. Beer and bread probably weren't too far behind.

With sourdough, though, the story gets more complex because yeast don't work alone but rather in tandem with lactic acid bacteria (*Lactobacilli*), a family of organisms that can survive and even thrive in the alcohol-rich and highly acidic environment that the yeast produces. These bacteria create a range of sharp and mild acids that influence the taste of the loaf, the texture of the interior crumb, the appearance of the crust, and the loaf's longevity, since they delay staling. In a marvelous relationship, the yeast and bacteria work together, for the yeast converts starch into the type of sugars that the bacteria can digest. The bacteria also expel carbon dioxide gas, helping the loaf to rise. Debra Wink, a home baker in Pittsburgh with a background in microbiology, explained to me that these organisms don't appear all of a sudden. The starter's ecology evolves, with one set of organisms appearing only to be supplanted by another as the culture matures and acidifies. To create an acidic niche for the most beneficial organisms in a sourdough starter, she uses pineapple juice to help the process along, though any citrus or even crushed vitamin C will lower the pH enough to achieve the effect. But, as with grapes, I've found this isn't absolutely necessary.

While yeast may be spread by wasps, lactic acid bacteria are also found in many places: in the mouth, in the digestive tract, on fruits and vegetables, in feces, and in compost piles. But they are not floating around "in the air," as I've also heard so often from bakers, and which I believed for years. Neither yeast nor bacteria survive long in open air, which is why it's unlikely that a traipsing bacteria or yeast cell will blow into your kitchen and inoculate your infant batch of sourdough starter. These organisms need to travel on some kind of agent—saliva, juice, insects, skin, fruit—but eventually they can become established in the microclimate of a bakery, or even brewery, and then, yes, they can be found in the air. But the science is clear: they aren't in your kitchen at the outset.

Scientists are just starting to tease out the origins of these microscopic cells, and they are finding strong evidence that they originate in the bowels of various animals. From there, they migrate into flour or dough. One study found that *Lactobacillus reuteri* in a rye sourdough matched a strain found in the entrails of rodents. Another species in wheat sourdough was identical to one found in the human intestine. Still other strains mirrored those found in the vagina. (This gives new context to the role of the seventeenth-century French *geindre*, mounting the dough in a fetid basement baking room as he kneaded the mass, sweating and sputtering and inoculating the substance with his various effusions. Maybe this made for a lively fermentation.) But lactobacilli are far more prevalent in the viscera of pigs, mice, chickens, and rats than in humans. Michael Gänzle, an authority on the science of sourdough at the University of Alberta in Canada, who coauthored the groundbreaking study on the intestinal origin of lactobacilli, told me that rodents likely infect the grain at the farm, mill, or bakery. Or they might arise, as one paper delicately put it, from "fecal contamination in the sourdough production environment."

Insects may also play a key role. In a South African study, thirty species of lactic acid bacteria were isolated from the guts of fruit flies, including those bacteria commonly found in sourdough starters. When I first heard about this study, it suddenly hit me that this may be the reason that fruit flies congregate above the starter bubbling away on my kitchen counter. They love the stuff. I actually created a fruit fly trap by putting ripe sourdough in a plastic container, covering it with plastic wrap and punching holes in the top. The fruit flies dive in like kamikazes and then perish. The reason: fruit flies lay their eggs when they smell ethanol from a fermented substance, for it signals that their larvae will have access to a complete diet of sugars, high-protein yeast, and even alcohol, for survival. Maybe they were the source of the bacteria in my sourdough. But when I put it to Gänzle, he told me that this hasn't been studied enough to get a definitive answer.

Sadly, these microbiologists destroyed a myth that I and so many bakers had accepted for so long: the idea that sourdough reflects a particular region. *Lactobacillus sanfranciscensis*, first discovered in 1971, for example, was long thought to be unique to San Francisco and gave the city's sourdough bread its tangy flavor. It's a nice story but the species has now been found globally and is among the most prevalent type of *Lactobacillus* in sourdough. Interestingly, it hasn't yet been found anywhere else in nature, aside from sourdough and the guts of South African fruit flies.

Ultimately, the bacteria that do take up residence in sourdough reflect the ecology of the substance. This, in turn, is determined by the amount of water in the starter, the frequency of refreshment, the ambient temperature, the type of flour, and how much starter is used to rebuild a new batch. Change these factors and the microbiota within the mix might change as well. Feed the leaven at a temperature between, say, 68°F and 80°F (20°C to 27°C), once or twice daily, and odds are about one in four that you will eventually get *Lactobacillus sanfranciscensis* in your starter. But if, like industrial makers of sourdough, you keep the temperature of your leaven at 100°F (38°C) and feed it every few days, far more acid-tolerant bacteria will arrive, such as *Lactobacillus reuteri*.

I've learned to manipulate sourdoughs to work with various flours, and I now believe that the starter has more influence on the flavor of the bread than the flour itself. That said, the type of flour used to feed the starter will affect the bread's taste as well. If you mix the sourdough with rye, it will taste more earthy and less grassy than wheat. If you mix the starter so it resembles a stiff ball, and keep it at a rather cool temperature of around 67°F (19°C), it will develop a tangy edge. That's because the bacteria producing the sour-tasting acetic acid will dominate in a cooler, stiffer culture. Produce a leaven that resembles pancake batter and ferment it at 80°F (27°C) and you will instead favor the production of lactic acid, which resembles the rounder notes of yogurt. The most extreme example I've encountered is a German Detmolder rye sourdough described in Jeffrey Hamelman's book *Bread*. The sourdough is fermented and refreshed at three different temperatures for varied lengths of time to influence the taste of the final loaf. There's no need to go to these extremes—you'd need a temperature-controlled cabinet to achieve such Prussian precision in making a sourdough culture—but it does help illuminate what a bit of flour, water, organisms, and fermentation can achieve. Whatever the method, if the starter is fed regularly and maintained at a consistent temperature,

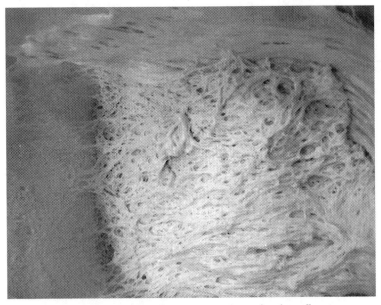

Ripe sourdough starter, made with white flour

the microbes will likely remain consistent, too. That is why scientists have found highly stable bacterial cultures when looking at bakeries' sourdough starters.

But the biota in my sourdough will probably not match yours, even if I gave you a bit of my starter to begin with and you lived down the block. So far, more than fifty-five species of *Lactobacillus* have been identified in sourdoughs, yet a study of nineteen Italian sourdough cultures showed that each was unique—that is, none shared the precise same mix of organisms. Another study found that cultures can even change when moved from one setting to another. Of course, this tends to undermine the romantic notion of keeping a culture alive for years, decades, even centuries, and passing it on, so that it spreads out, multiplies, but maintains its original essence. Bakers have relied on sourdough since antiquity and it's taken on mythic status. "Here, take some of my culture that has been kept alive for 250 years," someone might say, which is a lovely but meaningless gesture. A culture can be nurtured this way, but unless all the conditions mirror the original, it is unlikely to harbor the same combination of yeast and bacteria. Nature loves diversity, whether we like it or not.

Several years ago, I had the chance to meet New York baker Jim Lahey (the guy behind no-knead bread). I coveted the loaves he made at Sullivan Street Bakery and their light, airy quality. I would just rip off a piece and chew it as I walked down the street. The bread had an unforgettable texture and taste. When I met him, a few years after I first discovered the bread, I brought along a loaf for him to critique. This was in the days when my own starter, I realize, was rather weak and the loaves were dense, but he complimented me. When we walked through his baking room, I asked if he would share some of his sourdough—a request I've made to a number of bakers over the years. Like all the rest, he didn't hesitate. He reached into a bin and pulled out a golf-ball-size piece of sourdough, putting it into a pint container. He mentioned that it had originally come from Italy.

I took it home on the train and dutifully kept the starter alive for a couple of years, thinking that I was tapping into some secret colony of Italian microorganisms. I found, however, that it didn't perform any differently than other sourdough cultures I had made. I now realize that within a couple of weeks it had probably adapted to my kitchen microclimate and feeding schedule, picking up whatever wild yeast and lactic acid bacteria were already in residence because I baked frequently with sourdough. They probably beat out the original Italian relatives in the starter, or more likely, the pushy New Yorkers who had already displaced the Italians. The starter wasn't really the point, though, when it came to the light, airy quality I coveted in his breads. As I later learned (practice, practice), his bread had more to do with fermentation (using commercial yeast), hydration (a lot of water), and fabrication (gentle handling of a very viscous dough) than it did with the starter. Or, at least, that's what I concluded when I tried to reverse-engineer the bread.

So let's toss aside the myths about sourdough starters: that only San Francisco sourdough can be made in San Francisco; that you can nurture a culture from somewhere else that dates back two hundred years without changing it; that if your two-hundred-year-old starter dies, you will never get it back (there's a good chance the organisms that repopulate the new starter will turn out to be the same as before, all else being equal). Or that all the sourdough methods I tried worked because they were good methods (they probably were, but they might also have worked because wild yeast and bacteria were probably thriving in my kitchen since I bake with sourdough regularly). Starters are actually hyperlocal, with an ecology influenced by the hand of the baker, this farmer of microorganisms, and his particular feeding regime. And isn't that ultimately what local is? Making decisions within the confines of your bioregion, even if that happens to be a slurry of flour and water sitting on your kitchen counter?

In the early days of baking, however, I understood none of this. I just knew that if I took a quarter cup of starter out of the refrigerator and mixed it with warm water and flour, it would rise after eight hours or so. If I hadn't baked with the substance for a week or more, I'd feed it twice, or even three times, before I mixed the dough. By the end of that feeding schedule, I could tell the difference. The starter was more lively, it bubbled and made the difference between a lofty loaf and a dense one. I learned these lessons only by practice and observation, and in doing so, I generally veered away from what I was reading in books. In the end, the process led me to my house loaf: a mixture of white flour, whole wheat, and rye that might be called *pain de campagne* and has had a presence on our table for more than a decade.

It's not original, but it was clearly my bread, with a taste and texture that arises from those organisms that I've learned to cultivate so well. But this loaf had a rich lineage, a long line of influence, not only from the books of people like Nancy Silverton and Dan Leader, who have built businesses on the backs of their humble sourdough starters, but from a movement of artisan bakers. At some point, I knew I had to visit them and learn where my bread came from.

Sourdough Starter

⌒ Feeding a sourdough starter with
white and whole wheat flours and water

I actually dislike the word *sourdough*, because it adds a note of confusion, implying that the bread will be sour, or acidic. It can be, but I've had many "sourdough" breads that don't have any apparent acidity and instead exhibit rounder, deeper flavor notes of lactic acid, which I feel brings out the inherent sweetness in the grain. That's what I aim for in my starter culture.

To make a sourdough starter, remember, you are a farmer, not a cook! You are creating the conditions for your microscopic animals to live happily. If you keep that in mind, the process will go a little more smoothly. I use organic whole rye flour because it's an especially active medium for fermentation. It has higher levels of sugar than wheat to feed wild yeasts; it also has more amylase enzymes to break down starch and create yet even more sources of sugar for these tiny organisms. I also use raw (unpasteurized) honey as a nod to Pliny the Elder and because it's the most concentrated source of natural sugar found in nature. Plus the raw form contains wild yeast. One word of warning: Avoid the use of glass jars, unless you cover them loosely. If sealed, they can explode while fermenting.

Tools
    An 8- or 16-ounce plastic or ceramic container with lid
    Table spoon

Sourdough Starter Ingredients
    Organic whole rye flour
    Raw honey
    Filtered or spring water (so bacteria-killing chlorine is
        removed)

Mix 3 tablespoons (30 grams) lukewarm water (about 80° to 90°F) with 1 teaspoon raw honey. Add 3 tablespoons (20 grams) rye flour and let this sit in a covered container for 1 to 2 days. The amount of time depends on the ambient temperature. If your kitchen is cool, the organisms will be less active and you'll need more time. Ideally keep it at around 75°F (24°C). An oven with the light or pilot light on works well.

If you can maintain an ambient temperature of 75°F (24°C), this first phase will probably take a day, which would be the case on your kitchen counter in the summer. If you simply ferment it in a cold kitchen in winter, it will likely take two days. When you pass by the starter, give it a mix with a spoon every now and again: your animals like oxygen in the initial stages. If they are happy, you will begin to see tiny bubbles forming on the surface of the starter as the organisms belch out carbon dioxide. This should occur after 1 or 2 days.

At this point, add 3 tablespoons of rye flour, 3 tablespoons of water around 75°F (24°C), and 1 teaspoon of honey. Let it sit for 24 hours. Stir occasionally.

Discard half the starter. Add 3 tablespoons of rye, 3 tablespoons of water, and 1 teaspoon of honey.

Repeat this last step every 24 hours until the starter is bubbly and begins to rise noticeably. Once that happens, usually by day 5 or 6, you can stop adding the honey. The starter might weaken at that point (you've removed its sugar fix, after all), but proceed anyway. It will come alive again. When the mixture doubles in volume within 12 hours, you can think about making bread.

Here's the test to see if the starter is ready, after it has risen: carefully remove a bit of it (a tablespoon will do) and place it in a bowl of warm water. If it floats to the surface within a couple of minutes, you've got an active starter. If it sinks like a stone and remains under water, let the starter mature for another hour and try again.

This whole process might take a week or more, especially in the winter. With my kitchen hovering around 65°F (18°C), it took me two weeks to achieve a predictable starter, with feedings every one to two days. Once the starter is bubbly and active, you can switch to whole wheat, or a mixture of equal parts white and whole wheat flour, in place of the rye. You can also increase the volume by using, say, 20 grams of the mature starter and then feeding it with 100 grams flour and 100 grams water.

Troubleshooting

You might start out and get bubbles, but by day 2 or 3 it just looks dead. You have a few options:

First, keep going, and eventually the yeast and bacteria will reappear and the starter will rise. An active, robust culture is nearly impossible to kill, even if you do leave it around on the kitchen counter for a few days. So if you forget to feed it for a couple of days, don't throw it out—just soldier on and see what happens.

Second, you can replace the water with an equal amount of

pineapple or apple juice to raise the acidity level, which creates a favorable environment for wild yeast.

Third, start over. If you do decide to start over, try to acidify the starter by using juice in place of water or a pinch of vitamin C powder with the water for the first 3 days.

Fourth, use a pinch of commercial yeast (really, just a pinch between your thumb and forefinger) to jump-start your sourdough. Although it might feel like "cheating," there's really nothing wrong with this method. Once your starter becomes sufficiently acidic over time, the wild yeast and bacteria will outcompete the commercial yeast and your starter will be much the same as if you started out without it.

If all else fails, here is a guaranteed method: Ask for a knob of starter from a friend or local artisan baker (it helps to mention how wonderful their breads are). You might also get a few tips along the way. Feed it once or twice daily, by taking 20 grams of the starter and adding 100 grams flour and 100 grams water and leaving it, ideally at around 75°F (24°C) for about 6 to 8 hours. Refrigerate it an hour or two after feeding if you're not going to use it within the next day. If it is kept in the refrigerator for a week or longer, refresh it at least once before using it to rise bread. I often refresh it twice, just to ensure it's sufficiently strong.

Variations

I tend to reuse a very small portion of my existing starter when it's feeding time. I use 20 grams existing starter, 100 grams flour, and 75 grams water. This makes a stiff starter that rises slowly, especially in the winter. After 8 hours it can be used, and will tend to have a very mild lactic acid taste. If it's left to ferment longer, say, up to 16 hours, it will turn ever more acidic in flavor.

Chapter 3

California and the Country Loaf

I was leaving the gym on Capitol Hill one cold, wintry afternoon early in 2010 when I checked the messages on my phone. Alice Waters's office at Chez Panisse had called. "Yeah, right, who was this anyway?" I wondered, running through a list of potential pranksters in my head. It was improbable that one of the most influential restaurants in the country, run by a woman who had propelled the local foods movement, the trend toward school gardens, simple fresh cuisine, and more, would be calling me.

But when I called back, I got Waters's assistant, which was the first surprise. The second was that Waters would be hosting a charity dinner in Washington and wanted to serve my bread. Turned out the baker she'd had in mind couldn't make the event, so they had asked a chef in Washington, Barton Seaver, whom they should get. He had suggested me.

"We hear you bake the best baguette in D.C.," Waters's assistant, Sarah Weiner, said.

"Well, yeah, I won a contest," I stammered, "but, you know, I'm just a home baker. The most I've ever baked for was for Thanksgiving dinner, maybe twenty people. How many people are you talking about?"

She said they were hosting about forty people at a $500-a-plate dinner at Bob Woodward's house in Georgetown. The event was in a week. As she continued talking, I wondered whether I could actually bake that much bread, or whether I'd really want to. Up until that moment, a dozen years into my obsession, I'd baked only for my family and friends and my own curiosity; it was never meant to be anything more than that. Here was my chance to turn pro, and the first gig was with Alice Waters! "Yeah, can I get back to you on that?" I said.

The call was of course validating, even flattering, Alice being Alice. But it was not the kind of call I had been waiting for. All I had done was bake bread two or three times a week, and then begun to write about it. Even the baguette contest I participated in nearly a year earlier had more to do with putting my bread up against pros than turning pro myself. When cookbook author Joan Nathan said to me, "It's great you won, but what can you do with it?" I had no answer for her. It hadn't occurred to me to do anything at all.

But I did know of Waters's love of good bread, which almost seemed to equal her passion for a great salad. One of her earliest bakers, Steve Sullivan, had worked at Chez Panisse and went on to found Acme Bread, a notable bread company still going strong. (It was Sullivan, incidentally, who gave Nancy Silverton the idea of using grapes in her starter at La Brea Bakery.) Waters had also championed other bakers in the San Francisco Bay Area, like Chad Robertson at Tartine.

These bakers seemed part of a dynamic local bread ecology: they worked hard, trained apprentices, and in this way seeded more bakeries. Michel Suas, a baker who arrived from France in the mid-1980s and who started the San Francisco Baking Institute, injected another bout of energy by teaching many aspiring bakers. The Bay Area and nearby Marin and Sonoma counties might now be home to the richest concentration of artisan bread bakers in the nation, reaching a kind of culinary critical mass. But northern California wasn't alone. I'd found aspiring hubs along the coast in Maine, in Vermont and Massachusetts; in New York City; in Asheville, North Carolina, which in my unscientific estimation might have the highest per capita concentration of artisan bread bakers in the nation; in Portland, Seattle, and the Twin Cities and many more in places that I've yet to visit. Sadly, I wouldn't put Washington, D.C., on that list, though it does have a couple of standouts. I've found that where there is a dearth of good bread, you occasionally get a superlative baker holding up the flag, but it's rare. Mediocrity, in other words, can nurture its own culture because there aren't enough customers who demand a good loaf. The Bay Area, though, had great bakers in spades, in part thanks to Waters.

I had met a few of these bakers over the years. Their breads had little to do with San Francisco sourdough, for which the area is still known, and far more to do with what I'd call a post-sourdough movement—one that eschewed that acidic taste in bread, cultured mild-tasting *levain*, and in many cases baked in wood-fired ovens. It's an approach I've tried to master over the years—minus the wood oven. The goal is a loaf that you can rip into with your teeth, but which also has a soft, pliable interior crumb. It has a dark crust that crackles when you bite into it, and where the slashes, the *grigne*, burst open in an inviting way. This bread is imperfect but captivating, and I continue to view it as somewhat magical no matter how much I learn about the method.

I know, by now you're rolling your eyes, but the proof really is in the eating, or in the favorable comment from one of my daughter's nine-year-old friends. Breaking away from Lego to rip off a piece of a loaf, this young girl said, "Sam, I don't like bread. But I like your bread." She was eating a sourdough country loaf that had been fermented overnight—a simple, rustic bread that riffed on the West Coast tradition I'd picked up from bakers. Over the course of a couple of years, after my baguette expeditions and that unexpected call from Waters, I visited many of these bakers for the first time.

Della Fattoria, in Petaluma about an hour north of San Francisco, is one of these bakeries. It's known for its dark, Italian sourdough loaves baked in two massive wood-fired ovens and then sold around the region and at the bakery's café in town. The bakery itself sits outside of town, an open-air, shedlike building next to a ranch-style house where Kathleen Weber, who founded the business with her husband, Ed, lives. Turning up their driveway one sunny morning in mid-May, I found it hard to tell that the place was a business—it felt more like a farm with one-story buildings, a garden, and a long wooden table underneath a large oak tree, where popular ranch dinners are held. In this complex, it's easy to spot the bake house, with its screen doors, old wood plank floors, and smoke curling out of the chimney.

Kathleen Weber didn't start out as a professional baker, but rather a home baker like me. She had a healthy obsession about dough and often baked loaves, bringing them to friends' homes for dinner. Her guidebook at the time was Carol Field's *The Italian Baker*, a classic that has influenced many bakers. Weber then took the short step from baking recipes out of the book to building a wood oven on her deck, with Alan Scott. At the time, he was the most influential builder of brick ovens in America and he happened to live nearby.

You know this trajectory: she bakes bread for a chef's olive oil tasting event, eventually gets an account, and before long is working day and night to fulfill orders. Her husband, Ed, would fire up the oven at dusk. She would mix the doughs at night, baking them the next day. "I was on fire," Kathleen told me over a soup and sandwich at the couple's Della Fattoria Café, also in Petaluma. "I had things just come to me. Coming home one day I had Meyer lemons and rosemary in the car and thought they would make a wonderful combination." She mixed the two in olive oil, tucked them into a sourdough bread, which was slashed open just before baking, to reveal the oil mixture—a bit of sea salt crumbled on top. When I bit into it, I got a hit of citrus, salt, olive oil, and rosemary all at once. The bread's still one of her best sellers. In the beginning, she was having a tough time meeting demand, but Michel Suas of the San Francisco Baking Institute told her, "It's a good problem to have." He sent up one of his teachers, Lionel Vatinet, another superlative French baker, now at La Farm Bakery in Durham, North Carolina, who taught her to work faster. "He would hold a stopwatch while I was shaping loaves and with each one, he would have me cut the amount of time," Weber told me. Now the bakery's much bigger, with a team of four bakers and numerous accounts. Ed Weber often can be found manning the bread stand at the Ferry Plaza Farmers Market in San Francisco on Saturdays or tinkering with the two ovens in the open-air bake shed, which long ago replaced the oven on the deck outside their house.

Monday morning wasn't terribly busy when I arrived, and I couldn't find anyone around the bakery. So I just opened the screen door and let myself in to look around. The fires were roaring in the two brick ovens that line an outside wall, the bread-baking baskets that would later hold the rising bread were all neatly arranged on shelves, and the butcher block tables where the loaves were shaped were clean and empty, ready for the day's activity. Compared with other bakeries I've visited, this had the feel of an outdoor kitchen, though the volume of loaves would rival others I saw, from Paris to San Francisco. While I was snapping pictures of the weathered, soot-marked ovens, and the fourteen-foot-long wooden peels,

Richard Hart poked his head inside. He was then the lead baker, a Brit in his mid-thirties, who had trained as a cook in three-star restaurants in London but now was tending to wood fire, dough, and handmade bread.

We said hello and he immediately began mixing the day's doughs, measuring out *levain* into plastic bins, and then adding flour and salt, talking to me as he worked. He said he had burned out on kitchens in fine dining establishments, including one of Gordon Ramsay's in London. "So the portrait of him on TV, the abusive chef, it's true to life?" I asked. "Oh, yes," he replied. "If the sous chefs were not nasty to the cooks they were fired, and I just had it with that kind of atmosphere, I had to leave, it was making me evil. I started to get angry—and I'm really mild mannered." At a friend's recommendation, Hart first took a job at the vegetable-centric restaurant Ubuntu in Napa Valley, uprooting his family from London to northern California, and working forty hours a week instead of the seventy or eighty hours he had before. "I suddenly had all this time," he said. So he began visiting Della Fattoria on his days off, curious about their sourdough bread and wood-fired ovens. "I mean, you're baking bread like they did one hundred years ago, who wouldn't be amazed?" he said. "Regardless of what it took, I had to get a job here." Within a year, he had joined the bakery staff and soon Kathleen put him in charge.

Hart had an easygoing manner, but after a few days I could also tell he was incredibly hardworking. In this business, bakers are always moving from one task to another, and Hart never stopped. By the time the rest of the bakers showed up that first morning, the pace noticeably picked up. Multiple doughs that Hart had mixed were being shaped, nestled into baskets, or slipped into linen *couches* to rise. The dying embers were swept out of the ovens, then the hearth was mopped out with a wet towel at the end of a long pole. Everyone seemed to be working at a pace just short of a jog. They plowed through hundreds of pounds of dough, shaping them quickly into round *boules*, torpedo-shaped *bâtards*, and finally baguettes. I jumped in and helped form the loaf with rosemary, lemon, and olive oil, which was spooned into a slight well in the dough. Turning it over and rounding the loaf with my hands, I stretched the skin of the dough taut with my pinkies on the underside of the loaf. The oily mixture flowed through the loaf as I continued to shape it, eventually ending up on top, visible through a translucent skin of gluten. Under Hart's watchful eye, I kept at it. The dough felt familiar, pliable, and easy to manipulate. I made a few loaves and plopped them into cloth-lined baskets to rise. Hart wasn't displeased with the outcome. Or, I should say, I didn't screw up, which is what most bakers worry about when an outsider arrives to join in, an amateur no less.

When it came time to load the loaves into the oven, a dance of

Loaves rising in a *couche* at Della Fattoria

the peels began—"somewhere between a rodeo and ballet," as Kathleen Weber described it. Hart cranked up the Beatles' *White Album* on the boom box. Several long-handled peels that could hold three or four loaves were arranged side by side on the wooden table. A baker flipped over the baskets holding the fully risen loaves onto the peels, then quickly slashed them with a razor. A second baker, holding the peel, twirled the fourteen-foot stick a quarter turn, and thrust it deep through the two-foot opening of the oven all the way to the back, releasing the loaves with a quick tug on the handle. The smaller loaves were set closer to the opening, since they would bake the fastest. With each few peel loads, the baker pulled down a metal rod from an overhead rack and sprayed hot steam into the oven, which was now clocking an extremely hot 550° to 600°F (288° to 316°C). The steam allowed the crust to remain moist and pliable, so it could spring up before it dried out and set. Once the oven was fully loaded, the spring-hinged door flopped closed and the loaves baked away in the heat.

Not twenty minutes later, the reverse march would begin: the metal oven door was flipped open and the baker tapped each loaf to see if it was done. If it was, it made an unmistakable hollow and resonant knock. The loaves were unloaded, front to back, and slipped from the peel to the steel racks that lined the edges of the room. By now it was dusk, the sky outside the screen windows turning a dark and rich red, not unlike the embers that had burned away in the oven. The brick oven baked a thick and rich crust on the bread, almost chocolate in color, others like caramel. Even though the loaves had not yet finished cooling, I tore into a polenta bread, one Hart had discarded as too dark to sell. I wouldn't normally advise this, because the crumb takes an hour to set and can be a bit tacky before then. But still, I plunged ahead, biting into the bread with steam billowing out from the crumb. The loaf tasted light, and I got a hit of the sweet corn and the dark toasted crust.

Sitting in my guest cabin on the Webers' ranch that evening, munching on samples we had baked that day, I realized that this bread was a distant echo of my hand-shaped loaves. The flavor of the loaf was very close to mine (minus the crust, that is, which benefits from the massive heat of the oven), but the production method was way beyond me. I had tried wood-fired baking a couple of times but I hadn't really learned the method, and here at Della Fattoria I could only observe—the pace was far too rapid to just jump in and man the oven. To find something closer to a scale I was used to, I turned to another baker a half hour away in Sonoma who baked bread in his backyard.

I first met Mike Zakowski at the hulking Las Vegas Convention Center in the fall of 2010, where, as a member of the American baking team, he was participating in the semifinals of a bread competition held on the edge of a massive industrial baking trade show. With two teammates—Harry Peemoeller and Jeremey Gadouas, who focused on artistic bread design and *viennoiserie*, or Viennese-style yeasted pastries, respectively—the team was jockeying to represent the United States at the 2012 World Cup of Baking, the Coupe du Monde de la Boulangerie. While American bakers are far less celebrated than glitzy chefs with their TV shows, they do far better in these competitions. They shocked the baking world when the U.S. team took gold for its bread in 1996, then won again in 1999 and 2005. Meanwhile, the United States has never placed better than sixth in the preeminent chefs' competition, the Bocuse d'Or, despite a lot of support and media attention.

Under klieg lights, with booming music, surrounded by cheering bakers and friends, Zakowski knocked out a series of rolls, baguettes, and whole grain breads with artful designs that had to meet exacting specifications—in weight, presentation, and ingredients. When it was over, the U.S. team had assured its place in Paris for March 2012.

At the party that followed, I talked with Zakowski over a beer. His white apron and chef's toque were gone, replaced by a clean T-shirt and porkpie hat. I asked if I might look him up the next time I was in northern California and maybe bake with him. It was then I learned that he was working in a quite spartan and simple way, a world away from the glitz and pressure of competition baking.

The world of baking seems to attract free spirits, but Zakowski—who calls himself The Bejkr—stands out even among them. For one, there's that unusual spelling of his business. Then there are his e-mails, announcing "fResH pAin tOdAY" (*pain* means bread in French). But even among the most committed artisan bakers, few mix their dough by hand, because of the demands of production. Nor do they work in shipping containers they've plopped in their backyards. Nor do they have massive wood-fired ovens between the shipping container and backyard vegetable patch. Zakowski had all of this—much of it hand-built without permits when I met him—on a rental property! One or two days a week, he drove to the farmers' market in Sonoma to sell his loaves, smoke billowing out of a homemade brick pizza oven hitched to the back of his vintage delivery truck.

He had given up the grind of the baking trade after nearly a decade and a half, quitting his last bakery management job in Sonoma several months before I met him. But before he left, he used the bakery's facilities to make bread on his time off, so he could get his hands back in the dough and connect with people who bought his loaves at the farmers' market. He eventually plowed his savings into the backyard bakery and went solo, pursuing competitive baking at the same time.

·　·　·　·　·

One morning the following spring, I drove up to his place in the small town of Sonoma at seven A.M. to begin baking with him. When I arrived, I could swear it wasn't a wood fire wafting from the house but marijuana. I didn't say anything. It was early, and we only exchanged a few words. Zakowski offered me some herbal tea in a quart-size glass mason jar. When I asked if he had any coffee, he said, "I can't do coffee, gets me too wired." I wish I could say the same. I hadn't had any coffee yet, so was wondering when the predictable lethargy would kick in.

We walked out the kitchen door and into the backyard, past an old giant steel mixer and the trailer-hitched pizza oven, and entered the screen door of the narrow shipping container–cum–bake house. He had bought the converted container from a company in Oakland, which had paneled the inside and cut windows and doorways into the frame. Plumbing and electrical systems had been put in and a friend had laid the terra-cotta tile floor. Wooden and metal tables lined one side. Just opposite across the narrow corridor stood a six-foot-high rack of wooden shelves where the loaves were left to rise, or "proof," before they were baked. He had sinks to wash up sheet pans and tools, bags of grains and flour bins arranged neatly under the counters, and above the work area, near the window, a line of kitchen timers along the wall, each set to time the rising of a dough. A thermometer hung alongside. This way, he had the two most important variables in bread baking under control—temperature and time.

I stood off to the side and watched Zakowski weigh the flours and sourdough, setting the ingredients into bins. All the doughs were different. There was a *pain de campagne* with blends of whole wheat and white flours, a cracked Kamut bread, again with a mix of flours and Kamut grain that he coarsely ground in a hand mill; baguettes with white flour and a bit of wheat where some of the bran from the fibrous hull of the wheat kernel had been sifted out

Mike Zakowski in front of his drying rack

(known as "sifted" or "bolted" flour), and a few others—all of them with a blend of flours to get the flavor and textural qualities he sought. He was following a printed-out spreadsheet as he went, a common practice among bakers who can easily calculate the weight of ingredients with the click of a mouse. When all the ingredients were in their respective bins, he added water and mixed them by hand. While this might sound like a lot of manual work for a day's production of bread, it actually isn't. Zakowski swirled his hand and stirred the flour, water, sourdough, and salt until they were just combined and still lumpy, a process that took maybe two to three minutes. Then he snapped the plastic lid on the bin, set the timer for twenty minutes, and moved on to the next dough, repeating the process. He was using the ingredient of time to develop the dough—just as Delmontel's bakers had in Paris. By waiting for set intervals (cleaning up in the meantime, or checking the oven), he allowed the dough to develop on its own. If you do this by hand, you also avoid having to wash a mixer. I do all of my mixing in a large stainless steel or plastic bowl, with a $1 plastic tray from IKEA flung over the top as a lid. I simply wet and then shake the water off my hands before I begin, so my hands don't get sticky and full of dough.

After the first twenty-minute rest, Zakowski removed the lid and began stretching and folding the dough, which developed the gluten's springiness—a common technique bakers use that is far gentler than mechanical mixing, or even kneading with the heel of your hand. He grabbed an edge of the dough and pulled it out, then folded it so that it landed beyond the center line of the mass. He then stretched the opposite end and folded it over the first. He repeated the process on the two sides of the dough, so four sides were folded in all, then flipped it over, so the folded edges were on the bottom. A key part of the technique is to keep the dough intact in one piece, rather than ripping the strands of gluten. The resting period was also important, because during that time, the gluten has time to relax, forming a more cohesive and plastic substance. Each time he stretched and folded, he created new and stronger bonds. At the end of the process, the dough glistened like the slightly moist surface of a balloon. Now it would rise.

Over time, strengthening gluten feels like a stretchy rubber band that grows increasingly taut. The baking term for that is *elasticity*, which occurs as gluten proteins rearrange themselves in the presence of water and connect with each other, forming longer protein chains. With dough, though, you don't want just elasticity, because then the rubber band would break apart if you pulled on it too forcefully. So bakers talk about a second quality as well, *extensibility*, which refers to the dough's ability to stretch *without* springing back to its former shape. Dough needs a mix of both these qualities to make a superlative loaf.

These attributes reflect the gluten proteins that reside in wheat itself, known as glutenin and gliadin. Glutenin proteins are made up of long chains of amino acids that create elasticity and strong bonds. Gliadin proteins account for the stretchiness because they link rather weakly with each other and with the stronger glutenin proteins. If you've ever made pizza, you can see these gluten characteristics at work. When you pound the dough and flatten it, it often contracts when you try to stretch it out. That's elasticity, and people often make the mistake of continuing to tug at the dough to stretch it out, finding that it recoils into an even tighter, smaller shape. By pulling the dough continuously, the gluten actually strengthens and heightens elasticity. At this point, the best thing to do is to let the dough sit for five or ten minutes and let the gluten relax, which allows it to become more extensible again and thus stretch out.

Once the dough is developed, the third quality bakers look for is *tolerance*, or the ability of a loaf to maintain its shape. Think of the way a loaf can rise, hold its dome, and then spring up when it hits the heat of the oven. Without tolerance, the dough will simply collapse.

While the protein level in a flour is often used as a proxy for how strong the gluten will be, it's an imperfect measure. American artisan bakers generally seek out flours that have protein levels of 11 to 11.5 percent. Stronger "bread flour" can measure as high as 13 to 14 percent. But it's not only the quantity of protein that matters, but the quality. (Spelt, for example, can exceed wheat in protein, but can't hold its shape very well because it doesn't mirror bread wheat's mix of proteins.) Millers also blend flours to achieve a high degree of consistency, and I've found many brands of unbleached all-purpose flour work well in bread making. Higher-protein "bread flour" tends to create too tight of a crumb for my liking, though it's fine for bagels, pretzels, and pizza. Ultimately, though, protein levels can't be found unless you visit the flour company's Web site, and even if you do get the number it's only a rough measure, for it doesn't tell you about the ratio of glutenin and gliadin proteins that determines the spring and stretch of the dough. For that, you need to try the flour and see how the dough feels, which is why bakers like Zakowski always have their hands in the dough. In this craft, hands become knowledgeable.

By stretching and folding the dough by hand and letting time do its work, Zakowski arrived at a mix of both strong and weaker bonds, and so his breads contained the uneven holes that bakers so often crave. In a high-speed mixer, the weaker gluten chains break apart and stronger ones form, resulting in a more uniform crumb. Industrial operations might also use flour containing bleaching agents or ascorbic acid to forge stronger gluten bonds. This is why artisan bread makers for the most part eschew highly intensive mixers and avoid the additives that are the bane of industrially produced breads. By stretching and folding, Zakowski gradually built up the elastic gluten bonds, but only to a certain point. And, of course, that point—the moment to stop—is a judgment call. It comes only by feeling the dough and, in my case, making a lot of bad bread.

When I asked to join him and shape a few baguettes, I felt a bit of tension, but he let me have a go at it. Two of my loaves made it into the mix, barely; the third came out a bit too long, so he smiled and set it aside after it was baked. In competition baking, baguettes must weigh exactly 250 grams (8.8 ounces) and measure between 55 and 60 centimeters (21.6 to 23.6 inches). The judges don't compromise on these requirements, and neither does Zakowski. He once made sixty baguettes by hand each day for a few months trying to perfect them. He got good, he told me, but his technique has since gotten better. "The biggest challenge is speed," Zakowski said, speaking of the competition. "In training, you're constantly refining the process to make the bread as quickly and as efficiently as possible with the highest quality. And it's tough because it's a lot—a lot of product."

The fire roared in Zakowski's oven, located outside the shipping container, but then gradually died down. He wrapped a bandana around his face and swept out the ashes, filling the air with dust. Then he mopped out the hearth. Once that was done, the baking was straightforward. He placed the loaves on a canvas loader, and delivered them into the oven. Then he misted the inside with a garden sprayer to create steam, which helped the loaves to spring up. Each successive batch was baked in this way, and within a couple of hours all were done. The bread cooled on gorgeous racks made from the oak wood of recycled wine barrels, then he packed them into birch plywood boxes, which like everything else in his bakery had also been handmade.

From there it was a short one-mile trip in the vintage delivery truck to the farmers' market, where Zakowski set up his bread stand and pizza oven, complete with an awning. But we had one drawback that day: it rained incessantly, keeping customers away and sales sparse. Luckily for me, it meant I got to bake several *schiacciata*—flatbreads topped with a local hard cheese and seasonal greens—in the mobile pizza oven. They were delicious, especially in the chilly wet weather, but it was still a shame that the foot traffic was so light. "I usually sell out," Zakowski told me, but not that day. With the rain still pounding, we loaded the unsold loaves back into the truck and drove home.

I t was a full year later when the Coupe du Monde de la Boulangerie was finally held at the global baking trade show EuroPain outside Paris in 2012. I made a point to show up, taking the RER commuter rail line from Paris to just outside the airport. The competition itself was held at the far end of the convention center, so I walked by booth after booth of millers, baking equipment manufacturers, bak-

Mike Zakowski displays his breads at the Coupe du Monde de la Boulangerie

eries, ingredient makers, and the like, each trying to grab your attention with a baguette, sweet pastry, or blaring music. I kept walking through the vast hall until I reached the back, where a thick crowd of onlookers milled about in front of the competing bread teams. Though bread making isn't exactly a soccer match, an announcer was on hand, droning on endlessly. Meanwhile, the baking teams worked furiously to produce their breads and pastries, which were paraded in front of the spectators and dissected and tasted by an eminent team of master bakers, clad in white coats and toques, from around the world. I caught Zakowski's eye and waved, though he barely acknowledged it as he moved at a fast pace, arranging his just-baked loaves in a beautiful display in front of the team's workspace. I didn't stick around for the entire competition, since it was difficult to make out just what was going on from a distance, but at the end of the multiday affair, the judges came up with their decision: The U.S. team placed second, just after Japan, and only losing by a few points. Taiwan came in third. It was the first time that a European team failed to win a place on the podium, signaling perhaps that French bread is no longer very French. Some of the breads were available to taste, though I couldn't manage to squeeze through the throngs to try the U.S. team's. I did snag a piece of a Japanese brioche made with green tea and citrus that was sweet, and oddly green. It stood out just like some other jaw-dropping displays at the trade show. I took a couple of modest bites. It tasted kind of weird.

A couple of years later, Zakowski was still baking on his own but he did lose his backyard bakery. The lack of permits finally did him in. He's now baking at a friend's place in Petaluma and scouting other locations for his oven and shipping container, both of which, luckily, are portable. But he's still competing, keeping one foot in the farmers' market and the other in the Paris baking competitions.

. . . . .

As for my northern California sojourn, my last stop was Tartine, located in San Francisco's Mission District and widely known for its bread, pastries, and lines out the door. I visited several times over a couple of years, making a point to stop in whenever my work took me out to the city. Chad Robertson, who bakes the bread, and his wife, Elisabeth Prueitt, who oversees the pastries, worked in France early in their careers and then set up shop in Point Reyes Station, a small town about ninety minutes north of the Bay Area, and baked out of a wood-fired oven. Robertson joined the

PHOTOGRAPH BY CHAD ROBERTSON

Tartine country loaf

ranks of similar-minded artisans—but he distinguished himself by baking alone in a tiny place with an oven built by the legendary Alan Scott, who had also made the Webers' first oven. Robertson's bread quickly gained notice locally. I actually tried it, in the late 1990s, when a friend drove me out to the small town; we stopped and picked up one of his dark, crusty loaves and a log of cheese from Cow Girl Creamery, then continued on to Tomales Bay. Around the same time, Robertson appeared on the cover of *The Bread Builders*, a classic book about bread making and wood ovens (and a must-read for bread nerds). But he still wasn't known outside the region.

Eventually, the couple moved to San Francisco, helping propel the renaissance on Eighteenth Street in the Mission District, which has become a food-centric corridor in the city, with the locavore Bi-Rite Supermarket a couple of doors down, a handmade ice cream store across the street, and the Italian restaurant Delfina just next door. They grew into a more mature operation, with a full staff and a strong emphasis on prepared food served in a storefront café. Robertson also traded the wood-fired oven for a full-scale professional baking oven, with several decks, which was more practical in the city and, he argued, baked bread that was just as good.

Once the doors opened, however, demand for the bread soon got out of hand. Robertson had to resort to preorder reservations because the loaves sold out so quickly. "People would line up and then we'd run out of bread even before they got to the counter, so we had to do something," he told me. One obvious solution would have been to bake more bread. But Robertson was limited by the oven, because pastries were baking during the day. He also wanted to avoid working at night. (The bakers began rolling in around eight A.M., which is when many other bread bakeries are nearly finished for the day.) To solve the problem of unhappy customers and lack of supply, Robertson rationed the bread rather than alter the schedule and boost output. When the loaves start coming out of the oven at five P.M., those with "reservations" are found in an orderly queue waiting for their loaf.

When I went to Tartine to meet him for the first time, I, too, lined up like all the rest to buy one of the sandwiches. I chose sliced ham and melted Gruyère on their thick-sliced country bread, which is the signature loaf made with *levain*. Luckily, the line did not take long and I also found a seat in the crowded café. My meal was delicious, the cheese melting around the crunchy and slightly assertive bread, the ham pleasantly salty, but I couldn't finish it, because it was huge. Plus, I had a tart for dessert. It was a lunchtime indulgence out of proportion to what I needed, but, hey, this was work, and I had to investigate. As I ate my meal, I kept looking to the back of the shop, where I could see the oven and the bread bakers, a few feet behind the cash register. I soon spotted Robertson, wearing a T-shirt, and with a visor on his head. When I finished eating, I went over to say hello.

We shook hands and he showed me into the back where the bread was being made—the dough laid out like circular paving stones on a wooden table, resting before it would be shaped. I realized my timing was good: I might be able to jump in and shape these loaves, too, if Robertson let me. As we snaked from one part of the bakery to another, he asked me about the bakeries I had visited and the breads I was making. We soon pulled out our phones and were showing each other pictures of our loaves. This kind of camaraderie is quite common among bakers. Although many bakers I met were introverted, and interviews at times painfully spartan, Robertson wasn't withdrawn. But he wasn't blustery either. He was friendly, curious, willing to share. He also seemed entirely relaxed, though the place was hopping.

Then again, I was a writer who had come to visit with him—not a baker looking for a job. Richard Hart, the baker at Della

Fattoria, who, it turned out, was itching to move on when I met him, told me later that he began pursuing Robertson at Tartine. "I sent him numerous e-mails," he told me, "and I didn't get one reply. So I baked him a bread, but didn't hear anything. So I baked him another bread, and another, until finally I got a reply saying he liked it." That was enough. Hart was soon working at Tartine on his day off, determined to get a job at the place the same way he had at Della Fattoria. Eventually he joined the staff. Nathan Yanko, a distance runner who was Robertson's lead baker and a master of dough, told me he simply showed up at the shop after culinary school and got a job. It was his first baking gig, which might have been part of the attraction for Robertson: Yanko didn't have anything to unlearn. There were many paths into this place.

Now, why all the fuss about Tartine bread? Well, it's very good. It has a mild *levain* flavor with a hint of acidity, open holes in the crumb, and a magnificently crackling dark crust. All of these qualities reflect the long fermentation that's central to the Tartine method. While the ovens are tied up with cakes, tarts, and pastries during the day, the bread bakers are busy mixing and shaping their loaves. Then, when the ovens finally free up late in the afternoon, the bakers remove the loaves that have been rising in the walk-in refrigerator since the day before. They spill the loaves from their *bannetons*, or baskets, onto the canvas loading belt, swiftly slash them with a series of cuts and then load them into the oven. Then with the push of a button, they inject a blast of steam, and, in a highly unusual maneuver, turn off the oven, so that the falling heat approximates the wood-fired hearth on which Robertson was weaned. When the crackling torpedo-shaped loaves start coming out, they fill the bakery with toasty, chestnut aromas that are incredibly enticing.

Like so many methods that bakers adopt, Robertson began this two-day baking regime out of necessity. Years earlier, in Point Reyes, he couldn't handle mixing and shaping the dough, chopping the wood for his masonry brick oven, and baking all in one day—if he and Liz were going to have a life. So he stretched the process over two days. To make this extended fermentation work, he relies on a relatively small amount of what he calls "young" starter in the dough. This sourdough has risen only for a few hours so smells rather sweet, favoring lactic acids, rather than the sharper acetic acids that come in a more mature *levain*. When he first described this approach in *Tartine Bread*, I was surprised because most sourdough recipes call for far larger amounts of leaven. But there's no hard and fast rule about how much starter to add to a dough, though the differing amounts, along with their hydration and temperature, can dramatically affect the way the final loaf turns out. If he had used a greater amount of leaven in the dough, for example, and kept it at a warm temperature of 78°F (26°C), the bread would be ready to go into the oven in five to six hours after it was mixed—not twenty-eight or thirty hours. But it wouldn't have the complexity of taste, the dark crust, and porous crumb that makes the loaf a Tartine loaf. The relatively small amount of sourdough and the cool overnight rise means this dough needs a long, languorous fermentation, which is perfect if you're planning on mixing one day, baking the next, and yes, sleeping at night, as he was, in the cool climate of Point Reyes.

I found this method tricky to achieve in the summer swamp of Washington when blasting air conditioning lowers the temperature to only 80°F (27°C). Starters, especially liquid ones, can overferment in those conditions and develop too much of the acetic acid that Robertson's trying to avoid. My fix is to use a stiff leaven in the summer. All else being equal, this takes longer to ferment than a liquid sourdough starter and gives me a longer overnight window to achieve a mildly acidic flavor profile. Another way to slow down the leaven in the summer is to mix it with cold water and to add salt (but don't forget to reduce the salt in the final dough by the same amount). When it's really warm, I use that approach. The way to maintain your sourdough arises from your particular needs, desired flavor profile, and careful observation of the starter ecology. It really is like farming because you're nurturing these microlivestock in a way that reflects the local climate—and mine wasn't northern California. To get a similar taste, I had to do things differently.

Like that of most bakers I've encountered, Robertson's method influenced some of the things I did, but the real eye-opener came at the bakery itself, where, it might be said, the exacting guidelines went out the window. "All this stuff is done by feel, every step of the way," Yanko told me. "I mean the calculations guide us, but how the dough feels, how it rests on the bench, all of that determines what we do." Even the flour changes with the seasons. Just a couple of weeks before I'd arrived on one of my several visits, they had altered the blend of white flours from Central Milling in Utah that they use in the Tartine country loaf. "We're constantly changing things," Yanko said.

This flexibility is especially applicable to the amount of water you add to the dough, which increases as the dough is progressively developed. It echoes something that Pichard in Paris told me: "Add as much water as the dough can handle." What's too much? I saw that years ago when I was mixing a *ciabatta* loaf, that extremely moist Italian dough that creates huge airy holes. I had added so much water at the outset that the gluten never came together. I was stirring a soup in my KitchenAid mixer, and the gluten was just swimming around, not hooking up. I had added too much water, and all at once. Had I added the water gradually, the gluten would have had a chance to form its connecting bonds, and then absorb the additions of water.

"We hold back maybe 10 to 15 percent of the water," Hart told me one day at Tartine, "and then just keep adding it, because we mix by feel." As the dough mass is stretched and folded, they hydrate the dough even more, until it's a highly elastic substance that has sucked up as much water as a sponge. While this method is often called "double hydration," it's more like triple hydration or perhaps constant hydration at Tartine, since they add the water until the dough looks sufficiently gloppy, but still strongly elastic. What's enough? Well, again, that's a judgment call by the baker and in part depends on the flour one uses. In my case, I just keep sprinkling on a couple of tablespoons at a time, after each rest, and fold and pinch the dough until the water's absorbed.

Another surprise in their technique was in the final shaping of the loaf, which I got to try on my first visit to Tartine. It mimics nothing so much as origami. Usually, when shaping a loaf, you cut and weigh the dough for the size loaves you want, then gently fold it into a rough shape. This preshaping builds up a slight bit of tension in the skin of the dough, making it easier to manipulate into the final shape after a brief rest. Since Tartine's loaves are so fully hydrated, though, the preshaped loaf kind of collapses into a one-inch-thick pancake on the wooden counter during its resting period. Then, when it comes time to shape the bread, they do a series of folds, and folds upon folds. Their hands work quickly and automatically as they wrap the dough into an airy, taut package. It was far more intricate that any technique I saw in Paris—or anywhere else for that matter. Now, I could try to describe this folding technique, but there are so many pulls and folds, each stretching the skin of the dough around a loose and pliable interior, that a verbal description wouldn't do it justice. Robertson doesn't even bother mentioning it in his bread book.

But after watching him shape a few loaves at Tartine, I tried it on the butcher block counter. Robertson was standing beside me. The counter was nearly devoid of any flour, so you have to live with potential stickiness. (Beginning bakers make the mistake of throwing down flour, when the loaf starts to stick, but when you do so, the loaf can't "grab" the counter and achieve a taut skin. It kind of flops around instead.) I went to work, folding this way and that, trying to be quick about it. When my somewhat mangled loaf was done, he said it was "okay." He was kind. It was clear it would take a lot of time and practice to get this shaping technique down. "I've been doing it eight months and I still haven't got the hang of it," Hart told me during one of my visits. I could tell that he hadn't, because he didn't look particularly relaxed and fluid when he shaped the bread. It was the same with a visiting baker from Sweden. But at least they could accomplish the task. I couldn't. I even took a video of the technique to try to remember what they were doing, but even then, watching it repeatedly, it was still hard to

Nathan Yanko (left) and Chad Robertson at Tartine

figure everything out. You can't slow down or stop during the shaping process. If you do, your hands will be stuck to a gloppy mass. Every time I tried the technique, the wet, delicate dough stuck to my fingers or the skin of the dough ripped. It's an impossibly precise but relaxed technique in which your fingers—not your brain or eyes—figure how to manipulate the dough.

But here's the other thing about shaping: I've hardly ever seen two bakers shape loaves in exactly the same way, at least in the United States, where many bakers are self-taught or learn at the elbow of another baker. In Europe, there might be a higher degree of consistency because of schooling and formal apprenticeship. Some eschew the preshaping step, so I tried that for a while as well. Others insist on preshaping. I've concluded that there's really no one right way to shape a loaf of bread, but there are many wrong ways, which often arise from too much pressure or a misjudgment about the amount of flour on the shaping surface. By pressing on the loaf, the inept baker condenses the crumb, and ends up with something resembling a brick. With too little flour on the counter, the skin of the dough rips, releasing all the pressure you're trying to create. Too much flour, though, means the loaf just rolls around.

Ultimately, you need to stretch the outer skin of the dough without compressing the air bubbles that have accumulated inside. It's like containing a sponge with a rubber band. But achieving this is tough, and takes practice. Once you do get it, though, you'll see the skin is elastic and becomes even more so as the loaf rises, so that by the time it's ready to go into the oven, you can slash it swiftly with a razor. The slash will open slightly and you'll notice air bubbles inside the cut. Once it hits the steam of the oven and the loaf rises, the *grigne* will burst open. The look is aesthetically pleasing, a distinctive, dark crust surrounding an airy interior, which might describe the Tartine loaf.

But this is hard to achieve and can't be done if all the preceding steps haven't been properly carried out. As Tim Healea of Little T American Baker in Portland, Oregon, said to me when we were discussing this in his bakery: "Each defect along the way gets kind of magnified in the process." Proper shaping won't correct a badly fermented loaf. And bad shaping can ruin a properly fermented loaf. Each step needs attention.

W hen I got the call from Waters's office that day in early 2010, it was before all these trips to California. So the thread to this West Coast baking lineage really came through books, occasional tastings of bread when I was traveling, and practice. But I still was apprehensive when asked to bake for forty guests at the $500-a-plate dinner at Bob Woodward's house. I tried to figure out how much bread I would need to make and realized I could probably do it—five big loaves and several baguettes. I then called the baker and author Peter Reinhart, whom I'd met a couple of years earlier. "That's not a lot of bread," he said, and he encouraged me to give it a whirl.

So began my first gig as a professional baker. I quickly settled on breads I made time and again and eat at home—a *pain de campagne* (country loaf) made with sourdough and a mix of white, whole wheat, and rye flours; a *pane casareccio di Genzano*, an airy, white, big loaf crusted with wheat bran that I picked up from Dan Leader's *Local Breads*; and my baguettes. Then, I worked out a time line. I would need to begin Friday to have the breads ready on Sunday afternoon.

I started by feeding 50 grams (about a quarter cup) of sourdough starter Friday morning, the seed of the leaven that would eventually feed forty people. I refreshed this substance three times, building it in size so that by Saturday evening, when I needed the ripe starter to make my doughs, I had more than 1.5 kilograms of sourdough, filling a small plastic tub. With that steady feeding every

Pain de campagne dough, fully risen

eight to twelve hours, the starter was bubbling, itching to impregnate the dough. This itself was a good sign, for a robust starter will always make better bread than one that seems weak, slack, and slow to ferment.

That evening, I began weighing out the flour and hand mixing the dough. I combined the ingredients until the flour and water came together. Then I let the shaggy mass rest so the flour slowly soaked in the water, folding it at steady intervals to develop the gluten. By the end of the process, the dough was elastic and glistening with moisture. If you pull away a small piece and stretch it out with your fingers at this point, you should be able to see through it—the so-called windowpane test that shows when gluten is fully developed.

Now the magic began—the first rise, the source of flavor—and luckily it was a chilly night. Why was that important? Because when it's cool out, I often let my sourdough breads rise in an un-heated basement storage room that is about 55°F (13°C), about the same temperature as Tartine's walk-in refrigerator. That's the perfect temperature for a languid fermentation, when the sugars in the bread develop. Bakers buy proofing cabinets that cost thousands of dollars to retard loaves at this temperature. My solution was less precise, but worked fine. The Genzano and baguette doughs rose in the refrigerator, since they contained instant yeast as well as sourdough and I wanted an even slower fermentation. At seven A.M. on Sunday, I took the *pain de campagne* dough out of the cool basement closet and let it warm up for about an hour. I shaped three *boules*, letting them rise for two and a half hours, which was longer than usual but, then again, my kitchen was quite cool. In the meantime, I heated up the baking stone in my oven. Then I repeated this

Loaves for Alice Waters's charity dinner

with the Genzano dough, and then the baguette, shaping both of those doughs cold. (It's easier to shape highly hydrated doughs when they are cool.) The rise went well, and when the breads hit the baking stone, they were full of oven spring, rising upward in less than five minutes.

I finished baking at about two P.M. and let the breads cool, then delivered them across town to Woodward's house for dinner. Jean-Pierre Moullé, who was then the executive chef at Chez Panisse, was there to greet me. We talked briefly about the breads and I mentioned I was a home baker, not a professional.

"I know, but you did not bake these at home," he said.

"Yes, I did," I countered, and I noticed his eyebrow rise a bit.

For a home baker, there's always the moment of anticipation when the bread comes out of the oven and you wait for it to cool before tearing into it. With these loaves, I didn't get a chance to cut into them, to evaluate the flavor and aromas or assess the interior crumb or the density of the crust—all crucial to a decent loaf. But I trust they were fine, influenced as they were by a long lineage of bakers. Later that evening, at a party preceding the dinner, Alice Waters took me aside, bread lover that she is, and thanked me warmly. It was a nice moment and quite telling. I reminded her that I had interviewed her before, for a previous book, but she hadn't remembered—just another interview with a writer. From this moment on, though, she never forgot my bread. In the proceeding years, she has called me often when she had a charity dinner in Washington. To her, I'm a baker, not a writer. And you know what? That's just fine.

Pain de Campagne
(MODERATE)

Makes 2 loaves

Bakers often think in ratios, with the percentage of each ingredient measured against the flour, which is always 100 percent. They even do this in shorthand, as in, "What hydration level are you using? Oh, seventy percent." What that means is that the water in the dough amounts to 70 percent of the flour weight, or 700 grams of water per 1 kilo of flour.

But bakers also use devices to remember these ratios, and one that I found especially useful was the 200/400/600 ratio, with 200 grams of natural leaven, 400 grams of water, and 600 grams of flour. With 12 grams of salt, this ends up with two loaves weighing a bit over 600 grams each, which is a decent-size bread when baked.

I often keep this ratio in my head when making a simple loaf, with one caveat. I find the hydration level a bit low. So I start out with 200 grams of starter, and mix it with 400 grams of water and 600 grams of flour. Then, when I add the salt, I also add another 25 grams of water. During the dough-making process, I keep drizzling on water, so it really ends up more like a 200/450/600 ratio. With the extra water, the overall hydration of this loaf goes up to around 73 to 75 percent, but the whole wheat and rye flours tend to absorb copious amounts of water so it's not a loose, gloppy dough. I encourage you to alter the water slightly so you can see the differing effects on the crumb of the loaf, after it's baked.

Tools
    Bowl
    Rimmed baking sheet
    Rectangular baking stone
    Plastic dough scraper
    Colander and kitchen towel, in which the loaf can rise
    Baking peel or cutting board, to move the loaves to the oven
    Single-edged razor blade, *lame*, or knife
    Instant-read thermometer (optional)
    Cooling rack

Levain Ingredients
    100 grams unbleached organic all-purpose flour
    30 grams organic whole wheat flour
    100 grams water
    20 grams ripe starter

Final Dough Ingredients
    200 grams starter
    400 grams water (plus another 50 grams added in increments)
    70 grams organic whole wheat flour
    70 grams organic whole rye flour
    460 grams unbleached organic all-purpose flour
    13 grams sea salt

Olive oil, to grease the bowl

Semolina and flour, to dust the baking peel

Morning, First Day

Mix all the *levain* ingredients together and let it ferment for 8 to 10 hours, until the starter has domed but not collapsed. There will be extra starter left over once you remove 200 grams for the dough. Use this remaining starter as a base to refresh your leaven. (To refresh, mix 20 grams of the remaining starter, 75 grams water, 50 grams whole wheat flour, and 50 grams white flour; let it ferment 2 to 4 hours at room temperature and then place it back in the refrigerator.)

Evening, First Day

Mix the dough. In a bowl, mix the starter and 400 grams water until the starter is dissolved, though lumps here and there are fine. Add the whole wheat and rye flours and stir until combined. Then add the white flour and mix for 1 to 2 minutes, until the flour dissolves and forms a shaggy mass.

Make an indentation on top of the dough and add the salt and 25 grams water into this well, so that the salt can begin to dissolve. Cover the bowl and let it sit for 30 to 40 minutes.

Moisten your hands, then shake off the water. Stretch and fold the dough by pulling the dough out from the edges and folding in toward the middle. You want to stretch the dough out to strengthen the gluten but ideally don't rip the dough. You can also pinch the dough between your thumb and fingers to further incorporate the salt. Stretch and fold the dough in a circular pattern, pulling the dough out, then folding the edges toward the middle 10 to 12 times. Turn the dough over, so that the seams are facedown and the smooth side is on top. This entire process should take about 2 minutes. At this point you can add the remaining water, letting it sit on top of the dough until the next round. Cover and let the dough sit for 30 minutes.

Repeat the stretching and folding for another round. Pinch the dough with your thumb and fingers to help incorporate the additional water. By this time, you should feel some tension in the gluten, but be careful not to rip the dough. Once this process is complete, turn the dough over so the smooth side is on top. Let the dough sit for 30 minutes.

Having completed two rounds of stretching and folding, the dough should be elastic. You may, however, add one more round of stretching and folding to further develop the gluten, after allowing it to rest for 30 minutes.

Remove the dough and clean and lightly oil the bowl, or move the dough to a lightly oiled container. Cover and let sit for another 30 minutes, then place it in the refrigerator or in a cool basement room ideally no warmer than 55°F (13°C). Let the dough rise for 8 to 12 hours, though it can rise for as long as 24 hours. However, the longer this first rise lasts, the more sour the flavor will be.

Second Day

Place a rimmed baking sheet on the bottom of the oven and a baking stone on a rack in the middle. Preheat the oven to 500°F (260°C).

After letting the dough rise in the cool environment, you should see fermentation bubbles, and the dough should have at least doubled in size. If it hasn't, let it warm at room temperature for another hour.

Dust the counter lightly with flour and gently remove the dough with a dough scraper, letting the smooth top of the dough fall onto the counter. The sticky underside will now be face up. Cut the dough in half. (You can make two loaves simultaneously if they fit into the oven. Or refrigerate the remaining half the dough, then remove it and shape it into a second loaf after the first loaf is out of the oven.)

Preshape the dough. Stretch the four sides of the dough out and let them fall into the center. They can overlap. Then turn the dough over so that these seams are facedown. Dust with flour, cover with a light cloth or towel, and let the dough rest for 20 minutes.

Dust the counter with flour very lightly, then turn the dough over again so the seams are face up and the smooth side is on the counter. Stretch and then fold the edges in toward the center, so that you have an approximately round shape, which should take 6 to 8 folds. Apply light pressure in the center so the folds seal. Turn the dough over, so the smooth side is now face up, and, cupping your hands around the dough, use the outer edges of your palms and pinkies to stretch the skin of the dough and tuck it under the bottom, moving the dough in a circular motion so that you end up with a round shape. Try not to compress the loaf tightly, though the goal is to have a taut skin. (This last action takes time to master, so don't worry if it doesn't come out perfect on your first attempt—there will be many more loaves to come.)

Let the loaf sit while you prepare a colander lined with a floured towel. Then using the dough scraper to loosen the loaf from the counter, pick up the loaf and place the smooth side facedown on the floured towel in the colander. The seams will be face up. Cover with a towel and let the loaf rise for about 90 minutes, or until the loaf springs back slowly when you lightly press it with your finger. If it snaps back into shape quickly and leaves no indentation, it is not done rising, so give it another 20 minutes and try again. This is a judgment call, but it is better to err on slightly underproofing the loaf rather than letting it rise until it collapses on itself.

Dust a peel or cutting board with semolina and flour, or just flour. Turn the loaf out on the peel or board, so that the smooth side, which was on the towel, is now face up. Using a razor blade or bread knife, score the loaf with one cut, or in an X pattern, or in a square pattern, about ¼ inch deep. Angle the blade while you slash the loaf with swift, sure cuts. Don't dawdle, fuss, or repeat the action.

Transfer the loaf to the hot stone and close the oven. Then open the oven and pour ½ cup water into the baking sheet and close the oven, trapping the steam. Turn the oven down to 460°F (240°C) and bake for 30 minutes. Open the door briefly to release the remaining steam. Then turn down the oven to 420°F (215°C) and continue baking for another 10 to 15 minutes, or until the crust is dark brown. Turn the oven off and prop open the door slightly with a wooden spoon, leaving the loaf in the oven for another 5 to 7 minutes. Ideally, the loaf will have a hollow knock when you remove it from the oven, signaling that moisture has adequately dissipated in the loaf. Alternatively, stick an instant-read thermometer in the bottom of the loaf. The center of the loaf should read at least 205°F (96°C).

Let the loaf cool on a bread rack for at least one hour before cutting into it. Since this loaf is made with sourdough, it will last a long time. For the first two days, I simply keep it wrapped in a towel or in a paper bag, the cut side facedown. If there's anything left after that point, I keep it at room temperature in a plastic bag.

CHAPTER 4

Re-creating a Diverse Grain Pantry

In our kitchen, I have a huge wall cabinet across from an island counter where I mix bread dough. At one time, the cabinet housed only an electric circuit box surrounded by a lot of empty wall space. This design flaw was the result of a taciturn carpenter, and it lasted for years. But as my collection of flours and grains grew, I decided to colonize the space, so I added shelves. Now with the cabinet doors open, I can observe my holdings: The bottom shelf with bins of all-purpose white flour, whole wheat, and rye flours. Another shelf with polenta, coarse wheat bran, high-gluten flour, pearled Korean barley, and durum flour. On the top shelf, I have a small bin of diastatic malt powder, containing the amylase enzymes that help break down starch into sugar and fuel fermentation. There are garlic flakes, sesame seeds, and a box of Finax Swedish rye bread mix I picked up at IKEA one day. I haven't had the heart to just add water and bake it because it feels like cheating. In the refrigerator, I store more perishable items that I don't use as often and which might go rancid after months at room temperature: cornmeal and garbanzo bean flour; millet, buckwheat, brown rice, and more whole wheat flour; flax seed and wheat germ; spelt and oat bran; and a large Ziploc bag of Red Star instant yeast and another with Backferment, the organic German sourdough granules that a friendly baker sent me from Berlin. I have whole unmilled grains, too—the latest episode in my baking adventures. They sit in a nearby closet in gallon-size mason jars. There's hard red winter wheat and rye from Maryland, wheat and spelt berries from Maine, emmer wheat, and freekeh (spelt harvested while still immature, then roasted to a smoky flavor for Middle Eastern pilafs). These last two came from Klaas and Mary-Howell Martens, who are organic grain farmers in New York State.

Compiling this list scares me a bit, because it looks like a full-blown hoarding disorder, but that is not unusual when you get the bread-making bug. For professional bakers who need to produce a full line of breads every day, this wide variety of grains, and their variable performance, would be a curse. If there's one thing professional bakers need, it's *consistency*—that is, being able to reproduce the same bread time and again to the same high standards because that's what their customers expect. That's the bane of home bakers, whose results are so often inconsistent. The crust might be too hard one day, the interior too dense another. At times, you might get a marvelous flavor but the loaf will be compact. At other times, you'll get good loft and an airy light crumb, but there'll be an absence of flavor. Yet without this requirement for consistency, home bakers get something in return: the ability to experiment, to do a lot of R&D. For me, that's more fun, because it's in the trying, in playing around, that you arrive at something new. It might even be the result of a simple mistake, and then if you do nail it, well, hopefully you remembered all the steps. Then you can reproduce it, maybe even with some consistency.

There's an impulse, when baking with a range of flours, to make the types of bread that we're familiar with, because you can simply swap out one flour for another. But that can set you up for failure because flours often perform differently. One simple way to try a variety of flours, though, is to begin at the beginning, which

I got a taste of when I took a class with baker Jeffrey Hamelman in the small town of Norwich, Vermont.

Now, I've tended to avoid classes, mostly because they involve travel and can be costly. I'm content to try to work on breads by myself, or to talk my way into a bakery. But this class, held at King Arthur Flour, where Hamelman runs the baking department, caught my eye because it focused on wood-fired ovens. And it was during this class that I had a surprising epiphany related to all those diverse grains in my cabinet. It could be reduced to one word: simplicity.

The first thing we baked in the class was a flatbread, which had four ingredients: whole wheat flour, water, a bit of oil and salt, and no leavening. Hamelman had mixed up the dough several hours earlier and then let it sit, so that the whole wheat could fully hydrate. He then had us slice off small portions and roll them into balls. After they rested for a half hour, we flattened them into thin eight-inch disks, and folded the dough around a spicy tomato sauce Hamelman had whipped up with feta cheese and herbs. Then the fun began. We took giant wooden peels and slid the stuffed flatbreads into the hot, wood-fired oven, which was sheathed in stone and about eight feet deep. The heat emanating from the oven was enormous: my flatbread puffed up in about thirty seconds. After a minute I flipped it to darken the underside and then removed it to a piece of aluminum foil, wrapping it to keep the crust soft. The aroma in the classroom was intoxicating. Some students tore into their flatbreads before they were even cool enough to handle. I gave mine five minutes to cool down and then devoured it. It was among the best I've eaten.

Flatbreads were probably among the earliest breads, since all you need to do is grind grain and add water. Porridge was easier, no doubt, if you had a vessel to cook it in, but if you combined flour and water and simply flattened the dough in your hands and cooked it on a hot stone, it wouldn't be too far removed from the kind of bread I was eating that day with Hamelman. In fact, if you want to explore the flavor of a grain, this is one of the best ways to do it. At home, in the absence of a wood oven, I bake flatbread in a cast-iron skillet, then toast it directly over the flames, inspired by the simplicity of a master baker.

When you think about it, the diversity of my grain pantry—which I bought at the supermarket, by mail order, and from farmers—is pretty unusual in the roughly twenty thousand years that humanity has been eating cereals. If you go back, way before packaged flour was sold in supermarkets, and before the global grain trade, people had very little choice about the grains they ate. Instead, they ate what was grown nearby—and whatever was available at harvest time. It might have been wheat. It might have been barley. Or it might have been nothing at all, if the harvest failed.

These grains were propagated and culled by generations of farmers, chosen because they grew well in the soil and climate. Maybe they survived drought, thrived during pest infestations, or stood tall while a fungal rust disease decimated the rest of a crop, making them candidates to be saved and replanted the following year. Given the variety of challenges these premodern farmers faced, they were always looking for the best varieties and hedging their bets. When one grain variety failed, another might make it. So they were careful to plant a diverse population of seeds, or what are known as "landraces." These weren't the monocultures of today, where a single variety of wheat might dominate a state, or even a nation. Landraces consist of subtly different varieties, which would also vary from one place to another. These cereals were the

The flours in my cabinet

primary source of food once agriculture took hold, when people were eating two to four pounds of bread a day, with every meal, amounting to 80 percent of their diet. For these farmers, diversity wasn't the huge bounty of choice in my kitchen cabinet. Diversity was an insurance policy, and thus civilization's, for it meant at least some grain might make it to fill empty bellies from one harvest to the next.

Diverse seeds not only defined what the farm looked like, they also determined the bread, because the baker had to work with grains of varying quality. The result was a surprising variation not only in what was produced but also in what was done to stretch calories. If there wasn't enough wheat, which was the de facto case, bakers turned to fast-growing buckwheat, cold-tolerant rye, or high-protein millet. They ate cakes made from oats and barley, as in Scotland, since both grains were especially hardy in northern Europe. Or they mixed coarse bran into rye—so-called horse bread eaten when food was scarce. They added walnuts and acorns and spent grains from the brewery to stretch the loaf out. Chickpeas were ground up, as with *socca* flatbread, in southern France, where the thin batter is baked on a dome-shaped griddle, or with *farinata*, as it is known in Liguria. In Cyprus, fermented chickpeas became a foundation for wheat and barley loaves, and in ancient Rome, the flour from ground fava beans was made into a bread known as *panis lomentus*. Bakers might grind chestnuts into flour, as in Sardinia, when wheat shipments were interrupted. Later, a New World starch, the potato, became a major buffer against famine in eighteenth-century Europe as the population exploded. Maize or corn served this purpose as well, baked into the dense Portuguese *broa de milho*, which is made with rye. Corn-rye also proved crucial to the early American settlers, where it was known as "rye-injun bread," because wheat grew poorly in the southern New England climate.

But no matter where grain was grown, if scarcity struck, people moved down the ladder of preference from refined flours to breads made with whole grains and then bran. Starvation was a constant motivator, as in Venice in 1585, when bakers resorted to chestnut and bean flours. Or in Sweden, when rye *nödbröd* ("emergency bread") was made with lily roots, Icelandic moss, and rowan berries. When hunger beckoned, grape seeds, pine bark, clay, and often straw was mixed into dough, though the use of ground bones was likely a myth. Nothing was wasted. Stale bread was remilled and mixed into new loaves or made into porridges or puddings, or simply eaten, for descriptions exist of giant whole grain breads lasting six months or more.

The very concept of "stale bread" might have been unknown, given that famines occurred at regular intervals. Thousands struck Europe between 1400 and 1700. In seventeenth-century France, five famines struck in the course of fifty years—about once every decade—and bread prices shot up tenfold. The famines continued into the eighteenth century. More recently, in Russia, four million to seven million people starved to death in 1933–34, just a decade after nine million perished from starvation. Indeed, grain shortages have been the rule in history, which could lead one to conclude that grain diversity, while a good measure, wasn't obviously enough of an insurance policy to maintain a food supply. People ate whatever they could and hoped for a successful harvest the next season—that is, if they weren't forced to eat their store of seed, too.

Taste no doubt was a part of the equation, because some of these expedient choices became favored ones, defining a region's bread. But choice wasn't the driving force, subsistence was. These days, coming across a panoply of breads in an upscale specialty grocery store like Dean & DeLuca in Manhattan, the choice is almost daunting, from the darkest and hardiest Scandinavian ryes to sourdough French breads or their airy Italian cousins. While a link might be made between these breads and a particular country, the long-ago impetus to bake a loaf a particular way, to make it into food, has largely been forgotten. It was heavily determined by what was available, who could afford it, and what would prevent starvation lurking just over the horizon.

Diversity was advantageous in any number of ways: in protecting the food supply, in offering a wide variety of staples, and in the novel methods one applied to make these ingredients palatable. And these methods often came from a home baker, not a professional.

I suppose I come closest to this age-old problem of variability when I bake a loaf with whatever grains happen to be around, figuring out how to make them work. I do this most often with barley, spelt, and rye. The results have ranged from dense and gummy, when I first began baking with them, to remarkably good, with a flavor impossible to conjure from white and whole wheat flours. But these experiments took time. The only modern-day equivalent to the problems faced in the premodern era might be in the gluten-free baking now going on with corn, amaranth, teff, and buckwheat. All these grains take knowledge and practice to master. Inconsistency and unfamiliarity, when measured against the predictable yardstick of white flour, will leave you feeling almost dumb and incompetent. In the past, I wonder if bakers felt this way, too. Whether they were really dissatisfied, say, with a dense bread, or whether they craved it because density meant concentrated calories. Hunger again—it changes our perception.

D espite the higher nutritional value of whole grain breads, white flour has been prized since antiquity. Whole grain flour tends to be more assertive and at times bitter, though it can also have a deeper and more complex flavor, if you coax the dough properly in a long fermentation. If milled coarsely, the bran can end up as tiny flecks that remain on the tongue when you're eating the bread—pleasant to some, but not to all. But, again, these assessments need to be viewed in context, because whole grain flour was far easier to produce than white until relatively recently. Once you begin to mill the grains into flour, a number of technological and social questions arise, namely, how will you grind it and who will actually do the work?

In ancient Rome, *pistor*s ground the grain. According to Pliny the Elder, it was "generally known" that the *pistor* was a chained prisoner of war, often a rough foreigner, who spoke poor Latin. He was given a wooden mortar and pestle, reinforced with metal, and put to work. This was especially tough because the grain was spelt, a subspecies of wheat that has a hull which needs to be broken to release the kernel. (This is also one reason why spelt is expensive—

White and spelt flours, with flaxseeds

the grain must be hulled, adding one more step to the milling process and reducing the yield of the harvested kernels.) The *pistor* had another job, too: making pearled spelt, which involved rubbing the grains with chalk or sand to remove the bran so that the grain could be made into a staple porridge known as *puls*.

If, as I did, you want to see what a *pistor* was up to, here's what you do. Buy some wheat, rye, or spelt berries (which lucky for you will have already been hulled) from the bulk bins at a natural foods store and put a tablespoon or two into a mortar. Now crush the grains with a pestle. (There's no need to chain yourself while you do this, unless you're into that sort of thing.) The grains will jump around a bit so use a grinding motion, too. Within a minute or so, you will see white flour and flecks of darker bran. The white stuff comes from the endosperm of the grain and makes white flour.

It contains protein and starch. The hard outer coating is the bran, consisting of minerals, vitamins, more protein, as well as the insoluble fiber that passes through your gut, feeding your intestinal biota along the way. The germ, or embryo of the seed, is made up of oils and nutrients, though you can't see it when you grind the grain. What amazed me when I first tried this hand-milling technique was just how easily the endosperm split into a white, flourlike powder. The starch doesn't have the fibrous material to hold it together, so it just dissolves, with very little work. The bran, which evolved to withstand brief bouts of rain, aridity, and pests, is much tougher. If you taste a bit of this meal you've created, you'll notice the bran is gritty; the flour fine. But crushing the grain was just the first step of the *pistor*'s toil.

Now comes the hard part, which is to remove those brown flecks of bran from the white flour. I kept pounding the grain, hoping the bran would break down into as fine a substance as the starch. No such luck. So I turned to the next obvious solution, sifting. Flour was sifted through reed baskets in ancient Egypt. In milling operations, I've also seen flour sifted through a taut, vibrating cloth, or a series of progressively finer mesh screens, separating the bran and white flour. I poured mine into a flat, circular sieve and shook. That took out a bit of the bran, but obviously the sieve wasn't fine enough because most of it got through. So I tried a finer mesh. Then I tried cheesecloth. Now imagine all these tasks, pounding, grinding, and sifting, for entire days with a chain around your ankle—you get the idea. To do this work on any scale would be enormous, and by scale, I mean enough flour for a few thousand loaves, not one or two tablespoons.

Try this out and you will realize why the earliest bakers made whole grain breads. Millers went through the laborious task of sifting, or bolting, flour only if someone was willing to pay them enough money and if they had slaves who did the work. (It's been argued that agriculture was the foundation for socially stratified societies, and in this one example, you might see why.) Eventually, hand milling evolved into horse-drawn mills, giving the *pistor* a break. The slaves eventually became the bakers, who were celebrated in Rome. But even in this ancient era, there were many grades of flour, from the finest white, to white with a bit of bran, to coarsely milled flour, to the lowest castoffs of bran saved mostly for livestock, which is still the case today. Those who ate these dark brown coarse loaves, made of barley and bran, were often the poorest of the poor.

There was a centuries-old stigma attached to such dark bread as well as attempts to mask its nature. Jewish bakers in eastern Europe would sift fine rye meal over dark rye and barley loaves so that they looked, well, more white. This might have been the origin of marble rye, that mixed dark and light loaf still sold today. But there was also a historic recognition that whole grains were healthier. As Pliny said: "Among the ancients, too, it was generally thought that the heavier wheat is, the more wholesome it is." Hippocrates, the Greek historian, thought barley aided health. He wasn't wrong, considering the high level of beta-glucans, or soluble fiber, which inhabits not just the bran but the endosperm of barley and has the benefit of lowering blood cholesterol, tempering blood sugar, and reducing the risk of heart attacks and strokes. No wonder barley sustained soldiers and gladiators in ancient Rome, who were known as *hordearii*—barley eaters.

But, Hippocrates and other outliers excepted, viewing whole grains as healthy gained prominence only once the diseases of modern life blossomed. Now of course we are barraged with the full panoply of health benefits from eating whole grains despite the fact that so few of us approach the recommended daily amount. Throughout history, whole grains were the default loaf. It's easy to overstate this irony now—the poor ate the healthiest bread!—because this was true only to a point. Take into account that coarse flour could contain insects, rodent droppings, dirt, perhaps small stones and straw, and it becomes clear why people valued the more expensive, sifted stuff. Whole flour might have been more healthy, but much of it was fit only for livestock. Plus, white flour wasn't valued only for its social connotations of purity; it was also a more concentrated source of carbohydrates that the body metabolizes more quickly into energy. Bran has other essential nutrients, and protein as well, but its fiber passes through the body. That's why white flour has about 9 percent more calories than the same amount of whole wheat. Then there's the taste quotient: because amylase enzymes in saliva convert starch to sugar in the first stage of digestion, white flour tastes sweeter than whole wheat. Yet even white flour could be subject to adulteration with toxic whitening agents, especially during wheat shortages. That's why the regulation and policing of millers and bakers has been an enduring concern since at least the Middle Ages.

This idea of white bread as preferred and aspirational arises through history, so that in seventeenth-century Paris, laborers would choose three pounds of white bread to four pounds of whole wheat. In one instance, a prison riot broke out in Paris in 1751 when the inmates rejected dark bread, hurling bottles at guards. Historian Steven Kaplan, who relates these incidents in his works, does say that while Parisians favored white bread, they were also viewed as extravagant by the rest of the nation. "Everyone understood that the whiter the flour, the smaller the number of people who could be fed by a given amount of grain," he writes. With bread the main source of calories, sifting out the bran lost 30 to 50 percent of the kernel, depending on the mill and the sifting method. That meant everyone had to share the white flour that remained, with the aristocracy first in line. Unlike Parisians, peasants in the French countryside weren't about to waste half of what they grew and so ate a combination of wheat, rye, and barley well into the nineteenth century.

Sadly, this waste continues today, if you consider the vast amount of calories, essential minerals, and nutrients in the bran and germ that get tossed aside in the milling of white flour, which extracts only around 72 percent of the kernel. With every 100 grams of wheat bran left behind, 216 calories are discarded, including 16 grams of high-quality protein. Along with the bran, the nutrient-dense aleurone layer of the endosperm is rejected as well. In a food-scarce world, where wheat provides one fifth of calories, not only is a vast amount of food being wasted, but the most nutritious part is being siphoned off for livestock.

But whole grains have long been a hard sell. After the French Revolution, the constituent assembly proposed a *pain d'égalité*—a loaf defined as three quarters wheat, one quarter rye, with all of the bran intact. It was anything but cake. No one would eat aristocratic white bread in a democracy. But even more telling, Kaplan told me, *pain d'égalité* was never adopted because the ingrained preference for white flour in French society could never be broken, even among those who largely ate whole grain breads. *Pain d'égalité* was more ideal than reality, and white bread truly remained the aspirational loaf, even among those revolutionary peasants who could not afford to eat it.

If millers, however, could produce white flour on a massive scale and thus bring down the price of white flour, then the egalitarian impulse could be fulfilled at least in the consumer realm. That's what happened by the late nineteenth century, with the advent of mechanical roller mills that easily separated bran, endosperm, and germ. Bakers could now rely on a consistent supply of refined white flour and everyone could eat white bread. Customers looked forward to consistency and predictability, rather than variability, and they would come to fight for it.

This shouldn't be a big surprise. Remember the TV episode where Seinfeld offers an old lady $50 for the last loaf of Jewish rye she bought from the New York bakery, then grabs it and runs down the street when she refuses? People don't want variation, inconsistency, excuses, or a different loaf. They want their bread, and they want it now. Mariah Roberts, who runs the lively Beach Pea Baking Co. in Kittery, Maine, told me a story about a customer who was fuming after the person ahead of him bought the last four loaves of her most popular bread, a delicious *fougasse* with rosemary, olive oil, and coarse salt. He was unwilling to even consider another choice for his Thanksgiving dinner. So he cursed out the woman in front of him and stomped out of the store.

From this vantage point, diversity becomes a defect, a source of inconsistency that's unpleasant on the palate. So wheat was bred to produce more consistent results in the bakery as well. Though some might pine for this loss of biodiversity—all the rare landrace wheat varieties, now known as heritage or heirloom wheat—the triumph of more productive wheat varieties and the day-in, day-out consistency that could be achieved was nothing short of revolutionary in the history of grains. If wheat was uniform, bakers no longer had to figure out what to do with flour of varying quality. They would not have to adjust their recipes dramatically for different harvests. Bread lovers would not have to shift among a diet of coarse grains, barley, bran, and beans to supplant scarce wheat. Bakers and consumers now had something far more expedient: a steady supply of white flour that made uniform loaves and the luxury to eat wheat as one *part* of the meal. Bread became a choice rather than the main source of caloric energy.

As a result, so many staple grains—buckwheat, barley, spelt, rye, einkorn, emmer, millet, and tens of thousands of landrace wheat varieties—that people consumed for centuries ended up in the modern world as little more than a curiosity; they eventually became specialty breads that only recently are making a comeback. These grains are grown on a very small scale today, with the vast majority of diverse varieties sitting in frozen gene banks as a repository for specialized grain breeders. Well, either there, or on the shelves of bakers like me.

While bread is now consumed globally, the origin of the cereal grains is rather narrow. Grasslands cover about 40 percent of the earth's surface, but the distant relatives of the wheat fruit we eat arose in the Fertile Crescent—an arc that runs from Israel, Jordan, and Syria through southern Turkey and into Iraq and western Iran. Wild wheat and barley along with grinding tools dating back 23,000 years were unearthed in a settlement on the shores of the Sea of Galilee. There were also signs of bread making at this site. The oldest evidence of grain consumption, though, appears about 105,000 years ago, from a cave in Mozambique in which sorghum residues were found on stone grinding tools. Nomads first began gathering these grains in the wild, though wild wheat kernels—the plant's fruit—presented a challenge if they were to become food.

The brittle seed heads on which wild wheat forms—known as spikes or ears—naturally shatter when they mature, allowing the kernels to spread on the ground so that the plant can grow again. This was an evolutionary advantage for an annual like wheat but not a culinary one for humans. After the spike shattered, a person would need to scoop the grain up from the soil before it sprouted and spoiled. If you are a gardener, used to bending over a plot, you can appreciate why gatherers may have sought the grain before it shattered, or selected seeds from rare mutant plants with intact ears. If you happened to come across a chest-high wheat plant with mature grain attached to the stalk, you wouldn't have to bend down and pick up tiny seeds on the ground. You could snap the stalk just below the ear, put the grains in an animal skin bag, and take them back to your settlement. You might even save some seed, planting it the following year. This was the beginning of the domestication of wild wheat.

Nonshattering wheat had another advantage absent in most wild wheats: it had a hull that split open, releasing the kernel when it was threshed. This mutant trait—known as "free-threshing wheat" and a clear sign of domestication—first appears in settlements dating back 9,500 years. Other ancient wheats and barleys that shattered in the field had tough hulls that had to be removed to get at the kernel inside, and removing the hull was tough work—the job of the *pistor* in Rome grinding away at spelt. So, the evolutionary mutation of free-threshing wheat meant less work. Curiously, the domestication of wheat wasn't a straight line that favored these traits, and many hulled wheats were favored for centuries. Free-threshing wheat, for example, evolved *before* hulled spelt, which means that humans didn't always view hulled grains as a disadvantage, perhaps because they liked the taste or had slaves to hull them.

These domesticated traits could be easily selected because wheat self-pollinates, with wheat pollen fertilizing the plant's flower before it opens and blooms. That meant these early farmers could grow the varieties they wanted without worrying about nature mixing in inferior traits from other plants through cross-pollination. (Although wheat does cross-pollinate, it happens only rarely.) Nearly all the earliest crops at the dawn of agriculture in the Fertile Crescent were self-pollinators, which makes sense, because it allowed farmers to, in effect, design the plants they wanted. But this domestication process was messy, uneven, rather than appearing suddenly in a Neolithic "revolution," as archeologists once imagined.

This is apparent in the domestication of wheat, the first signs of which began around 10,500 years ago, according to studies of charred seed remains. Archeologists have realized that it took another millennium or so for various domesticated traits to become dominant. So what took so long? George Willcox, an archeobotanist at Archéorient, CNRS–Université Lumière in Lyon, France, and one of the principal researchers on these findings, suggests that crops failed repeatedly, forcing farmers to return to wild sites where they would gather new seeds. Or they would consume their entire grain supply, because food was in short supply. Domestication accelerated only once these farmers began to plant their crops farther away from wild wheat fields.

This process occurred at multiple locations in the Fertile Crescent, with diverse grasses. In southeastern Turkey, Neolithic farmers gathered wild einkorn and emmer wheats, then cultivated it. In other settlements, rye and a type of buckwheat appear. Farther south, near present-day Jordan, emmer wheat was favored, and to the east, settlements sprang up in the fertile valleys along the Euphrates and Tigris rivers, where emmer and barley were grown. Grain cultivation also sprang up to the west, in central Turkey and in Cyprus.

From left: freekeh, rye, red winter wheat, spelt

Something else happened as well. At a well-preserved 11,000-year-old Syrian site known as Jerf el Ahmar, on the banks of the Euphrates River, archeologists identified sickle blades, grain storage vessels, saddle querns for grinding grain by hand, and ample remnants of wild barley and rye along with preserved mice droppings (perhaps providing a source of *Lactobacillus*). Even a kitchen was excavated with stone basins, a hearth, and three querns, which would allow people to grind grain side by side. At this site, wild grains and lentils, along with game, were the main sources of sustenance.

While archeologists long thought that the advent of farming caused hunters and gatherers to settle down, forming communities, villages, and eventually complex societies, this theory has recently been questioned, because long-standing sites have been located without any signs of agriculture. One gathering spot in southern Turkey, Göbekli Tepe, which dates back 11,600 years, has the world's oldest known temple, with intricately carved pillars decorated with gazelles and wild boars, snakes and scorpions. The people who built this site had no pottery, for it hadn't been invented, nor draft animals, for livestock had not been domesticated, yet they were able to move sixteen-ton rocks and might even have brewed wild grain beer in stone basins. They built the first known monuments in human history, practiced art and religion, perhaps while enjoying a wild einkorn wheat brew, but they still were hunting and foraging to feed themselves in massive gatherings.

The site remained important for more than two thousand years, maybe the Neolithic rave or Burning Man of its day. Eventually, archeologists speculate, these religious gatherings created a demand for food that could be met only by farming. Coincidentally, Göbekli Tepe is just sixty miles from the Karaca Dağ mountain, where the closest wild ancestors of domesticated einkorn wheat are found. It is also near a site in Turkey where people began farming about

9,250 years ago—which coincides with the ascendance of Göbekli Tepe. Did this farming settlement twenty miles away provide food for the worshippers? Did the religious gathering create an impetus to begin farming? Perhaps the two developments—religion, farming—were related, or maybe not. As Klaus Schmidt, the archeologist who has been studying the site for two decades, told *National Geographic* magazine, less than 10 percent of Göbekli Tepe has been excavated. Who knows what future secrets remain buried?

The early farmers, unsurprisingly, planted crops that did well in their locale, since the temperature, amount of rainfall, and even soil type in the northern reaches of the Fertile Crescent differed from those in the south. They sowed grains near where the wild grasses grew, but also in areas that were free of them, which points to seed trading or sharing and human migration—the process that eventually took wheat into Europe and Asia. Along with ancient wheat, barley, and rye, these farmers grew flax, chickpeas, and lentils, as well as peas, fava beans, and bitter vetch. Goats soon joined the mix. Figs, pistachios, almonds, and grapes, which grew wild in the region, were domesticated, too. These crops were the earliest landraces, adapted to microhabitats, selected by farmers, and grown for generations. They were, to put a contemporary spin on it, local food, or maybe ultralocal, because their very existence was intertwined with the soil and climate in which they grew.

The wheat was also highly diverse, made up of many species, in contrast to the wheat we eat today. Einkorn wheat (*Triticum monococcum*), which is barely grown these days, has one of the simplest genomes among wheat, with just two sets of chromosomes (known as a diploid). Though it boasts more protein than modern bread wheat, it's a low-yielding hulled wheat, which may explain why, after becoming established in southern Europe through medieval times, it fell out of favor. Recently, einkorn has had a minor renaissance among organic farmers, such as in France, where it is known

—— White and emmer flour loaf

as *petit épeautre*. You can find loaves made with einkorn in a few Paris *boulangeries*.

Emmer wheat (*Triticum dicoccum*) evolved from two wild grasses and has a slightly more complex genetic structure than einkorn, with four sets of chromosomes (known as a tetraploid). With barley, emmer became the dominant grain in these Neolithic settlements and also a staple in Egypt, where it was used in bread and beer making. Along with einkorn, emmer was grown in the first farming settlements in central Europe, dating back 6,500 years. It has a unique smoky flavor that adds an earthy note when blended with other flours. On its own, I find it a bit overpowering, though that may just be the variety I'm using. The genetic remnants of emmer can now be found in durum wheat (*Triticum durum*), the primary high-protein wheat used in pasta making.

Bread wheat (*Triticum aestivum*), or what is commonly called "wheat," is the most complex of all these grasses, with a genetic code that's five times larger than the human genome. Bread wheat was the offspring of emmer wheat and a species of wild goat grass (*Aegilops squarrosa*), a spindly weed found in a wide-ranging area of the Near East. The genetic contribution of goat grass was especially important to wheat, because it improved wheat's gliadin proteins, which allow dough to stretch out without breaking. As a result, a *pizzaiola* can throw a thin disk of dough into the air, letting it expand without ripping apart. But a segment within gliadin can also trigger the potent and potentially fatal celiac disease.

Since wild emmer doesn't naturally grow near populations of wild goat grass, a chance hybridization likely occurred once domesticated emmer moved eastward with human cultivation, near the southwestern shores of the Caspian Sea. Once the two mated, the result was a hexaploid wheat with six sets of chromosomes—four from emmer, two from goat grass. Since the wild population of goat grass ranges northeast of the Fertile Crescent, bread wheat spread in an area north of Iran, stretching from Armenia to the western Caspian Sea. These wheats proved far more adaptable than their wild progenitors, and were able to survive the cold winters of northern Europe and the humid summers of Asia. So they spread, first into Georgia, and then into the Ukrainian and Russian steppe—the vast grasslands that extend as far as Siberia. Bread wheat also moved from Iran into Afghanistan, eventually becoming a staple in India, and then migrating to China. It now accounts for 95 percent of all wheat grown today, with durum making up the remaining 5 percent.

Ancient wheats, now relics, are cultivated on a very small scale, though they are having a culinary resurgence. Spelt (*Triticum aestivum* var. *spelta*) is one of them, known by Romans as *far* in Latin, hence *farina*, meaning flour. Spelt has a sweet, robust flavor that I find superior to whole wheat flour, which is why I suggest blending in a bit of it for those beginning to bake with whole grain flours. While some believe that gluten-sensitive people can tolerate spelt because it's "not wheat," be wary. Spelt is a subspecies of bread wheat. It does contain gluten and some varieties have been hybridized, that is, crossbred with other nonspelt wheat varieties, to improve baking quality.

When considered as a whole, the wild grasses that produced these domesticated wheats had a great deal of diversity. But even so, farmers had to choose what diverse traits they wanted and which seeds would be saved. Given this annual practice of selecting and propagating seeds—this one doesn't shatter, that one is bigger, these did well during last year's drought, this one makes better beer or bread—it's no wonder that the story of wheat breeding reads like the biblical passages of who begat whom, from the earliest wild wheat to the most modern varieties. It's one long lineage of seed selected, saved, bred, and passed on until the oldest, original varieties were largely lost to time. Now, if a major portion of the wheat crop perishes—a not unreasonable fear, given the periodic outbreak of virulent wheat diseases—humanity will find itself short of food. If humanity perishes, domesticated wheat will disappear and be overtaken by wild grasses with ears that once again shatter. Plants never stand still—a fact that became clear when I began to look into one of the "heritage" wheats that created the breadbasket of the Great Plains, which is where I'll turn in the following chapter.

While writing about the origins of wheat in the Fertile Crescent, I serendipitously got an e-mail from Mary-Howell Martens offering to send me some of the ancient wheat she and her husband, Klaas, grow at Lakeview Organic Grain in New York. I have known the Martenses for many years, and was aware of their work, but had never tried their grains. So I made arrangements for a friend to pick up the samples at a farming conference the Martenses were attending in Pennsylvania.

When I received the delivery, I couldn't quite believe my good luck. There were bags of whole hull-less oats, spelt, emmer wheat, a red winter wheat, a beautiful white wheat, a variety of heritage corn known as Wapsie Valley, and smoked spelt (freekeh). They sat around in mason jars for a while, a bit intimidating, but then I went to work and ground the emmer wheat with a countertop stone mill.

I made a simple flatbread, without any leavening, using the method that Jeffrey Hamelman had taught. It can hardly be called a recipe because it simply contains flour, oil, water, and salt. I let the dough sit for several hours, then rolled it out and cooked it on a cast-iron griddle. Then I moved it directly onto the flame. After charring it a bit here and there, I spread a little butter on it—and ate it with lentils and a salad. With a glass of beer, I toasted my Neolithic ancestors.

Emmer Flatbread

(EASY)

Makes 12 flatbreads

The hardest part about this recipe is getting hold of emmer flour, which is pretty rare and can be pricey. But if you do find it, dive in. I tried this recipe with 100 percent emmer flour, but found the taste too assertive, so I mixed it with an equal portion of whole wheat flour. (If you want a milder version, mix the emmer with white flour, but cut back on the water slightly.) Although the recipe calls for the dough to sit for as long as 8 hours, you can use it far sooner, though the flecks of bran may be more noticeable.

Tools
    Bowl
    Plastic wrap
    Plastic dough scraper
    10-inch cast-iron skillet
    Rolling pin
    Spatula (optional)

Flatbread Ingredients
    200 grams whole wheat flour, plus more for the work surface
    200 grams emmer wheat flour (if unavailable, use whole wheat)
    265 grams water
    2 tablespoons vegetable or olive oil, plus more for the bowl
    7 grams salt

Morning

Combine the flours, water, oil, and salt in a bowl until they come together into a mass. Cover and let sit at room temperature for 20 to 30 minutes while the flour absorbs the water.

Transfer the dough to a lightly floured work surface and knead for about 5 minutes by pushing down on and spreading the dough and then folding it over on itself. It should be smooth and elastic. Form it into a ball and place it in a clean, oiled bowl. Cover with plastic wrap and let the dough rest for 4 to 8 hours.

Afternoon or Evening

About 45 minutes before you want to bake, spread out the dough on a lightly floured counter, cut the dough in half with a dough scraper, and roll it into 2 logs. Cut each log into 6 pieces. You should have 12 pieces of dough that weigh about 55 grams each; evenly distribute any leftover dough.

Shape each piece into a ball. Let the balls rest for 30 minutes at room temperature under plastic wrap.

Place a cast-iron skillet over medium-high heat and let it heat up for several minutes.

Mean while, liberally flour a work surface. Flatten a dough ball and dust it lightly with flour, then use a floured rolling pin to roll it out as thin as possible (7 to 9 inches in diameter), rotating the disk to keep it even. If it resists, let it rest for a few minutes and continue rolling again. Cover the disk with a towel. Repeat with the remaining dough.

When the skillet starts smoking, gently lift a disk of dough. Place it in the skillet, cook it for about 30 seconds, and then turn it over with your fingers or a spatula for another 30 seconds. Remove the skillet from the flame and, holding the flatbread by its edge, put it directly on the fire. Keep moving it in a circle so that it doesn't burn, then turn over and repeat. The bread should be blistered and dark in spots.

Remove the flatbread and cover it with a towel or aluminum foil to keep it from forming a crust. (Dot it with butter and fold it in half if you like.) Repeat with the remaining disks of dough. Serve warm. These can be made in advance and stored in a resealable plastic container on the counter for a couple of days. But they are best eaten fresh.

Socca Américain
(EASY)
Makes 4 pancakes

I first made *socca*—a chickpea flatbread eaten in southern France—in the wood-fired oven class with Hamelman. We poured the liquid chickpea batter into a preheated metal pan that had been doused with a good deal of olive oil and thrust it back into the oven. It was done in a few minutes, and we cut it up and scarfed it down.

The second time I came across *socca* was in David Lebovitz's *The Sweet Life in Paris.* I had great success cooking it right under the broiler in a cast-iron pan. For this version, I tweaked the recipe in a nod to the Americas, and added just a bit of cornmeal. Now, my French friends may be rolling their eyes, but it does add a sweet flavor to the chickpea flour. This batter is very liquid, so don't try to thicken it up. Make sure you let it rest for a couple of hours (even overnight in the refrigerator) so that the legume and corn flours really hydrate. You can cook it under the broiler, but I also got stellar results just heating up a cast-iron pan on the stove, swirling around olive oil until it's just starting to smoke, then pouring in the batter. I cooked it until brown on one side, which takes about 2 minutes, then flipped it over for another minute. Maybe it's just a chickpea-corn pancake.

Tools
    Bowl
    10-inch cast-iron pan
    Spatula
    Cutting board

Flatbread Ingredients
    160 grams chickpea flour
    40 grams fine cornmeal or corn flour
    430 grams water
    3 grams salt
    ¼ teaspoon ground cumin
    4 tablespoons extra virgin olive oil

Mix together the flours, water, salt, cumin, and 3 tablespoons of the olive oil. Let the batter rest for at least 2 hours, covered, at room temperature, or overnight in the refrigerator.

Heat the cast-iron pan on a high flame, drizzling in the remaining 1 tablespoon of olive oil, so that it covers the whole surface. Just as it begins to smoke, pour in enough batter to fill the pan. Swirl the batter so it fills the pan to the edges, and turn down the flame to medium.

After 2 minutes check the underside with a spatula to see if it's brown. When it is, carefully flip the *socca* over and cook the remaining side for about 1 minute.

Slide the *socca* onto a cutting board, drizzle with high-quality extra virgin olive oil, and cut it into 4 or 8 pieces. Eat immediately.

CHAPTER 5

Turkey Red: Heritage Grains and the Roots of the Breadbasket

Rewind to 1912: A fifteen-year-old Kansas boy named Earl Clark noticed a plant with unusual black wheat kernels on his family's farm, so he saved three of these seeds and kept them to plant again. Clark, who went on to become a renowned wheat breeder in Sedgwick, Kansas, found that these seeds matured more quickly and produced a bountiful crop, so he continued to propagate them. Named Blackhull, the variety spread, accounting for a third of the Kansas wheat crop by the 1930s. Clark went on to breed eleven new varieties, such as Red Chief, which was more erect and vigorous than Blackhull and thrived in poor soil. It became a popular variety in southern Kansas in 1944. Clark then crossed Red Chief with another variety from which a single plant was selected—KanKing—found growing amid weeds. Released to farmers in 1952, KanKing was then crossed back with another offspring of Red Chief. Their progeny, a white wheat selected over eight generations, was released as Clark's Cream in 1972. White wheat has a milder flavor than more common red wheat, because it lacks the dark pigments in its bran. It is primarily exported to Asia, where its light color is favored by noodle makers. Clark's Cream also became popular with Kansas wheat farmers who still plant it today. I have a bag of the flour sitting on my kitchen shelf and I blend it with freshly milled corn flour and spelt to make a marvelous sourdough waffle. I normally wouldn't think twice about it—

it's just "white wheat," after all—yet its lineage can be traced all the way back through a dozen selections to black-hulled seeds plucked from a Kansas field by an observant teenager a century ago. One plant, one field, one kid, in the most important wheat-growing region of the country, all the way to my waffles.

When I talked about Clark with Mark Nightengale, the manager of a farmer-owned flour milling company in western Kansas called Heartland Mill, he told me that he had tried to grow all of Clark's varieties on his family's 3,000-acre farm. But they could not yield as much grain as modern wheat varieties nor tolerate intensive mixing—the giant mixers that make today's soft, pan-loaf breads. As a result, many of these once-dominant varieties had fallen out of favor by the 1950s, as industrial bakers sought out higher-gluten wheat that could withstand industrial fabrication. The only one of Clark's varieties that Heartland still milled was Clark's Cream, which is where I bought the flour.

Kansas cropland

As I grew more curious about the wheat I baked with, I began to look more closely at its origins—first, in the ancient grains of the Fertile Crescent, and then with the more recent varieties that came from the Great Plains. I wanted to get beyond the façade of "flour," which makes one bag seemingly indistinguishable from the next and obscures the plants and seeds that create this staple. The more I looked, the more fascinating this story became. As wheat breeds evolved, what had been left behind? What tastes and attributes were lost in this headlong push to the wheat we eat today? And what was gained?

As it turned out, Clark had plucked that black-hulled grain from a field of Turkey Red wheat, a diverse landrace population grown in Ukraine. This seed came to Kansas with Ukrainian Mennonite immigrants who arrived in 1873, fleeing religious persecution and lured by the prospect of farmland from the Santa Fe Railroad Co. The railroads at that time were laying tracks across the Great Plains, settling farmers and transporting grain to the nascent commodity markets of Chicago, which swallowed it up and then shipped it out to New York, Philadelphia, and Europe. These farmers settling the Great Plains were never "local" in the way that we understand the term today: their very presence in the latter half of the nineteenth century was made possible by railroads, grain traders, markets, and millers. Turkey Red wheat became prevalent in this locale because the Ukrainian steppe matched the climate and soil of Kansas and the immigrant farmers who brought it in sacks had the knowledge to sow it.

This was hard red winter wheat, which was relatively rare in the region before the Ukrainian Mennonites settled there. It became the early foundation for much of the wheat grown in Kansas to this day. Hard red winter wheat is particularly important for artisan bakers because it has protein levels in the range of 10.5 to 12 percent and is suited to gentle fabrication, such as hand shaping. Home bakers should seek it out as well. This isn't too difficult, since many "all purpose" flours are milled from it.

What makes this wheat "hard" is a relatively high percentage of protein, which is necessary to raise a loaf of bread (one old method of testing the grain was to chew on the wheat kernel to see how "hard" it was). The phenolic compounds in the bran, which appear brown or dark red in color, give whole wheat flour its slightly bitter and nutty flavor. It's known as a "winter wheat" because the crop is sown in the fall, then undergoes a period of vernalization, when prolonged exposure to cold temperatures causes the plant to go dormant. In the early spring, when the days grow longer and the temperature warms up, the plant's reproductive stage is triggered. It resumes growing, then blossoms and bears its fruit, the wheat kernel. Once the seed dries on the stalk, usually in the late spring or early summer, the harvest begins.

Turkey Red wasn't the only wheat grown in the Great Plains in the nineteenth century. Another variety, Red Fife, was dominant in the northern plains. It was thought to have originated in Danzig, Poland, and was shipped via Glasgow to a Scottish farmer in Ontario, David Fife. He and his wife, Jane, were reputed to have bred out the seeds of a single plant grown on their farm in 1842 (in contrast to Turkey Red, which consisted of a diverse landrace population). It was the first hard spring wheat grown in North America. Unlike winter wheat which is sown in the fall, spring wheat is planted as soon as the soil is dry enough in the spring and grows continuously until harvest. Since it doesn't need a period of dormancy, it was suited for the northern plains where the winters are often too harsh for fall-sown grasses. It also produces a much higher-protein flour of around 14 to 16 percent that creates terrifically strong gluten, suitable for bagels, high-volume pan breads, and intensive mixing machines in industrial bakeries. Although Red Fife became a relic, it has recently been revived by Canadian farmers and currently has something of a cult status among artisan bakers, even more so than Turkey Red.

Unlike the northern plains, Kansas, Nebraska, and Texas were better suited to growing winter wheat varieties. So here, Turkey Red supplanted the wheat varieties that early settlers brought with them from the humid East, which didn't adapt well to the plains. Since Turkey Red matured early, it could be harvested before devastating fungal rusts appeared in the summer, which could wipe out spring wheats. Still, it took nearly three decades after its introduction to spread widely. Since much of the seed came from immigrants, there wasn't a sufficient supply. Mills accustomed to softer, or low-protein, wheat only bought Turkey Red at a discount because it was much more difficult to grind. It wasn't until milling technologies advanced—with roller mills—that Turkey Red took off, helped along by the newly constructed rail networks and a burgeoning global grain market. By the early twentieth century, when Turkey Red was near its peak, it had supplanted all previous varieties. At this time, less than 8 percent of the nation's wheat varieties could be traced back to the 1840s. By 1919, Turkey Red represented 99 percent of the winter wheat crop in the United States and remained dominant until 1944, when it was overtaken by higher-yielding varieties.

From our vantage point, Turkey Red is an extremely rare heritage wheat, cherished because of its taste, story, and small-scale cultivation. But at its height, it was the modern wheat of its day and had actually supplanted earlier eastern varieties, many of which are now lost to time.

Learning this history, I knew I had to visit Heartland Mill, so one crisp fall day I flew into Denver International Airport, then drove east in a rented gray minivan. I had been to Denver dozens of times, but I had always driven toward the Rocky Mountains, never away from them.

Interstate 70 was a straight arrow out of Denver, with slight curves and subtle hills. As I entered the plains, rangeland and crop fields rolled on for miles, broken up only by the occasional gas station–mini-mart, fast-food restaurant, or chain motel. In one small dusty location, I spent the night at a motor lodge with a neon sign, where I was greeted by a woman in a sari and the rich smell of Indian food wafting out of the office kitchen.

Early the next day, I got back on the highway and continued heading east, into the rising sun. I was nervous about my whereabouts, but with acres upon acres of grassland and a straight road as far as one could see, there weren't many options. I plowed ahead. Eventually, I exited the highway and took a right, heading due south on a two-lane road cutting through a region recently planted with winter wheat. The clouds parted in the distance—the light shining in a kind of "Hallelujah!" moment—so I stopped and got out of the van to snap a picture. The only sound I heard was the wind sweeping across the vast grasslands.

A few hours later, I rolled into Marienthal, Kansas. It wasn't so much a town but a collection of buildings: a tall grain elevator, a few small wood-frame houses, and the slapdash buildings that housed Heartland Mill, all positioned around the railroad track that ran east–west.

Mark Nightengale, a robust man with a firm handshake, greeted me in the kitchen of the small white wooden house that serves as the company office. We sat down at a table, and over coffee, he told me the story of how his grandparents fled Ukraine for Kansas. In his telling, I could see the *culture* in agriculture, for his family's story was also the story of Turkey Red wheat, the rise of the breadbasket, the settling of the plains, and the growing of wheat for a hungry nation.

Marienthal, Kansas

While Nightengale went on—regaling me with details about cousins in Germany, where the Mennonites originated; tales of starvation on the Ukrainian steppe; and wheat and religion and the promise of a new land—I mentioned in passing that my father's family, the Fromartzes, had hailed from Kiev, which is also in Ukraine. They were Jewish immigrants who ended up in Brooklyn. Nightengale perked up at this. It was as if a bond had been forged right there over the kitchen table. He focused his steely eyes on me, one religiously persecuted immigrant offspring to another, and I knew right then this trip would be worth it.

His grandfather broke sod with a steam engine and plow, then planted a quarter section, or 160 acres, with Turkey Red wheat. Three generations on, the farm had expanded to nearly 3,000 acres, and had followed the wave of modern agriculture, using synthetic fertilizers, chemical pesticides, and whatever new wheat breed was released, planting wheat year after year. By the 1980s, though, the conventional regime was taking a toll, in compacted soil that couldn't hold water, in stunted plants, and in the need for ever more external nutrients because the soil was being mined. The crop was sold into the commodities market, which meant "we'd take the grain to the feedlots and they'd feed it to livestock, or it would get exported," he said. Farmers were under pressure from rising debt, sour land deals, and big equipment purchases. Then grain prices plunged in the early 1980s. A huge number of farmers left the land.

"You need to remember, in the late nineteenth century in western Kansas, there were more people living here than there are today," he said. Nightengale responded by returning to farming the way his grandparents did, rotating crops, seeking out manure and compost to rebuild the depleted topsoil. He avoided chemicals. It was cheaper, after all, and the stuff was toxic. By the late 1980s, these practices began to pay off in higher grain weights and better grain quality, but Nightengale said the wheat wasn't reaping anything extra in the commodities market. So Nightengale and several other farmers following a similar path started to peddle their grain at natural foods trade shows, where buyers had begun to ask about organic whole grain flour. Seeing an opportunity, the farmers, who were nearly organic already, decided to start a flour mill. Nightengale told me they thought it might be a way to keep young people—their kids—from leaving the area.

In a corner of a trailer, which housed Heartland's grain testing operation—overseen by his son—Nightengale reached under a table and pulled out a small eight-inch stone mill. "That was the first mill," he said. It didn't last long. They gradually expanded into the operation I visited that day—a huge building housing grain cleaning machines, a refurbished late-nineteenth-century roller mill, and a few giant stone mills. The plant was noisy, because every machine inside vibrated, shook, whirled, and blew. They were everywhere, so it was hard to hear Nightengale's full description of the operation, but we pressed on, winding between the equipment, up narrow metal staircases, traversing steel balconies and around pipes that ran this way and that all through the building.

Near the beginning of the process was a gravity table that shook the grain over a screen at a slight angle, allowing the seed to fall down a grain chute and separating the rocks, sticks, and chaff which were channeled off to another bin. "This is exactly the way the Egyptians did it," Nightengale said. Well, not exactly. Where two people used to shake a screen to winnow the seed, now there was a vigorous, noisy machine to do the work. From there, the grain flew through a dizzying number of cleaners and blowers and a magnetic chamber to remove any metal; it ran through pneumatic tubes circling the ceiling. Before it entered the yard-long cylinders of the roller mill, the grain was also "tempered," or moistened, several hours so that the bran would more easily split from the endosperm. Once inside the mill, grain passed between two steel rollers spinning in opposite directions, crushing the kernel and removing the bran. The grain was then sucked through a vibrating sifter and shot down to another set of rollers and ground again. At the end of the process, in which the flour passed through seven pairs of rollers in a matter of seconds, there was a bin of white flour, and others filled with wheat bran and germ.

But that was only part of the operation. Other batches of dry grain were channeled to thirty-inch stone mills, where the kernels were ground together rather than separated as in the roller mill, making whole wheat flour. For one product, the flour was bolted—that is, the milled whole wheat flour passed through a fine rotary screen so the coarsest bran flecks could be removed. Heartland calls this Golden Buffalo flour, which consists of only 82 percent of the kernel rather than 100 percent as in whole wheat. "Bolted flour" has been valued for millennia, because it's a kind of halfway point to whole wheat, containing some of the bran and germ, but not all of it. You lose some of the nutritional benefits but it's less assertive than whole wheat flour and may yield greater loft. This so-called high-extraction flour is common in Europe, though hard to find in the United States, unless you seek it out from specialty mills or professional suppliers. In supermarkets, home bakers are left with basic choices: either roller-milled white flour, which has no bran or germ (and consists of about 72 percent of the kernel), or 100 percent whole wheat.

Turning a corner, Nightengale hollered, "We've probably got one of the biggest collections of machine belts in western Kansas." He pointed proudly to row upon row of rubber belts aligned on a wall for the milling machines. These machines were refurbished, bought from outmoded mills that the grain giants had shuttered and sold off as scrap. Heartland's Allis-Chalmers roller mill was manufactured in the 1890s, then partially rebuilt in the 1940s. But after Nightengale bought it, the rollers were stripped, sanded, and reassembled from the inside out. Two-story-high grain silos that looked like rocket boosters came from an Archer Daniels Midland mill that had recently shut down. "The hardest part was getting them here," he said. Once they were erected on a concrete slab, his team welded a metal building together around the outside of the silos so Heartland had a warehouse to store flour. Everything he showed me had been bought used, overhauled, rebuilt, and recycled. Nothing was new, except maybe those machine belts.

"You have the talent to do this kind of thing?" I asked, surveying this vast arena of secondhand machines, gizmos, sifters, and even buildings they had built by hand. "Well, we're all farmers and farmers have to be good at a lot of things," he replied. Nightengale had learned it all on the job, from textbooks, or from talking to milling experts, with trial and error. What drove him forward were bakers who wanted superlative flour and the local farmers who wanted to sell it to them.

Among those flours was Turkey Red wheat, which was brought to Heartland in 2009 by Thom Leonard, a baker who had a passion for the grain. Leonard told me he had first come across it in 1977, when the wheat's centenary was celebrated in Kansas. Leonard then found the few farmers who still grew the wheat and added it to the lineup at his highly regarded WheatFields Bakery in Lawrence, Kansas. More recently, he worked with farmers and Heartland to expand its cultivation and milling. But it was still an extremely rare crop in the state, owing in part to its lower yield. Leonard has since moved on to Athens, Georgia, where he has opened Independent Baking Co., but he still has a Turkey Red loaf in his lineup.

Since it's an "identity preserved" flour, Heartland doesn't blend its stone ground Turkey Red flour with any other type of wheat to correct for the natural variations that may appear from year to year. Randy George, who owns the Red Hen Baking Co. in Middlesex, Vermont, and who has baked with the flour for several years, told me he routinely alters his Turkey Red dough, because the flour varies so much. It sounds a lot like premodern flour, before the onset of specialized wheat breeding and blending created highly consistent products.

When I tried baking with it, that's exactly how I found it. The bolted Turkey Red flour was more tricky to work with than, say, Heartland's Golden Buffalo flour, whose gluten develops quite predictably. The Turkey Red required much gentler handling to avoid ripping the skin of the dough and it was quite extensible, or stretchy. But I found that if I didn't make the mistake of letting the loaf rise too long, it would hold its shape nicely. The lactic and acetic acids in the starter definitely helped strengthen the dough. The loaf didn't end up as a hard brick, nor did it have the assertive tannins you sometimes find in 100 percent whole wheat bread. It had a light internal crumb and the mild hint of caramel, which, with the slight acidic punch of the sourdough, made for a pleasant taste. It was, in short, quite good flour, and soon I was adding Turkey Red flour to my baguettes, making a long, rustic-looking loaf with a single slash down the length of the loaf.

Later that day, on our way to visit one of Heartland's farmers, we drove out past a huge Cargill feedlot, with tens of thousands of black cows being fattened for slaughter fenced in on a muddy, stinking hill. A massive pile of corn feed two stories high and as big as two football fields lined the side of the road. Then, we came upon the cows' inevitable by-product: row after row of cow manure cooking into compost, the heavy scent wafting down the road long before we approached. I had never seen the heartland of industrial agriculture, but you can't miss it once you arrive. It's not only the eighteen-wheelers hauling animals, feed, grain, and hay down narrow highways between fields of wheat but also feedlots filled with cattle and the unmistakable smell of their waste.

We drove into the middle of the vast composting operation, and while we were taking in the view of these giant, six-foot-tall rows of manure, a worker released a hose and water spewed out down the roadway toward Nightengale's truck. The fierce wind hurled the water toward us, now mixing with the thick muck of manure on the ground, splattering the windshield with a wave of brown gunk. Nightengale turned on the wipers. "Guess I'll have to get a carwash now," he said. We turned around and roared out of that mess, the stench filling the cab of the truck.

But as noxious as this feedlot manure was, at least this animal waste would be composted and spread on wheat and corn fields as an alternative to chemical fertilizers, rebuilding the soil in which these crops grew. This isn't an endorsement of these factory livestock farms—which traffic in disease and rely on the copious use of antibiotics—but I can think of no better way to dispose of their vast hills of manure once they are there.

We drove over to Karlan Koehn's farm, which Nightengale said was "nearby." In farm country, such terms are relative. About forty minutes later we arrived. Koehn's father, brothers, and their kids were all gathered around a tank-size combine that had broken down, interrupting the corn harvest. It was hot, the yard full of flies. Koehn apologized that he couldn't take me for a spin in the machine, so instead brought me inside a large barn where women in white-and-blue bonnets brought in trays of sweet iced tea and homemade oatmeal cookies. We talked about the wheat he grew, which he was gradually shifting to organic methods, though it accounted for only 280 acres of a 4,000-acre farm. He was drawn in, he said, because "it seemed like our weeds were getting more resistant to the herbicides." Plus, it wasn't a sacrifice. He told me one field of irrigated organic wheat yielded 100 bushels an acre, topping his conventional fields and double the state average. This result tugs at the often-stated narrative that organic farming methods, which eschew chemical fertilizers and pesticides, always yield far less. Koehn, who was by no means a die-hard organic farmer, attributed the results to the use of compost, but he still found the bountiful yield surprising and perhaps an aberration.

There was another, more subtle reason he was moving in this direction. "It was intriguing to have a quality product, grown on our farm, being consumed by people and milled by our neighbors," he said. The alternative was to send the wheat to the grain elevator, and from there into the global food chain. "We never know where it ends up," he said. So, even here, in this great expanse of farmland, among the most productive wheat fields in the world, the farmer yearned for a personal connection, though he could never be "local" in the sense of the farmer who sells at my farmers' market in Washington, because local demand would never match his vast supply.

Koehn wasn't growing Turkey Red wheat, but rather the modern varieties released by university breeders and then put into production by seed companies. Much more productive than the old wheat varieties, such as Turkey Red, these new wheats seemed like a winning formula, but then, in the 1970s, scientists began to warn that these plants were awfully similar to one another, narrowing genetic variability. By breeding this highly productive wheat and then planting it in widespread monocultures, a basic food staple might become vulnerable to a devastating epidemic. It was the same old worry that had bedeviled farmers for millennia. The insurance policy for the food supply—plant diversity—was missing.

A wake-up call came in 1970, when an epidemic of southern corn leaf blight struck the hybrid corn crop in the United States with intense speed. Worried about the implications of such a knockout blow for other staple foods, researchers at the National Academy of Sciences acknowledged that there had also been a "genetic erosion" in wheat. "The breeder, who means well, is destroying by his actions the genetic base for a new generation of varieties," one researcher wrote.

This risk of vanishing germplasm results anytime breeders select a chosen few from a broad population of plants. Certain plants may exhibit robust disease resistance, a larger kernel, reduced risk of lodging (in which the plant droops over so is more difficult to harvest), earlier maturity, and the like. But if these plant selections are cultivated in a monoculture, pests and diseases can evolve to attack them. Once the varieties lose resistance, they become, in effect, an all-you-can-eat buffet for the newly evolved pest.

Aside from corn leaf blight, severe disease epidemics struck wheat in India.

In Russia, a widely planted wheat variety also failed, forcing Moscow to secretly import wheat from the United States for the first time in the 1980s. To prevent this kind of repeated food crisis, which distantly echoed famines of the past, resistant plants needed to be developed—and hopefully faster than threats evolved. But if the pool of genetic resources upon which breeders depended for their work narrowed, they would have fewer resources at their disposal: these "resistant" plants would have a built-in vulnerability.

Ironically, this "genetic bottleneck," as it's known, was an unintended effect of the Green Revolution—a massively successful wheat breeding effort which took off in the 1960s and created high-yielding varieties to feed a growing world population. At the core of the program were semidwarf wheat varieties, so called because of their fat seed ears and short stalks, which were first bred in Japan in the 1920s. Researchers seeking higher productivity crossed a Japanese dwarf wheat variety, thought to have originated in Korea, with another wheat from the Mediterranean. Then this variety was bred with Turkey Red wheat to create the grandmother of modern wheats, Norin 10. (When I learned that modern wheat descended from a Eurasian cross, and one with Japanese and Ukrainian roots no less, I began to feel some weird natural kinship to these plants, for essentially they mirror my own Japanese–Ukrainian Jewish heritage.) These short-stature plants were less prone to falling over in the field and could also devote more of their energy to producing grain instead of fibrous stalk, making the plant more efficient. Discovered by U.S. wheat researchers during the postwar occupation of Japan, these semidwarf wheats were refined at Washington State University and then became the foundation for modern wheat bred by Norman Borlaug, the father of the Green Revolution. In the 1950s, even before the arrival of these new varieties, Borlaug's work in Mexico produced a dramatic increase in wheat yields—the amount of wheat grown per acre—of nearly 6 percent per year. Then he shifted to the semidwarf varieties that came via Washington State, and after several years and many failures, the gains kicked in again. Yields of these semidwarf varieties rose nearly 5 percent per year in the 1960s and '70s.

These compact varieties thrived with a regime of synthetic fertilizers, irrigation, and pesticides, eventually becoming so productive that Mexico became self-sufficient in wheat. Mostly spring wheats, they quickly spread to other areas of the world, such as South Asia, Latin America, the Kansas fields of the United States, and Australia. They were less suited to dry land areas, where cereal grasses first evolved, though by the 1990s breeders had adapted the semidwarf varieties to these regions as well. During the Green Revolution, global wheat yields increased by about 1 percent a year, which meant that countries like India and Pakistan could feed a growing population.

Borlaug eventually won the Nobel Peace Prize for the work and was credited with saving perhaps one billion people from starvation. But after the mid-1970s, yields began to stagnate. And something else was happening as well—what wheat geneticists called "a narrowing of genetic diversity coming out of the breeding pipeline relative to that going in."

By the 1990s, the vast majority of spring wheat grown in developing countries originated at the International Maize and Wheat Improvement Center, the research center that housed Borlaug's work, known by its Spanish acronym CIMMYT (pronounced *Sim-mit*). If the seeds did not come directly from CIMMYT, they came from national agricultural programs relying on CIMMYT's germplasm, its seed bank. In this way, CIMMYT was at the forefront of breeding high-yielding varieties that, as one scientific paper put it, "replaced the landraces in great swaths across the world."

The adoption of modern spring wheat was particularly significant, because it accounts for about two thirds of all wheat grown in developing countries—mostly by small-scale farmers for local consumption. By 1997, 97 percent of all spring wheat landraces had been replaced by modern varieties.

This lack of diversity in wheat wasn't limited to CIMMYT seed lines. European wheat varieties, which showed a great deal of diversity from the 1840s through the 1960s, narrowed considerably as hybrid varieties replaced landraces. By 1993, the National Academy pointed out, landraces were all but being ignored because they had little apparent value, and yet it warned that those landraces might hold the key to future environmental stresses—a particularly prescient point as global temperatures rise. As it turned out, the Green Revolution wheats CIMMYT developed in Mexico suffered in years when temperatures rose above average. This is now a growing concern as global warming progresses. In developing countries such as India, models project that rising temperatures could stunt the wheat crop and threaten the food resources of hundreds of millions of people. In North America, forecasts project that wheat farming will shift to the north, with amber fields of wheat extending into Alaska by 2050 as temperatures continue to rise. Letting diverse landraces languish, or even vanish, was like playing Russian roulette with the food supply—twice—first from the standpoint of disease vulnerability and second from climate change.

CIMMYT heeded these warnings in the 1990s, and began looking anew for genetic material in wild grasses. Recall that wheat descended from the initial selections made by Neolithic farmers around ten thousand years ago. Bread wheat itself arose from the happenstance interbreeding of these farmers' emmer wheat with wild goat grass weeds. To bring more genetic diversity into modern wheat, researchers looked anew at the wild goat grass cultivars. They crossed them with lines of durum wheat—the pasta wheat that emmer evolved into over many centuries—trying to re-create versions of the original bread wheats, but with new genetic material. To increase diversity and develop certain traits, wheat breeders were adding genes from wild grasses that were closely related but never interbred into the wheat genome. These were not genetically engineered plants; the breeders used conventional breeding techniques to create these hybrids. But these novel creations are known as "synthetic wheat," because they represent an unprecedented genetic stew. They then crossed these creations with elite breeding lines of wheat, and further mated them with local cultivars in China and other countries. With this work, CIMMYT researchers have boasted that wheat now has more diversity than before the Green Revolution, making the wheat crop even more productive, especially in conditions of extreme heat and drought.

But how does this lab-induced biodiversity compare with landraces that evolved in farmers' fields, over millennia? Nearly all the seeds on which breeders depend are now held in "doomsday" seed vaults designed to protect the world's store of genetic material, or more accurately, the food supply. The most infamous site, the Svalbard Global Seed Vault, sits below four hundred feet of solid rock on a frozen Norwegian island above the Arctic Circle. CIMMYT alone holds one tenth of the world's crops and has more than 168,000 different varieties of wheat, barley, rye, and wild grasses, which are the foundation material—the germplasm—from which to breed new plants.

Even scientists worry this invaluable seed stock isn't quite the same as maintaining biodiversity in nature, because biodiversity can't simply be reduced to a library collection. The very word *biodiversity* means not only genetic variation but variation in the landscape and among species. So if you breed a new wheat plant and then seed it in a monoculture, across an entire nation, you're essentially undermining the kind of biodiversity you're trying to re-create. And this is occurring globally, as the latest and most popular wheat varieties are released and then planted across wide swaths of land. The practice by farmers of selecting seeds for microclimates—as Earl Clark did with Blackhull wheat, or as farmers did with their landraces—falls dormant. The natural selections and happenstance adaptations that occur in the field go by the wayside.

Meanwhile, wild grasses—another source of biodiversity—are vanishing. "More and more land is used for farming in order to grow commercial crops to feed the increasing human population. Extensive herding has led to overgrazing and erosion. The last primary habitats of wild stands will soon be destroyed. We are close to losing a valuable source of genetic diversity that could help plant breeders to provide food for future generations," a team of archeologists wrote in 2010. This worry isn't just theoretical. In 2013, wheat researchers identified a gene in ancient Turkish einkorn wheat that conferred resistance to a devastating fungal rust disease, known scientifically as Ug99, that has wiped out wheat in East Africa and Iran and threatened to spread globally. Another resistant gene was found in wild goat grass. Once identified, those genes could be bred into new wheat varieties, creating resistance to this new scourge.

This is just the latest example of how relic and wild wheat species provide the genetic keys to preserving wheat. In other words, the future of one fifth of the world's food supply may reside precisely in the genes of wild grasses or the least productive landrace wheat varieties, with the worst bread-making qualities, which is why these grasses have been ignored, even trampled upon, for a century or more, at humanity's peril.

The lack of diversity doesn't just have implications for farming or the food supply. It may be related to gluten toxicity as well. While the broad array of "gluten sensitivity" issues has only recently been defined by physicians, let alone understood, celiac disease, which affects about 1 percent of the population, has been the focus of sustained research.

For those people with the disease, gluten acts as a trigger, causing the immune system to misfire and attack itself. The targets frequently are the microscopic folds, or villi, of the intestinal wall, which once damaged can no longer absorb nutrients into the body. Classic symptoms include diarrhea, intestinal pain, and signs of malnutrition. Atypical signs, such as tiredness, depression, osteoporosis, migraine headaches, muscle or joint pain, anemia, delayed growth, and even schizophrenia, are also associated with the disease.

Although celiac disease was first described by a Greek physician in the first century, gluten was only identified as the culprit in the mid-twentieth century. More recently scientists have located the most troublesome proteins, which reside in the gliadin segment of gluten. If you put your baker's hat back on, you'll recall that gliadin proteins are crucial for dough's extensibility—that is, its ability to stretch out without snapping back like a rubber band. Gliadin contains a specific segment of proteins—or chain of amino acids—that prompts an immune response in about half of all people with celiac disease. Gliadin's sister protein, glutenin, which adds strength or elasticity to dough, isn't an innocent bystander, for it, too, can prompt an immune reaction, but it occurs less frequently.

Because wheat has been the subject of intensive selection and breeding, geneticist Hetty van den Broeck, at the Wageningen University and Research Center in the Netherlands, wondered whether modern wheat differed from older varieties in a way that would prompt more expressions of celiac disease. Did the toxic gliadin protein fragment—known as an "epitope"—appear more frequently in modern wheat than in ancient landraces? A paper by a team of Norwegian researchers in 2005 had sparked this line of inquiry, as it identified einkorn and durum wheat that lacked this specific disease-triggering epitope. But they hadn't looked extensively at modern and landrace wheat varieties.

"Before we started the analysis we didn't have a clue how prevalent the celiac disease epitopes would be in modern and old varieties," van den Broeck told me. So she tested thirty-six modern European varieties and compared them with fifty landrace and ancient wheats, from regions as distant as the Middle East and Ethiopia—admittedly a small sample considering the tens of thousands of wheat varieties, but still large enough to get a meaningful result. What she found was that the toxic fragment was far more prevalent in the modern varieties. "This suggests that modern wheat breeding practices may have led to an increased exposure to celiac disease epitopes," she and her coauthors wrote in the *Journal of Theoretical and Applied Genetics* in 2010.

While she didn't locate any wheat varieties that lacked the toxic sequence, there were varieties where the epitope was minimally present, even among a few modern wheat lines. Van den Broeck suggested that if breeders focused on these less toxic varieties, they could eventually produce less toxic flour for people genetically susceptible to celiac disease. "Breeding was always done for baking quality, or yield and pest resistance, but there's never been breeding done for the presence of CD epitopes," she told me.

This is admittedly a challenging task, because gliadin proteins are essential to bread making. Think about it: if you're breeding wheat and stumble on a variety that produces an especially light loaf, then you're going to make sure other wheat varieties share the same characteristics. So breeders are sure to crossbreed this trait into the hybrid wheat they develop. Given this selection criterion, it isn't too surprising that modern wheat shares a basket of similar traits. But van den Broeck's findings suggest that less toxic wheat varieties may one day be available, in part because scientists now know where this prevalent toxic gluten fragment arose from: it came from the gliadin proteins transferred thousands of years ago from wild goat grass, when it mated with emmer wheat.

This suggests that wheat species that lack these genes—einkorn wheat, for example—would lack these toxic gliadin fragments, too. But that turns out to be ambiguous. While some studies have found that einkorn wheat can be tolerated by patients with celiac disease, other studies have found toxic protein fragments in the grain. "Einkorn does have epitopes, just less of them," van den Broeck explained. "It's not as if you can just get rid of one protein and the story is over. That is what makes it complicated to find a wheat variety suitable to all patients."

But that hasn't stopped geneticists from trying. Recent papers have pointed to some early success at "silencing" the toxic fragments through genetic manipulation. These modified grains yielded only a minor response from immune cells involved in celiac disease, but this research is at a very early stage, and the work is fraught with complications, since so many proteins are involved and so many wheat varieties exist. "It's not something you can do on a Friday afternoon," van den Broeck said. The question she's pursuing is whether the less toxic lines can be hybridized into modern wheat, lowering exposure to the disease-causing proteins. Perhaps then the switch for celiac disease would remain in the "off" position, at least for some people susceptible to the disease.

Translating this rather arcane line of genomic cereal science into a choice for bread or flour is exceedingly difficult. Ancient varieties of wheat are highly diverse, so even if you could locate some landrace wheat—that is, untouched by the breeding efforts of the Green Revolution—it's a crapshoot whether you'd find a variety that reduces the likelihood of a gluten reaction. While einkorn wheat has been tested on people with celiac disease, it hasn't been widely studied. I've heard a lot of anecdotal evidence from bakers about gluten-sensitive customers raving about the digestibility of this spelt bread or that ancient wheat variety, when fermented with sourdough. But these are anecdotes. These toxic gluten fragments have been studied only in relation to celiac disease, not with the much wider range of "gluten sensitivity" disorders, which might operate in a very different way in the human body. The precise way that gluten interacts with these other vague disorders is still largely unknown.

From van den Broeck's work, however, it is clear that landrace and ancient wheats had more diversity, at least when it comes to these protein fragments. In the premodern era, the staple diet was more diverse as well. When harvests were bountiful, people might gorge on wheat. But the next year, they were eating barley, rye, chickpea, or chestnut flour and trying to avoid famine. In one valley, wheat might have been higher in protein. Over in the next valley, it might have been lower. One year, the wheat might have yielded strong gluten. The next, it might have been damaged by summer rains, unleashing protease enzymes that compromised these gluten proteins. The upshot: one's lifetime exposure to these wheat proteins was probably as inconsistent as the food supply. That's not the case today, at least in places in the world where we have a bountiful supply of food. Diversity wasn't reduced only on the farm but in cereal foods as well. As van den Broeck's work shows, the breeding of more uniform wheat cultivars had implications for the modern diet—and perhaps for disease as well.

While I was muddling through this research on wheat breeding, I stumbled across the work of Eli Rogosa, a self-styled guerrilla seed breeder in western Massachusetts, who was growing ancient landrace wheat, such as einkorn. I filed it away as a curiosity, but as I talked with farmers, breeders, and millers, her name kept coming up. Some described her as passionate, even mystical, but whatever the case, she was clearly driven by a mission to restore

Eli Rogosa holding one of her heritage wheat varieties

wheat diversity and was growing a vast number of landrace wheats on her small farm and then selling the seeds to farmers. I thought that was fascinating, given everything I was reading about biodiversity, for here was a rare case of a farmer working outside the specialized world of seed breeding and pursuing the work on her own.

Rogosa isn't trained as a botanist or geneticist, so she's an outsider, but this gives her a perspective that others inside this close-knit world might not have. In a world of largely privatized breeding, Rogosa seems like a modern-day Johnny Appleseed, nurturing wheat varieties that have nearly vanished from agriculture and then spreading them around.

When we finally spoke, she gave me a brief rundown of her work. She had collected nearly extinct einkorn wheat from Druze farmers in the Golan Heights; visited with farmers in France, Italy, Germany, and Greece; passed through the former states of eastern Europe, and been to the Caucasus in the Georgian Republic, helped along by research grants from the European Community and various gene banks. Her quest was to collect rare landrace wheats from farmers who still cultivated them.

"They are almost apologetic about planting these wheats," she told me. "They'll say, 'We're growing modern wheat, but this is what my grandfather gave me.' And then they show me a little spot off on the corner of a field where they keep the landrace," she said.

When I visited her one fall day in 2011, torrential rains had just drenched the Northeast, causing a creek to crest its banks and wash out the road to her farm in western Massachusetts. The Northeast hadn't seen devastating flooding in decades. Rogosa had made it through the storms, and the fields where she had recently planted wheat were moist but not flooded. But as I looked over her small, modest farm, I wondered, "This is where the future of biodiversity lies?"

In her clapboard home, a cast-iron woodstove in the living

~ Sheaves of wheat in Eli Rogosa's home

room burned bright. Around the sofa, where her partner, C. R. Lawn, the founder of a Maine seed cooperative, Fedco, sat, were sheaves of wheat, tied neatly together, with the seed heads splaying out. The wheat was also stacked on wooden chairs, strung up on walls, piled in corners, and hanging from the ceiling. Some had fat bursting seed heads, while others had thin rows of seeds. Some were golden in hue, others dark brown, with long beards, or needlelike hairs, protruding from the ear. If there was any doubt about the vast array of wheat, one need only pay a visit to Rogosa's living room to see a sample. She had made this her life's work, but in the process, it had taken over the place where she lived. Aside from the bundles of wheat, she had boxes filled with seed from the world over. She later explained that wheat had a kind of other-worldly appeal. She talked about the "energy" and "life force" in the plants. Anyone who has ever planted a seed and watched it sprout might feel that way, though for Rogosa, with her frizzy hair, wire-rim glasses, and loosely fitted farmer's attire, the plants seemed to express something essential that had been lost. Now she was trying to bring it back. "I'm Jewish, I'm into history," she explained with a laugh.

Her work had actually begun in Israel, where she had lived for fifteen years, working with Arabs and Israeli Palestinians on organic farming and sewage treatment projects. While there, she began looking for local flour to bake with and realized that nearly everything for sale was imported from the United States. Alarmed, she visited an Israeli gene bank to find out where local wheat was grown. She found out there wasn't much, which was curious because she knew this was the area where wheat originated. "I ended up writing a proposal and I became the coordinator of this collaborative to restore ancient wheat in Israel," she said. Through the water and farming projects, she had met Palestinian, Arab, and Jewish Ethiopian farmers who had saved their seed. These were the landraces she collected for the Israeli gene bank. "They saw it as conservation," Rogosa said, but she saw the work as something more.

Back home, she began growing these ancient wheat varieties and found they were especially tolerant of extreme weather, and thrived without irrigation. These landraces were selected by farmers long before synthetic fertilizers and pesticides came into use, so were also better suited for organic agriculture. Rogosa spaced the plants far wider than usual, at twelve inches, rather than the tight spacing of intensive modern farming, relying in part on techniques described in nineteenth-century farm manuals. "You get these huge plants, up to six feet tall, with a lot of tillers," she said, referring to the side shoots on which seed ears also develop. "They need room to grow." When they were spaced closer together, the plants were more compact, with fewer tillers, which meant fewer seeds to select. She also mated these ancient varieties, trying to adapt them to the Northeast. "That's one of my varieties over there," she said, pointing to a thick sheaf of wheat hanging on her kitchen wall, its huge seed heads drooping over. These large plants had deep root systems, which could tap water sources in drought. Modern wheat has shallow root systems well suited to irrigation, but without a source of water, they might perish. "Unless we have flexibility and resilience, which comes from diversity in our gene pools," she said, "we don't have capacity to adapt."

As she said this, she was dropping seeds into small plastic envelopes that she planned to distribute at a farm conference in Maine. She encouraged me to take some home and plant them in my community garden plot in Washington. She riffled through her collection of boxes on a desk, choosing seeds that she thought might do

⤙ Seed samples and catalog on Eli Rogosa's desk

well in the mid-Atlantic. She gave me seeds grown by biodynamic German farmers; another selection from Ukraine; a French variety, known as Rouge Bordeaux, and another from France known as Mélange; and Canaan Rouge, a Maine variety bred from the Rouge Bordeaux and adapted to the Northeast. I thought she would charge me, since these small packets are quite pricey on her Web site. But she refused. "I'm happy to share my seeds with you," she said. "We're all looking for artisan bread, but the artisan grains are this enormous missing link that no one person can renew and restore." She hoped I would join the movement.

So on a warm fall morning in late October, I visited my garden, located just south of a freeway in Washington, D.C., about a mile from the U.S. Capitol, and sowed the landrace winter wheat that Rogosa had provided. I might have been the only one growing wheat in the nation's capital. I seeded two twenty-five-foot rows of Canaan Rouge. Then I planted two more rows of the French varieties she passed on to me, the Rouge Bordeaux and Mélange. I spaced the seed about six inches apart, which is quite wide, but Rogosa assured me that wider spacing would mean more vigorous growth. I returned every week as the weather turned cooler, and was disappointed. Only a handful of seeds had managed to germinate. Was it a problem with the seed or were animals eating it? Over the years we'd had a visible urban rat population in the park, plus it was filled with birds.

After an e-mail exchange with Rogosa, I went back and planted more, this time after soaking the seeds in water so they might have a better chance of germination. By November, it was getting colder at night. Of the seeds that did take root, the plants were now about three inches high. Once they grew a bit more I'd mulch them with hay for the winter in order to keep the weeds at bay. The next summer, I thought, I'd be harvesting wheat, though of what quality I did not know. I had dazzling visions of my Capital Wheat. If I did well, I'd have around ten pounds of grain, which could make several loaves.

By the next spring, the wheat was growing vigorously, and by May the plants had sent up tillers, the strong stalks on which the seed head forms. They were three to five feet tall and quite beautiful, especially the French Mélange. They had huge green husks of grain on an ear that was seven or eight inches long, pushing upward from red-tinged vegetative grass. It looked like the wheat harvest would arrive in a month, and though I had only about fifteen to twenty plants, I would definitely yield enough grain to make bread. The true urban farmer, I felt proud. Along the way, I reconnected with Klaas and Mary-Howell Martens of Lakeview Organic Grain in upstate New York. They estimated the harvest date from the pictures I posted on Facebook. All was going well.

Then one day I arrived at the garden after about a week's absence and those beautiful French varieties that I had so patiently nurtured looked as if they had been attacked. Instead of standing erect, the stalks were bent to the ground. The seed heads were denuded of any grain. I felt a little panic—this was my wheat!—and I wondered if these landrace varieties were defective in some way. I had just spent the week reading about the shattering traits in ancient wheat, and these looked like they had matured and then split open, the seed scattered on the ground, near the base of the plant. Would I now, like a Neolithic hunter and gatherer, scoop up the grain? I bent down and took a few of the grains in my hand, but on closer inspection it was clear there were no grains. All I could see were the split-open hulls. I could not find one seed in that handful, or in another. They had all been eaten!

I looked around the now empty garden. A few sparrows flew by, a blue jay, and then I noticed the massive amount of bird life around me. This was surely a welcome sight in an urban garden, but they, too, had to eat. Maybe my wheat was their dinner. Or perhaps it was rats, climbing up the stalks from the ground. A few people in the garden who had grown corn had faced similar trials. Beautiful, bursting ears of corn one day; the next, the cob denuded. The pests had good taste and knew exactly when to strike.

The next day I returned and found still more damage and realized I had lost well over half of my wheat crop. The animals were targeting the largest seed ears from the most vigorous plants. Desperate, I tied reflective metallic tape, which shimmers in the sunlight, around the stalks to scare away birds. I had found that this works well, especially with tomatoes, which also can be a frequent object of avian desire.

Once again, I posted pictures on Facebook of the loss. Klaas thought it might be mice as well as birds. Mary-Howell recounted how they once lost one hundred acres of organic soybeans a week before harvest in a hailstorm and were forced to plow under the crop. "We can't begin to convey the devastation, the horror, the disbelief, the loss," she wrote. "However, for years afterwards, the nitrogen level in that field was great!" (That's because soybeans fix nitrogen— an essential plant nutrient—from the air to the soil.) When I told another farmer friend about my loss, he simply paused and said, "Welcome to the world of farming."

So much for my grandiose plans of growing Capital Wheat. Now it was clear that I would not have my ten pounds of grain to bake with, only a handful or two that I could grind, or perhaps soak overnight and then mix into a dough. The loss made me think of those prehistoric farmers. Had they lost half their crop to birds, they might have faced food shortages and been forced to return to the wild grasslands to gather more seed. Or what about those farmers throughout the ages who faced successive famines? I had lost my crop, but luckily I didn't have to depend on it for food. I could go to the supermarket and buy flour, or begin making a dent in the large mason jars of grains sitting in my kitchen—the emmer, einkorn, spelt, rye, barley, red wheat, white wheat—all of which, in my particular place in the world, was accessible. Measured against humanity's relationship with grain, I was an outlier, for this staple was plentiful in my pantry. That toll I faced in the garden was far more often the norm in the past ten thousand years—scarcity.

The impetus to prevent such shortages and breed ever more productive varieties led the world away from crop diversity. But aside from the agronomic consequences of these decisions, there were culinary ones, too, in the qualities of flour itself. Airy white bread was the marker for every important decision along the way, from seed to milling to fabrication. And while "whole grain" breads have recently grown more popular, they often try to approximate white bread in look, taste, and feel, at least at the supermarket. It is not even clear how much whole grain these "whole grain" breads contain, for this has never been regulated by the Food and Drug Administration. But why use whole grains to approximate white flour? Why not bring true diversity back to our cereal diet? I had an inkling of these possibilities growing up with the breads of New York, but to explore this question further I knew I had to visit a place where whole grains weren't a novelty, or a health choice, or masquerading as white bread. I had to visit a place where whole grain bread was simply bread. And that's what took me to Berlin in the winter of 2011.

Turkey Red *Miche*

(MODERATE)

Makes 2 loaves

I actually learned about the history of Turkey Red wheat before I tried it, which underscores the oft-stated trope that the story makes the food. It wasn't until I returned home from my visit to Heartland Mill that I bought Turkey Red wheat, choosing the stone ground bolted version in which the coarsest bran is removed.

This recipe reflected the particular batch of Turkey Red I received in the fall of 2012. When I order the flour again, the quality will probably differ, so I'll end up adjusting the amount of water and *levain*. That's the challenge—and joy—of working with identity-preserved grains. The batches vary from year to year, which means you need to keep adjusting.

This recipe closely follows the *pain de campagne* at the end of chapter 3, the main difference being that it has a higher percentage of whole grain flour. In the absence of Turkey Red flour, you can use whole wheat flour, but try sifting out the bran through a sieve.

The result will be more dense, and you may have to add a bit more water. Plus it won't quite taste the same. Turkey Red is quite hardy and rather assertive, reminiscent of the tough life the early settlers faced on the Great Plains.

Tools
    Bowl
    Plastic dough scraper
    A bowl or colander lined with a kitchen towel, in which the loaf can rise
    Rimmed baking sheet
    Rectangular baking stone
    Baking peel or cutting board, to move the loaves to the oven
    Single-edged razor blade, *lame*, or knife
    Cooling rack

Levain Ingredients
    120 grams bolted Turkey Red flour
    80 grams water
    20 grams ripe starter

Final Dough Ingredients
    120 grams unbleached all-purpose organic flour, plus more for the counter
    480 grams bolted Turkey Red wheat flour
    200 grams starter
    425 grams water (plus another 25 grams added in increments)
    13 grams sea salt

Evening, First Day

Mix the *levain* ingredients together, cover, and let sit for 8 to 10 hours, until the starter has domed but not collapsed. There will be extra starter left over once you remove 200 grams for the dough, which you can use to refresh the remaining starter, as described in the *pain de campagne* recipe.

Morning, Second Day

In a bowl, blend the white flour and Turkey Red flour together. Add golf-ball-size bits of starter to the flour and 425 grams of water. Mix with your lightly moistened hand until combined, 1 to 2 minutes. Make an indentation on top of this shaggy dough, and into this well add the salt and 25 grams of water so that the salt can dissolve in this pool of water. Cover the bowl and let it sit for 30 minutes.

Moisten your mixing hand again, then shake off the water. Then stretch and fold the dough in the bowl by pulling the dough out from the edges and folding in toward the middle, circling around the dough as you do so. You can also pinch the dough between your thumb and fingers to further diffuse the salt. Stretch and fold the dough 10 to 12 times. Turn the dough over, so that the seams are facedown, and the smooth side is on top. This entire process should take about 2 minutes. Cover and let the dough sit for 30 minutes.

Repeat the stretching and folding for another two rounds, always ending with the smooth side on top and resting for 30 minutes between rounds. I usually do three or four sets of folding, depending on the needs of the dough. Let it rise for about another hour— I find that this first rise, including the time it takes to complete the folds, should take 3 to 4 hours.

Afternoon, Second Day

Dust the counter lightly with flour and gently remove the dough with a dough scraper, letting the smooth top of the dough fall onto the counter. The sticky underside will now be face up. Cut the dough in half. You can make both loaves at once if they fit into the oven, or refrigerate half the dough to bake it later.

Stretch out the four sides of the dough and let them fall into the center. They can overlap. Then turn the dough over so that these seams are facedown. Dust with flour, cover with a light cloth or towel, and let the dough rest for 20 minutes.

Dust the counter with flour very lightly, then turn the dough over again so the seams are face up and the smooth side is on the counter. Stretch and then fold the edges in toward the center, so that you have an approximately round shape, which should take 6 to 8 folds. Apply light pressure in the center so the folds seal. Turn the dough over, so the smooth side is now face up, and cupping your hands around the dough, use the outer edges of your palms and pinkies to stretch the skin of the dough and tuck it under the bottom, moving the dough in a circular motion so that you end up with a round shape. Try not to compress the loaf tightly, though; the goal is to have a taut skin.

Prepare a bowl or colander lined with a floured towel. Using the dough scraper to loosen the loaf from the counter, pick up the loaf and place the smooth side facedown on the floured towel in the bowl or colander. The seam side will be face up. Cover with a towel and let the loaf rise for 60 to 90 minutes, or until the loaf springs back slowly when you press it lightly with a finger.

One hour before you are ready to begin baking, place a rimmed baking sheet on the bottom of the oven and a baking stone on a rack in the middle. Preheat the oven to 500°F (260°C).

Place ½ cup hot water in a measuring cup.

When you're ready to bake, dust a baking peel or cutting board with flour, and turn the loaf out onto the surface, so that the smooth side, which was on the towel, is now face up. Using a single-edged razor blade, *lame*, or knife, score the loaf four times to make a square on the top of the loaf. Angle the blade while you slash the loaf in a swift, sure cut about ¼ inch deep.

Transfer the loaf to the hot stone and close the oven door. Open the oven again and pour ½ cup of water into the baking sheet. Immediately close the oven, trapping the steam. Turn down the oven to 460°F (238°C) and bake for 20 minutes. Then turn down the oven to 440°F (227°C) and continue baking for another 15 to 20 minutes, or until the crust is dark brown. Turn the oven off and prop open the door slightly with a wooden spoon, leaving the loaf in the oven for another 5 to 7 minutes. Ideally, the loaves will have a hollow knock when you remove them from the oven. Alternatively, stick an instant-read thermometer in the bottom of a loaf. The center of the loaf should read at least 205°F (96°C).

Let the loaf cool on a rack for at least 1 hour before cutting into it. Store it in a paper bag or wrapped in a towel for up to two days, cut side down, and then move it to a plastic bag. You can also freeze the loaf in a plastic bag. When ready to use, let it defrost, then crisp the crust in a 400°F (205°C) oven for 5 minutes.

CHAPTER 6

A Rye Journey to Berlin

After I had been making loaves with white flour for a while, then loaves with a bit of whole wheat, I decided to move on to rye breads. After all, I had distinct memories of rye as a child, though mostly in the form of Levy's Jewish Rye. Levy's was a hybrid product—an assimilated bread, you might say—which merged eastern European rye with the familiar airy softness of American white bread, and ended up with a light slice studded with caraway seeds that at best hinted at the possibility of true rye bread. That said, the story behind the bread is quite telling.

Levy's was a true Jewish bakery when it was founded by Henry Levy in 1888. It served an Orthodox Jewish clientele a mix of rye, challah, bagels, and rolls. But after World War II, as Jewish communities and tastes dispersed, the bakery fell on hard times and then went bankrupt. Seeking to resurrect the business, its receiver engaged one of the true Mad Men of Madison Avenue, an advertising executive who felt the brand would survive only if it moved out of the Jewish community. The memorable tagline was born: "You don't have to be Jewish to love Levy's real Jewish rye." Along with the airy reformulation meant to appeal to broader tastes, it rescued the company. Levy's ended up becoming a bit like the General Tso's chicken of Jewish rye (though even its bankruptcy receiver felt the new rye was bread "no Jew would eat"). That wasn't true, however: it was the rye I often ate as a child and I found it made particularly good toast.

Real rye breads were anything but light and airy, which I discovered when I went with my father to the Lower East Side or Flatbush in Brooklyn, where the bread was dense, chewy, tasty, and dark. Another close family friend, Sol Yurick, a novelist who grew up in the Bronx, had a real taste for "corn rye"—a misnomer because it doesn't have corn in it. It's derived from the Yiddish *kornbroyt*. *Korn* simply means grain, and *broyt* (or *Brot* in German) means bread. While the corn rye Sol bought at a deli in Brooklyn wasn't whole grain, it did have a very tight, chewy crumb, with a thick, crisp crust that was quite pleasant. Visiting the Yuricks in the Park Slope neighborhood of Brooklyn as a teenager, I recall that Sol would take the fat, shiny loaf out of a paper bag, cut off thick slices with a long bread knife, and then smear his slice with a thick slab of butter. He would eat the bread, roll a cigarette with the tobacco he bought at a Ukrainian smoke shop on the Lower East Side, and then have a smoke with a cup of muddy black coffee. What could be better?

Stanley Ginsberg and Norman Berg point out in their book *Inside the Jewish Bakery* that historically rye "was the mainstay of the Jewish diet." Rye thrives in the colder regions of Europe and grows well in marginal soils so was a cheaper option for those who could not afford wheat. Ginsberg and Berg write: "Bread could consist entirely of rye or of rye and some other flour—often barley or buckwheat, but rarely wheat. In the shtetls of what is now Belarus, Jews ate *plovnik* made from a mixture of finely and coarsely ground rye flour. In Poland and Lithuania, they ate sourdoughs like *gebatlt broyt* (about 55 percent rye flour) and *razeve broyt* (about 95 percent rye flour); *sitnice*, a light brown bread of mixed wheat and rye, and *kornbroyt*, or corn rye, which survived the journey to America and became a Jewish bakery mainstay." The exception, of course, was challah, made with eggs, oil, and wheat, on Friday for Shabbos.

Now, when I began to make rye breads at home, a few years into baking, I didn't have a firm idea of what they would be like, other than the distant memories of the breads from my childhood in New York. Most of the artisan breads that were becoming the rage in the nineties had a French or Italian lineage. If a bakery happened to have a rye bread, it was often a mild rye with caraway seeds—the artisan riff on Levy's perhaps. But when I tried a few recipes, the loaves I made had a fantastic, sharp, tangy taste that were a world away from Levy's. They were closer to the dark ryes I had had as a kid, and were almost a meal in itself.

Still, these early attempts at rye were trying. The grain was unfamiliar because, lacking gluten, it performed very differently from wheat. When I tried to knead the grayish-colored dough by hand, it was impossibly sticky. Dough would get caught between my fingers, cover my palms, and sit like a flat blob in my hands. When kneaded on the counter, it stuck there, too. So I resorted to my KitchenAid mixer and kept mixing and mixing because when I pulled at the dough, it would just tear off, rather than stretch, as I thought it should. Where was the elasticity, the spring? I had no idea what was going on, so I turned up the speed of the mixer and dumped in more white flour so that I eventually achieved a gluten structure that was familiar. Recipes pointed out that rye doesn't perform like wheat but that didn't help me much. So I ended up making ryes, but often ones with a good deal of white flour.

Like my early stabs at the baguette, this was discouraging, and I left these loaves behind for a time. But, as I began to dive into whole grain flours, I knew I had to return to rye and figure it out. I wanted to capture its remarkable, almost addictive taste, which I find superior to whole wheat flour. And what better way to learn about rye, in all its varied possibilities, than to visit a place where rye was at the pinnacle of the bread culture—Berlin?

I talked about this idea with Jeffrey Hamelman, a rye aficionado who worked in Germany early in his career. He suggested that I talk with a woman who had taken some baking classes from him, and who did a stint at a bakery in Berlin. Through a few e-mails and phone calls, I got the name of Weichardt Bakery, which specialized in whole grain breads made from freshly milled flour. Relying on Google Translate and the generosity of a German-speaking friend, I composed an e-mail and sent it. Luckily, the bakery manager spoke English and wrote that they were game to have me. We arranged a date—after their holiday rush. So, one chilly day in January 2011, I flew to Berlin, to learn how to make rye bread.

While I was excited about the trip, a part of me was uneasy. After all, I was visiting Germany to connect with Jewish bread—bread that came out of an eastern European culture, the Jewish portion of which was annihilated. My father had also fought in World War II (in the Pacific, not Europe), and I have friends whose relatives perished in Nazi concentration camps. While contemporary Germany is more closely associated with images such as the fall of the Berlin Wall, and all-night youth techno raves, for me, having never visited before, it dredged up much darker associations. For a long time, I had never had a desire to visit Germany, and I still know people who avoid the country. So, when I did decide to go, I flew a couple of days early, because I wanted to be sure to take in a few sites and memorials. One of the first stops would be the Jewish Museum.

Now, winter is a terrific time to travel. It's inexpensive, and the hotels and museums are relatively empty. On the transatlantic flight, you might even get a row of seats to yourself in economy. It might be gray most of the time, and the wind might bite, but it feels appropriate if you're making the rounds of all the Holocaust-related memorials in Berlin—and there are quite a few. Taking the Berlin subway, the U-Bahn, from my hotel, I got off at Kochstraße, or Checkpoint Charlie, which is now just a gatehouse in the middle of the road. There's no hint of the former wall at this spot. From there, I walked the several blocks down to the Jewish Museum, which is housed in a grand old mansion in the former East Berlin.

While I had planned to visit the museum for a couple of hours, I ended up spending the entire morning, making my way through the multifloor exhibit that painstakingly detailed the vast scope of the Jewish experience in Germany, which for centuries vacillated between assimilation and exclusion and led to mass extermination. One particular print from the twelfth century stood out—an illustration from the Middle Ages of Jewish bakers burning Christian babies in an oven. It was the kind of myth that caused Jews to be ousted or killed, and was ironic, considering how history turned mythology on its head. But the exhibit interestingly did not dwell on the Holocaust, which almost seemed like an exclamation point in this long historical slog.

In the modern wing of the museum, the Holocaust Tower designed by Daniel Libeskind depicts this moment architecturally. It is eerily effective—a thick door through which one enters a small angular cement room that went up and up, a window of light at the top of the unheated structure. I stood there for a few moments in the cold, the silence echoing through the narrow room, and then I pushed reassuringly through the door to reenter the museum.

After completing the tour of the exhibit and eating a pleasant lunch in the cafeteria, I walked several blocks through the neighborhood—filled with socialist-era apartment blocks, stunning pop-art wall murals—to the Typography of Terror Documentation Center, housed in the former headquarters of the Gestapo. Although revisiting this history was exhausting, I felt like I had made some peace.

What was so fascinating was how ubiquitous this history was in Berlin. The memorials seemed to be everywhere. There was no escaping the past.

The next morning, I rose early, had breakfast at the hotel's buffet, where the whole grain rye wasn't half bad, then walked the several blocks to Weichardt Brot. It was located in Wilmersdorf just off Berliner Straße, past a school, kabob take-out joint, café, supermarket, grand apartment buildings, and all the things you'd expect in a residential neighborhood. I turned off the main street and walked up to the bakery, which occupied two shops—one where customers were already lining up for their bread and a storefront next door where stone mills ground the whole rye and wheat into flour.

Heinz Weichardt, who trained as a pastry chef, founded the bakery with his wife, Mucke, in the early 1980s. He runs the business from a tiny, cramped office at the back of the shop. The couple were passionate about whole grain baking and biodynamic farming, a subset of organic agriculture founded in Germany which is much more prevalent in Europe than in the United States. Now, there are mystical aspects to biodynamic farming—which involves planting by lunar cycles and preparing nutrient sprays for fields and compost piles—but the upshot was that the grains they bought were of high quality. Since they viewed the rye and wheat as vital and nutritious, they believed the flour should be ground on the stone mills the same day the loaves were baked.

This is a debatable point among bakers, since white flour, at least, benefits from oxidation that occurs during aging, helping gluten to strengthen. But Weichardt and other bakers I've come across argued that freshly ground whole grains were the richest nutritionally, a point which is borne out by the science. Also, given the breads they were making, gluten strength wasn't an issue. Freshly milled flour also has an unmistakable taste and smell, reminiscent of a field of freshly cut hay, which you'd notice if you ever walked through Weichardt's milling room. Most of their breads were also naturally leavened, risen with Backferment, a sourdough culture popular in Germany and produced with biodynamic ingredients.

Dirk Eimer, the English-speaking manager of the bakery, had told me to come at 8:30 A.M., after the second shift of the day had started. The store had row upon row of wooden shelves bursting with the day's bread, all of them dark whole grain loaves, some covered with sesame, sunflower, or caraway seeds. I approached the harried woman working the counter, but at the last minute, forgot the German phrases I had practiced. The poor woman was at a loss to understand what I wanted, especially with other customers

Stone mills at Weichardt Bakery

waiting in line. So, I left and returned to the hotel, where I looked up the phrases I needed, and came back. With my remedial German, I was finally able to tell her why I was there. She immediately showed me into a floury baking room where Karl, Freddy, and Klaus, with whom I would spend the next several days, were busy shaping loaves. Eimer, who looked to be in his thirties and was the only one dressed in street clothes, walked in and said, "You're late!" When I explained what had happened, he laughed and said, "Ah, you need to learn German."

Indeed. One of the repeated challenges of this project was learning, observing, and absorbing lessons without the benefit of a common language. The Weichardts, for example, spoke hardly a word of English, so I was dependent on Dirk to translate for me. But, as I've observed before, bakers are not the most voluble or expressive characters I've met, nor does a spoken explanation really match the lesson you get by observing and then plunging in with your hands.

After I changed into my baker's whites, I watched the three work quietly. The rye dough was dark and grainy, nothing like wheat flour. Freddy, a young woman just out of baking school, turned to me and said, "Here, do you want to try?" and she flung a piece of dough to me across the counter. The technique worked like this: Freddy would spread a generous amount of whole grain flour across the butcher block work surface and then pick up a piece of dough that Klaus had weighed on a scale. Using her left hand as a guide, she rolled it around with her right hand, so that it barely touched the counter. Every now and again she swept her hand through the coarse flour, so that the loaf wouldn't stick. When the dough formed into a ball, she placed both palms on top, gave it a roll, back and forth, so that it turned into a fat log. Then she picked it up and placed it in one of the steel loaf pans on a shelf. It took maybe fifteen seconds.

Trying to mimic the movements, I picked up the dough she had thrown my way, but the shaping technique was so unfamiliar I was immediately in over my head. The loaf stuck to the counter, my hands became full of dough, and the impossibly loose, gooey, grainy mass was doing anything but forming into a neat ball.

Freddy stopped and watched me.

"What, you do not know how to do this?"

"Well, that's why I came . . . to learn."

She didn't roll her eyes, but then, she didn't have to. She just went back to work.

I sat out a few rounds as they dumped more and more dough on the counter. Karl, who was in his late fifties, worked with an economy of motion, as if he had been doing this a long time, and shaped two loaves at a time, one in each hand. He also spoke perfect English. So, while I was standing around watching, he pulled me aside and asked me to brush the bread pans with melted butter, "but not too much." All I could think was, "This is why I flew to Berlin, to grease bread pans?" But then, I wasn't doing anything else.

With that task done, the bakers quickly filled the pans with the rye dough, covered them with a thin sheet of plastic, left them to rise, and then went on to make more. Now Karl had me jump back into the fray, and working quite slowly, he showed me how to manipulate the dough. After several tries, I got it. The loose mass formed into a ball and I kept enough coarse flour underneath to keep it from sticking. The key was constant movement. If you stopped for a second, or if you were deliberate and considered, it wouldn't work. The dough would stick. You had to work quickly. Plus, I had to leave behind everything I had ever learned about shaping, since it all applied to wheat dough, not rye.

The loaves I formed that day weren't perfect, but Karl reassured me that they were okay. The dough would spread out and fill the

Three types of rye loaves

pan as it rose, doubling in size, and all the imperfections would be gone by the time they were ready for the oven. He was right. Thirty minutes later, this incredibly fast-rising dough reached just under the brim of the bread pans and we loaded them—four pans welded together, so that they weighed twenty pounds or more— into the hot oven, dousing them with steam. They baked at a relatively high temperature of 550°F (290°C) for about twenty minutes, then Karl removed them with thick oven gloves and shoved them onto another level of the deck oven where it was 390°F (200°C), where they continued baking for another forty minutes or so. When they were dark and toasty smelling, he took them out of the ovens and dumped the loaves out of the bread pans. Then he grabbed a long steel wand off the wall and blasted the top of the loaves with hot steam, causing the crust to shine and toppings, like cumin, sunflower or sesame seeds, to better adhere to the surface. Putting on a pair of thick gloves, I helped move the loaves to a wooden drying rack.

This went on all morning until the six-foot-tall bread rack was full. There was *Roggenweizenbrot*, which was a favorite of mine and literally translates as rye-wheat-bread; *Ganzkornbrot*, a whole grain loaf with *Schrot*, or cracked rye; *Kräuterbrot*, a rye with cumin, fennel, coriander, and nettle; *Kümmelbrot*, which was plastered with caraway seeds; *Vierkornbrot*, with rye, wheat, oats, and barley; and many other loaves. One of the last ryes we made was a giant 2 kilogram (4.4 pound) Weichardt "Special," with rye and wheat, which was hand-formed rather than risen in a loaf pan and included flour made from leftover bread. This day-old bread was cut up, dried in a low oven for an hour or more, ground up and then mixed into the dough. (Jewish bakers used a similar technique, known as *altrus*, soaking the leftover bread in water for the next day's dough because "nothing was wasted," according to *Inside the Jewish Bakery*.) This adds a deeply satisfying rich taste to an incredibly dark loaf, which is why it was called the Special.

At the end of the morning, we had finished baking the pan loaves, but we were still steaming ahead. We moved on to enriched doughs made with butter that we braided into *Zöpfe*, which look similar to challah. I hadn't done much braiding previously, so Karl taught me a three-strand braid made into a kind of cone-shaped loaf, and then a six-strand braided loaf. After a couple of days braiding dozens of loaves, the work felt automatic, as if my hands were leading me along. If I thought too much about it, though, I would inevitably screw up (which is what happened, of course, once I got home). Finally, we shaped this same dough into hundreds of *Kinderbröten*, or small rolls which the bakery gave away to children visiting the shop after school.

Despite all you hear about Europeans and their relaxed working hours, I found the pace just shy of brutal. After the first day, I started to arrive at 6:30 A.M. and hit the ground running. No one in the bakery even took a lunch break, though at one point Karl sliced up a rye, showing me the under-counter refrigerator where I could find a bit of cheese or sausage. There wasn't even a place to sit down (which made me painfully aware of how accustomed I was to sitting all day) so I just grazed while standing up. When one task was done, we moved on to another, and that went on until the day was over. No wonder most of the bakers were in their twenties or thirties. The work was grueling, especially for someone who usually baked, at most, a few loaves a day, not hundreds.

"It's really hard," Karl admitted. "I can't do it every day, or if I did I wouldn't have time for anything else." In the evening, he played jazz bass, so he worked the last shift of the day which began at 8:30 A.M. But that meant he also had the main task of cleaning up after everyone else. At fifty-seven, he was on his knees with a hand broom carefully sweeping flour out of every crack and crevice. I swept, too, with a broom, but it was clear I wasn't getting every crumb off the floor. So later, I also got down on my hands and knees. It was kind of humbling, this sweeping and scraping of hardened bits of dough off the floor. But then, I'd said I wanted to work in a bakery. This came with the territory.

Karl, with sweeping silver hair and a warm smile, told me he grew up in Austria and never wanted to be a baker, but his stepmother pushed him to do it because that way he would always have something to eat. "Given what she'd known during the war, it seemed like the best choice," he said. He didn't like the work as a young man—he couldn't go out with friends at night—but it offered a way to leave home, since bakers would give him a room, often board, too. So he apprenticed around Austria and Germany, ending up in Berlin in the 1970s, which then, as now, had a vibrant youth culture. He'd take months off from work and hitchhike

Heinz Weichardt (left) and Karl Steffelbauer
in front of the oven

through Turkey and Afghanistan, a popular path at the time, which often led to the ashrams in India. "Afghanistan was a beautiful place then," he said wistfully. "And the hashish was very good." He finally met up with Heinz and Mucke Weichardt a few years after they opened their bakery and has been with them ever since.

In a photo I took, Heinz and Karl are sitting in front of the oven, staring straight into the camera. "My old friend!" Karl said, when I showed him the picture. For Karl, it seemed, baking was second nature; just one part of his life.

. . . . .

One afternoon, I stayed a bit later than usual because Karl was mixing up the Backferment for the night shift, which would arrive around midnight. They made new batches of this starter from a package of granules about once every six months, then fed the sourdough twice a day. Sekowa, the German company that makes Backferment, mixes together organic wheat, corn, chickpeas, and honey, ferments the substance, and then dries the leaven in granules and sells it in packages. It favors mild-tasting lactic acid and is quite popular among German bakers of organic breads. Home bakers can also buy it in natural food stores.

At Weichardt, the starter was incredibly active, though that might have been due to the freshly ground rye, which has an excess of both fermentable sugars (rye exceeds wheat in this regard) and amylase enzymes (which you'll recall convert starch into sugar). In fact, I've found that freshly ground whole grain flour is like high-octane fuel for sourdough, which is why I add it to my starter when it appears a little weak. The stuff perks right up. In any case, when Karl mixed up the starter in the afternoon for the coming night shift, he dumped two premeasured bags of freshly ground whole grain rye and wheat into the mixer, perhaps ten kilos (twenty-two pounds) in total, added three big buckets of water, and then a small pitcher of starter. I was skeptical this small amount of starter would ferment such a large batch of flour, but he assured me it was enough. The ingredients were mixed together, covered with a loose plastic sheet, and then left to ferment in the giant steel mixing trough for about eight hours, for the bakers who worked through the night.

The night crew then baked breads with this leaven and mixed more Backferment for the morning shift, which I got to see when I arrived. The rye-wheat mixture was thick and full of porous holes, like a sponge. It also had a sweet, grassy aroma, not at all acidic or alcoholic. We added more rye flour and wheat to the

Weichardt Bakery's recipe book

leaven to make the final dough, though in this case the word "flour" might be a bit misleading. Much of it was quite grainy, so that it appeared more like coarse whole grain breakfast cereal. We added water and salt and then turned on the mixer. This was a single-arm mixer, with the steel arm bent at the elbow. The arm would sweep down into the dough, grabbing some of mixture as it rose up, then letting it fall and flop over on itself. Compared with the most mixers I've seen, it was incredibly slow. If you took a spatula, or your hand, and slowly mixed a batter by raising and lowering your arm, the result would be much the same.

Seeing this process was an important lesson, for I realized that the mixer was very gently incorporating the ingredients, rather than developing gluten strength, as with wheat flour. The porridge-like dough slowly combined into a loose, grainy mass with hardly any springy elasticity. After twenty minutes or so in the mixer, the dough held together in a cohesive mass, but really didn't look too different from the way it began. I realized I had to stop thinking about gluten when working with rye. Yet the curious thing about rye is that it *does* turn into bread. It does rise and it does get holes, even if small ones. The question I had was, how?

Rye grain, not surprisingly, differs quite dramatically from wheat. Its fiber soaks up an enormous amount of water, but it also has pentosan, a gumlike sugar which is far more prevalent in rye than in wheat and which also absorbs water. Rye proteins as a result go begging for hydration, and without sufficient water, they cannot rearrange themselves into anything like a gluten network. On top of that, rye has only a fraction of the glutenin proteins found in wheat, which are the source of elasticity and springiness, so rye can't create the kind of gluten network that allows wheat bread to expand.

Without gluten, rye falls back on starch and that gumlike pentosan to form a loaf. When mixed with water, they turn into a kind of foam that traps carbon dioxide during fermentation. So the bread does indeed rise. Then when the dough finally hits the hot oven, starch granules expand and soak up water, causing some granules to burst open and form a viscous substance. Think of the way flour thickens when heated in a pan with water to make gravy. Known as "starch gelatinization," this occurs in rye at 125° to 150°F (52° to 66°C). At the same time, sourdough microbes belch out ever more carbon dioxide gas into this viscous, gelatinous substance. Once the starch cools again after the bread is removed from the oven, the starch and pentosan form a semicrystalline structure known as "retrograde starch"—or liquid starch that has cooled and set. This becomes the bread's crumb.

In wheat loaves, starch and pentosan are more like supporting actors in a crumb structure dominated by gluten, so you rarely even hear about them. But with rye, the bit players get the starring role, and they do their job admirably; that is, if they can avoid one big nemesis: amylase. These enzymes work like mad, breaking down starches into sugars, and wreaking havoc on the interior crumb you're trying to create. Since amylase isn't deactivated until 170°F (77°C), it has ample time to target the gelatinizing starches, destroying the crumb in the oven even before it's fully formed. The result is that the interior of the bread can become a gummy mess. When you cut into a loaf that has suffered a dreaded "starch attack," the bread knife will come out covered in brown gunk. It's unpleasant, believe me. But the way to switch off these enzymes and ensure that your crumb will turn out just fine is to make the bread with sourdough, for its acidity keeps amylase in check and allows starch gelatinization to proceed. That's why rye bread is traditionally made with sourdough. Without it, the loaf will end up more like porridge.

So here's a tip: if you ever make gummy bread, which can be quite common in whole grain baking, increase the amount of sourdough in the recipe. Peter Reinhart, whose book *Whole Grain Baking* has one of the best discussions of enzymes I've come across in a baking book, usually pre-ferments about half the total flour in a recipe in the sourdough starter. Compared with most recipes, this proportion of sourdough is quite high, but it does the trick. The amylase is snuffed out.

Aside from deactivating this enzyme, sourdough improves the

quality of whole grain bread in another important respect. It mitigates the damaging effect of bran, which can degrade gluten and the connections it forges with starch. During fermentation, sourdough converts bran fibers into soluble polysaccharides, those long chains of starches that can contribute to the formation of the crumb. But to get this result, the bran needs a sufficiently long fermentation of eight to twenty-four hours. "It turns a negative element into a positive one," the sourdough researcher Michael Gänzle told me. This is why you should always make whole grain bread with sourdough.

But here's another counterintuitive tip: make sure your whole grain flour isn't milled too finely, because it may interfere with the formation of gluten. While I've often heard from bakers that bran "cuts" gluten—implying that finer bran wreaks less havoc—this seems questionable. Cereal scientists suggest that the enzymes and chemicals in bran inhibit gluten, and exposure to these substances increases the more finely the bran is milled. Studies show bread volume goes down noticeably with finer bran. So don't be afraid of coarsely milled whole grain flour: it may produce a better rise. At least it did at Weichardt.

Now, the Weichardt rye-wheat loaf tasted grainy, full of deep and earthy flavors. The Backferment, being mild in nature, meant that the freshly ground grains weren't masked by any harsh acidic overtones. This bread also had a kind of resistant chew when you bit into it, with flecks of bran and grain, making for a varied texture. With a schmear of butter, the bread was quite satisfying, but at most, I could eat two pieces sliced extremely thin, no more than a quarter inch wide. Karl told me that he sometimes had a slice of rye in the morning, and that was it. One slice didn't do it for me, but two would keep me going for a long time. The bread fueled a very slow burn.

Whole grains, as it turns out, do metabolize slowly, though to understand that we have to jump beyond the taste buds and into the nether regions of the alimentary tract. The scientific literature is replete with the benefits of whole grain fiber, noting the speed of "intestinal transit" and higher "fecal bulking weight" (that is, the stuff spends less time in the colon so there's less chance of disease-causing cell mutations). Among the health benefits we hear so much about, whole grains lower cholesterol and reduce the risk of cardiovascular disease. They also modulate blood sugar levels, not just when they are eaten but also for the following meal—so a bowl of oatmeal at breakfast slows the metabolism of carbohydrates at lunch. Refined carbohydrates, like white bread, work very differently, quickly converting into glucose and causing blood sugar levels to spike. This, in turn, causes the pancreas to pump out more insulin, which channels these sugars to the body's cells. Over time, on a diet high in refined carbs, insulin resistance can kick in and eventually may lead to type 2 diabetes, where blood sugar levels soar. Whole grains temper this entire chain reaction, because fiber doesn't convert to sugar but instead moves through the entire intestinal tract. Coarsely ground grains magnify the effect, because the digestive tract has a tougher time extracting the carbs.

In this equation, sourdough fermentation helps, too. Lactic acid slows the pace of starch digestion, while acetic acid prolongs the rate at which food passes through the intestine. This one-two punch from sourdough is so powerful that white sourdough bread raises blood glucose levels less than whole wheat bread made with yeast, despite its higher fiber content! In this way, sourdough tempers sugar shock.

But sourdough does something else quite beneficial, transforming rapidly digested sugars into nondigestible fibers. These fibers, known as exopolysaccharides, pass undigested through the stomach and into the body's colon. Once there, they become food for bacteria, which gobble them up and turn the large intestine into a fermentation crock. These fibers are known as "prebiotics," because they feed the biota that live within us. Along with resistant starch—or starch that hasn't been digested—and plant fiber, gut bacteria ferment this fibrous feedstock and multiply.

Although colonic fermentation may not sound appealing, it helps keep us alive. One of the beneficial by-products of microbial fermentation is short-chain fatty acids, which lower cholesterol and facilitate the absorption of electrolytes. As athletes know, electrolytes are especially important to maintaining hydration. But perhaps most important, these gut microbes reduce inflammation and in so doing may play a protective role in preventing ulcerative colitis, irritable bowel syndrome, even colon cancer. One study published in the spring of 2013 found that when people were fed a multigrain diet, their gut microbial communities flourished along with the compounds that fight inflammation. While studies have been inconsistent on the relationship between whole grain consumption and, say, lower risk of cancer, an eleven-year European study of 470,000 people recently concluded that fiber plays a protective role. The bottom line of this research: you want to keep your colonic fermentation tank bubbling away.

There's an elegance, too, in this ecological relationship. Sourdough microbes, which, as you'll recall, likely originate in the intestines of rats, pigs, chickens, fruit flies, or humans, find their way into dough; once there, lactobacilli eat carbs and belch out carbon dioxide and create exopolysaccharides; when we eat sourdough bread, these fibrous compounds flow through the stomach and to the colon; once there, the microbes that inhabit our intestines gobble up these fibrous fermented food products and create fatty acids that help us live. It's one big happy circle of microbial ecology, fueled by fermentation inside the body and out.

One more potential benefit of sourdough must be mentioned, which relates specifically to celiac disease and to the anecdotal reports I often hear about sourdough bread being easier to digest. Over the past decade, scientists have found that certain strains of lactic acid bacteria can degrade gluten to the point that it is undetectable. That is quite a feat, for it suggests that sourdough digests gluten and in this way could potentially make wheat less toxic for gluten-sensitive people. One of the foremost scientists behind this work, Marco Gobbetti, head of the Department of Plant Protection and Applied Microbiology at the University of Bari in Italy, told me that it wasn't simply "sourdough" that did the trick, as in the sourdough that's sitting on my kitchen counter. Rather, the handful of microbes he's selected were the most powerful gluten-digesting creatures his lab could find in more than one thousand sourdough starters in Italy.

I was curious about the origins of the idea. I mean, why even test sourdough for its ability to degrade gluten? "The idea for this research actually came from my father, who said and still says that the sourdough bread made by his grandmother was much better than the bread we eat today," Gobbetti told me. I refrained from interjecting that his father must be a smart man. "In some instances, when he had digestive problems, he felt better by eating this bread. Obviously, the observation was anecdotal. But that's where the idea came from." I almost laughed. Of course, the source of this scientific inquiry arose from bread made by an Italian grandmother!

At the beginning, Gobbetti thought nothing would come of the work, but he went ahead nonetheless. The results turned out to be surprising. Not only was his lab able to use this specially prepared sourdough cocktail to degrade gluten to below the EU "gluten-free" standard of twenty parts per million, they also fed bread made with gluten-degraded flour to celiac patients who in short-term studies showed no adverse reaction. Baker's yeast, the lab found, had no such properties. The researchers in Gobbetti's lab recognized this difference explicitly, noting that the fast fermentations common in industrial breads weren't doing anything to reduce the disease-related cereal proteins in wheat. Maybe, I asked Gobbetti, the historical loss of sourdough-fermented breads made people in general more vulnerable to celiac disease? He admitted that was an interesting hypothesis but it hadn't been substantiated in any epidemiological studies. Those types of studies would be difficult to conduct unless you could find a population of people who exclusively ate sourdough bread.

When I asked him whether the sourdough I used in my own kitchen would have a similar gluten-degrading effect, he stressed that his lab had identified a special team of lactic acid bacteria. "What we do with these bacteria to break down gluten *cannot be done at home*," he said, stressing the last part of his statement. Still, I pressed, thinking that even my sourdough would have some power over gluten, even if minimally. After all, wasn't it his father's folk wisdom that set him down this path in the first place—that his grandmother's sourdough bread was easier to digest? Gobbetti eventually did concede that my sourdough might have some slight effect on gluten, it was just uncertain how much. Maybe it was 0.1 percent, maybe 10 percent, of what they were achieving in the lab; it was all speculative and depended on those little microbes I had in residence, how long my fermentations lasted, and even the type of wheat I used. Overall, he stressed, "Don't try this at home." Homemade sourdough will not produce gluten-free bread, though I do accept the anecdotal evidence that it may be easier for some to digest.

All of this research makes clear that sourdough microbes can alter the nutritional profile of bread. The more I looked, the more I found. Studies have shown that sourdough fermentation can maintain the level of thiamine (vitamin B_1) found in whole wheat bread, even after baking. Certain strains of lactic acid bacteria can boost the level of riboflavin (vitamin B_2) by two to three times. As if that weren't enough, sourdough breaks down phytic acid, which is concentrated in the innermost layer of bran and blocks the body from absorbing beneficial minerals also found there, such as iron, calcium, magnesium, and zinc. Yeast and baking powder lack this power to neutralize phytic acid, which means mineral absorption declines when you make whole wheat bread with these methods. (Mineral deficiencies aren't a problem in wealthier parts of the world, but in poorer countries they constitute a major health problem.) Now, I'm not knocking your morning bran muffin made with a leavening agent such as baking powder, because you still get the intestinal benefit of fiber. But with sourdough-fermented whole grains, the bacteria neutralizes much of the phytic acid in the bran and frees these essential minerals to be absorbed by the body.

White flour, of course, lacks many of these benefits. Because milling removes the bran and the germ, vitamin E, vitamin K, and a range of minerals—calcium, magnesium, phosphorus, potassium, zinc, copper, manganese, and selenium—are depleted as well. A few nutrients, such as iron, thiamin, riboflavin, niacin, and folate, are added to white flour through "enrichment," but even these additions don't make up for the wide range lost in the bran and germ. Add in zippy yeast fermentation and the result is a loaf as devoid of taste as it is of the many nutritional benefits I've just described.

One day, Heinz Weichardt was talking to me about the nutritional superiority of using freshly ground whole grains and Backferment in making bread. In retrospect, there was quite a bit to support what he was saying. But Weichardt didn't need a nutritional label or a health claim to persuade customers to buy a loaf. Customers were not seeking a colonic aid, or a fiber boost. They were just buying bread. *Roggenweizenbrot* may have had a whole range of health benefits from its freshly milled whole rye and wheat grains, but at the end of the day it was just a good loaf: dense, yes, but almost addictive once you started eating it. At its apogee, food should sustain the organism, by tasting good, by feeling good in the mouth, by satisfying you, and by giving you sustained energy. Weichardt's bread scored on all those counts.

Sadly, such loaves are still few and far between in the United States. As I visited San Francisco's Tartine bakery over the course of a couple of years, Chad Robertson was moving more assertively into whole grains, influenced by rye bread he had encountered in Denmark. His bakers were constantly experimenting with grains like barley and emmer and his cooks at Bar Tartine had built a menu around thinly sliced grainy rye, known as Danish *Rugbrød*. Yet, when I visited the restaurant for lunch, there weren't yet lines out the door. Those could be found around the corner at the Tartine bakery, where people were clamoring for the country loaves, made with sourdough and the more familiar white flour. But maybe that will soon change. I've come across a handful of bakers in various parts of the country making eastern European–style loaves. One in Brooklyn makes Latvian-style ryes. Another in New York makes Finnish Ruis loaves that are grainy and quite good. In New Haven, WholeG sells terrific German-style ryes at the farmers' market, but truthfully, these whole grain bakers are few and far between. Hopefully, like heirloom tomatoes in the 1980s, they will soon have their day.

So, in Berlin, did I find that dense, rich, dark rye bread I ate as a kid in New York? I would have to say no. These German breads were different, with far more rye than I think I've ever encountered and also greater variety, but they were a distant echo of what I had eaten. There were other unexpected connections with my Jewish culinary roots, like the braided *Zopf* I made with Karl. If you didn't know better and were visiting Weichardt Brot on a Friday, you might mistake it for challah. Then, walking through Prenzlauer Berg in East Berlin one Saturday morning, I came across a crowded farmers' market where several stands were selling smoked and pickled fish. I associate these foods with Russ & Daughters on New York's Lower East Side, Zabar's on the Upper West Side, and the Sunday brunches of my childhood with my family in Brooklyn. *Sprotten*, a bite-size smoked whitefish that you eat whole, and the pickled herring would have made any Jewish appetizing store in New York proud. Another day, I visited the famous KaDeWe department store and rode the elevator up to the giant food emporium. I stood in line behind a modestly dressed working man who bought a pickled herring sandwich and I swear inhaled it. I went for the smoked mackerel, which was quite rich, oily, and oddly familiar.

All these delicacies were virtually identical to ones I associated with New York Jewish food—the food my dad loved. But what I didn't expect was to hear his words. One day, when I was standing in the bakery with a few of the bakers, Mucke Weichardt said in the midst of a conversation, *"Verstehst du?"* as in, "Understand?" I picked out the word because the pronunciation sounded so much like the Yiddish my dad would use: *"Farshteyn?"* With one word, an entire world came rushing in, for I hadn't thought about the way he used that phrase in years. And then I began recalling a few of the Yiddish words he would use. I mentioned this to Karl and we began trading Yiddish and German equivalents. And so here I was braiding *Zopf*, not challah, listening to German, not Yiddish, and eating pickled herring in Berlin, not New York. I had this overwhelming sense of connection to my past, in Berlin of all places, with its profusion of Holocaust memorials. It turned out to be the most surprising thing about the trip.

· · · · ·

By now you can probably guess what happened. I came home and began working on rye bread. The first problem I ran into, though, was the coarse rye flour. Most whole rye is pretty finely ground, but I knew that I wanted a mixture of coarse and fine flours. The only brand I found that came close to coarsely milled was from Hodgson Mill. I also bought a grain mill attachment for my KitchenAid mixer that could easily produce *Schrot*—the grainy flour. Finally, I needed loaf pans, since the short-fat ones I had on hand were better suited for zucchini bread than rye. I found some Pullman loaf pans in a King Arthur catalog that when filled half-way took about a kilo of dough. This was a big change for me, for I had never baked pan loaves. In fact, I'd looked down on them for years. But I realized it's not really about the pan, it's about the bread. And you can make terrific rye bread in a pan because the shape helps support weak doughs like rye.

As for Backferment, I did get a package through the mail from Karl, and it tasted quite mild in flavor just as it did in the bakery. But I liked my own sourdough, too, so I used both, at different times for the rye breads, and probably ended up with an amalgam of microbes—who knows? The final over-the-edge step, several months into baking with rye, was to buy a small countertop stone mill, so I could mill all the flour I needed, not just the *Schrot*. (Of course, I ended up buying a German-made KoMo stone mill, which while sporting an iPad-like price tag will hopefully last ten years or more—and unlike an iPad, will never need an upgrade.)

With all of these elements in place, I began working on my loaf, a mixture of 70 percent rye and 30 percent whole wheat. It came together pretty quickly and was far easier than the baguette. I kept in mind the lessons about easy mixing and relied on my hands to do the work. I found that if I continually moistened my hands in water, the surface of the dough would remain slippery, not sticky. So I took to mixing and folding the dough in a bowl by the sink, wetting my hands under the faucet and then shaking off the excess so I didn't incorporate too much. I still used the fold-and-rest method, though since gluten wasn't involved, I didn't stretch it out. I would mix every five minutes or so, for a minute or two. After three or four rounds, the dough seemed fine. Since ryes ferment so quickly, the first rise usually took forty-five minutes to an hour, then I'd form the loaf as best I could using the method I learned at Weichardt and drop it into the oiled loaf pan, dusting the top with a good coating of rye flour. Even if it was misshapen, it would invariably flatten out, fill the pan, and rise evenly. While the dough filled only one half of the pan going in, within an hour, sometimes less, it was at the top. At that point, the floured surface would begin to crack open like ice. I'd then bake it, first at a high temperature with steam, then at a lower temperature, just as they did at Weichardt, for a total of sixty or seventy minutes.

Now the important part: once it was done baking, I'd let the loaf rest for at least twenty-four hours, though the interior of the crumb really improved after thirty-six hours. It takes that long for all the starch to fully set. Karl had told me that the Weichardt Special lasted seven days and I found that to be the case with these homemade ryes as well. They keep well, because they soak up so much water and because the sourdough inhibits mold and bacteria. It was quite amazing really, cutting through a thick crust after a week and finding a moist interior. It's yet another reason to bake with rye: it not only fills you up and burns slow but lasts a long time without going stale. In terms of staying power, nothing quite matches it.

With rye under my belt, I had one task left—to explore locally grown grains, which had begun to reemerge spottily in farmers' markets and in bakers' breads. It was the latest thrust in the locavore movement and perhaps the most difficult to grasp, for unlike a tomato, we've learned to think of flour as just flour. As I began to explore this thread, one baker in particular caught my attention. Maybe it was the picture of his windmill, the small village where he lived, or just his bread. Whatever the case, I knew I had to visit with him and so in spring 2012 I returned to Europe, this time to southern France.

Roggenweizenbrot
(DIFFICULT)

Makes 1 loaf

Roggenweizenbrot (literally, rye-wheat bread) was my favorite loaf at Weichardt Brot. It has a mixture of coarse and more finely ground rye flours, which I made by mixing equal parts of Arrowhead Mills organic whole rye flour and Hodgson Mill rye flour. To achieve a mild sourdough, which favors lactic acid, I've added a second rise, or build, to the leaven. Since there's such a high percentage of sourdough in the rye-wheat dough, it ferments quickly. The first rise takes 45 to 60 minutes and the final rise in the pan about 1 hour. If cooler than 75°F (24°C), it will proceed more slowly.

A key step in this recipe is to dust the surface of the dough entirely with rye flour, once it's in the pan. Most of the flour gets absorbed into the moist dough, so don't be concerned about getting a mouthful of flour when you eat the bread. When the dough rises sufficiently, the flour cracks open on the top, signaling that it's ready for the oven. This is a far more accurate gauge of rising time than anything else.

The bread also takes two days to make, with the bulk of the work accomplished on the second day. So plan for a six-hour window on the second day to make the bread. Since this loaf rests for a full day before you cut into it, truthfully, it's a three-day bread. If you start making the sourdough on Friday evening, you can cut into the loaf by lunch or dinner on Sunday.

Optional step one: This loaf is quite good on its own, but for a twist you might want to add freshly roasted spices. Lightly toast 1 teaspoon each cumin seed, aniseed, and coriander seed in a pan until fragrant, let cool and then grind them in a spice grinder.

Optional step two: When starting out, you might want to use 1 teaspoon of instant yeast as an insurance policy to help the loaf rise. But it isn't necessary if you have an active starter.

Tools
    Bowl
    Plastic dough scraper
    Rectangular baking stone
    Rimmed baking sheet, for the bottom of the oven
    Loaf pan measuring 9 by 4 by 4 inches (also known as a
        Pullman loaf pan)
    Kitchen mitts

First Starter Ingredients
    10 grams ripe starter
    100 grams rye flour mix (made of coarse and fine rye flours;
        see headnote)
    80 grams water at 80°F (27°C)

Second Starter Ingredients
    180 grams first starter
    100 grams rye flour mix
    80 grams water at 80°F (27°C)

Final Dough Ingredients
- 180 grams whole wheat flour
- 220 grams rye flour mix
- 11 grams salt
- 1 teaspoon instant yeast (optional)
- Ground spice mixture (optional)
- 360 grams starter
- 320 grams water
- Vegetable oil spray or 1 tablespoon melted butter

Evening, First Day

Mix the ingredients of the first starter together until combined and place in a covered bowl or container. Rye is very active, so you don't need a lot of starter to get it going, especially during a long fermentation. That's why there are only about 2 teaspoons of starter in this initial fermentation. Let it rise for 16 to 20 hours.

Second Day

The first starter will have risen and will contain a lot of bubbles, with a noticeably acidic aroma. Mix it with the ingredients of the second starter until combined. Dust the top with rye flour and cover the bowl. The starter will double in size within 3 to 4 hours and the rye flour on top will have cracked open. At this point, it's ready to be used in the final dough.

Final Dough

Place a baking stone on a rack in the middle of the oven and a rimmed baking sheet at the bottom.

Preheat the oven to 460°F (240°C).

Roggenweizenbrot

Combine the whole wheat flour, rye flour mix, salt, and the yeast and spice mixture, if using. Break up the starter with your fingers and add it to the flour. Pour in all the water. Then, using one hand—moistened with water—mix to combine. I find this is easiest if you have the mixing bowl right next to the sink, so that you run your hand under the water as soon as the dough begins to stick to it. If you wait too long, you will have a hunk of dough stuck to your fingers. (If you do get a hand full of dough, moisten the fingers of your clean hand and use your thumb and forefinger to remove the dough from the dough-encased hand, then rinse it again.) Mix until just combined, 1 to 2 minutes, and cover. Then let sit for 10 minutes so that the flours can hydrate.

At this point, the dough will be quite thick, almost like cookie batter. Wet your hand and then go at it again, squeezing the dough with your fingers and folding the dough over on itself. This should take 1 to 2 minutes. Let the dough rest covered for about 10 minutes, then repeat the action, adding more water so that the dough loosens up a bit. (While mixing, I will add 40 to 60 grams more water.)

The dough should be stiff but pliable. Cover and let it rise for 30 to 40 minutes, until it looks slightly more porous and gassy.

Lightly oil the loaf pan, or brush it with melted butter.

I find it easiest to shape the loaf in the bowl. Wet your hands and fold the dough toward the middle several times, so you have a round ball. Turn it over, so the seam is facedown. Then with your moist hands, roll the ball so it's kind of a loaf or football shape and about the length of the pan. Then with two hands, pick it up and gently place it in the pan. Wet your hands and smooth out the top, but don't worry if it's uneven: the dough will flatten out as it rises and evenly fill the pan. The dough should fill one third to one half of the height of the pan. Dust the top of the loaf with a generous dusting of rye flour and cover the pan with plastic wrap.

The timing of the final rise is crucial. You want the loaf to rise to within a half inch of the top of the pan. But more crucially, look for cracks in the flour coating. When they begin to appear, the loaf is almost ready for the oven. Let the cracks open a bit, until they are a quarter inch at the widest point. Depending on the temperature of your kitchen, this will take 50 to 70 minutes. If your kitchen is very cool, it might take longer. But remember, the cracks are your ultimate guide—not the time.

Preheat the oven to 460°F (240° C) with the baking stone on the middle rack and the baking sheet on the bottom of the oven.

When the loaf is ready, place the bread pan on the baking stone, pour ⅔ cup of water into the baking sheet, and shut the oven door. Bake the loaf at 460°F (240°C) for 20 minutes.

After 20 minutes, open the oven to vent the remaining steam and then lower the temperature to 390°F (200°C). Bake the loaf for another 40 minutes, turning the loaf around after 20 minutes if your oven tends to bake unevenly. Then turn the oven off and let the loaf sit in the oven for another 10 minutes, for a total baking time of 70 minutes.

Using thick kitchen mitts, remove the loaf from the oven. It should fall right out when you tilt the pan over. Place it on a cooling rack. Let the loaf rest for 24 hours before slicing it open. While it rests overnight, place a towel over it.

This loaf has exceptional keeping quality. I cover it with a towel for 3 days, then place it in a plastic bag and continue to eat it for a full week. Alternatively, freeze half of it in a plastic bag. Remove and defrost the loaf, though there is no need to reheat the loaf unless you desire.

CHAPTER 7

Local Bread in Cucugnan and Cobb Neck

I n southern France, the wind is known as the *tramontane*. It whips
from the northwest, flies over the snow-topped Pyrénées, and
blows across the bright sunny coastal region of France along
the Mediterranean. In the tiny hilltop village of Cucugnan, in the
Languedoc-Roussillon region, about an hour in from the coast, the
wind is known as *le vent de Cers*. It blows in a steady hum and howl
through the narrow streets of the medieval-looking village, and it
was the first thing I noticed when I arrived there one day in March.
At night, it's all you hear, slapping and growling and hissing outside. The wind blows through the old-growth vineyards in the Val-
lée du Triby, flies up the cliff peering over the western side of the
village and then hits a formidable windmill that rises out of the
craggy rock outcropping.

When Roland Feuillas and his wife, Valérie, bought the windmill in 2006 and moved to the village, only a portion of the brick-
work was still standing. Luckily, there were still workers in France
who rebuilt windmills, so Feuillas contacted a renowned carpenter
in this line of work. One morning, at the end of the project, after a
long night of drinking wine with the man, Feuillas awoke bleary
eyed to begin making bread at six A.M. He walked outside, looked
up and saw the carpenter, naked with his arms outstretched, bal-
anced on the huge wooden blades of the new windmill, facing the
wind from the valley below. "He was howling like a shaman," he
recalled.

Windmills, it seems, can have that effect. Feuillas and his wife had bought the mill after selling an educational software company with forty employees. "I was always on this," Feuillas said, holding up his cell phone. "Now it hardly rings." His passion was bread, but he didn't want to just "bake bread." He also wanted to grow the wheat, then mill it. He had looked through the south of France for a pristine location and settled on this area because no wheat was grown nearby. The fields had long ago been abandoned, so he didn't need to worry about pesticides drifting from neighboring farms. Here, he would plant long-forgotten French wheat varieties that had been gathered and shared among a small movement of farmers, or were sitting in gene banks. In one instance, he obtained just ten seeds of a variety known as Toussel, which he read had been favored by Louis XIII. He grew the wheat, harvested the grain, chose the fattest seeds, and planted them again. This planting and selecting went on for several years, with a number of different varieties. He also planted different varieties together so that they might breed with one another. He had eight original varieties in this kitchen biodiversity project, including two types of Toussel. Perhaps it was similar to the grain once grown in the region destined for the Cucugnan mill, which like all mills was controlled by the local throne. Holding up a handful of cream-colored, stone-milled flour, Feuillas looked at me and said, "This was the tax."

I had first heard about Feuillas from a home baker in Britain, Azelia Torres, who writes the thoughtful bread-baking blog "Azelia's Kitchen." When she posted the pictures of his bakery and windmill I knew I had to go. I was curious to see this one-man band who controlled the wheat, the milling, and the baking of his bread. With any scale, these activities are separated and with good reason: each takes a special kind of attention, and once you grow beyond a certain size, it's impossible to orchestrate them all. But since Feuillas made just a few types of loaves, rather than the dozen or more varieties you might see in a larger *boulangerie*, this wasn't out of the question. He relied on a thirty-inch electric stone mill for everyday use (when he wasn't cranking up the windmill) and he made his bread for people in the village, every one of whom he knew. The name of his enterprise seemed to say it all: *Les Maîtres de Mon Moulin*, The Masters of My Windmill, a play on a popular nineteenth-century French novel set in the town.

Feuillas is among a small movement of *paysannes boulangers* (peasant bakers) who grow their own organic wheat, mill it into flour, and make their bread. They remain outsiders in the baking industry. This is an especially tough career to pursue, because the state has strict rules requiring farmers to plant only seed sold by agricultural companies. Farmers who save their seed can sell their crop only if they pay an annual tax at the granary, and they can share varieties with one another only through a tenuous research exemption. The radicals of this world—for they are radicals, or at least on the agricultural fringe—read this as the state's way of protecting French seed companies in the face of much larger global competition, but it also marginalizes the farmer and *paysanne boulanger*. The rules also impair private attempts to preserve biodiversity and ancient wheat varieties on the farm. "Breeding your own grains is becoming more and more difficult legally," said Patrick de Kochko at Réseau Semences Paysannes, a group at the heart of this movement, though the farmers have kept at it for now through loopholes and exemptions.

Being on the fringe of the baking trade meant that Feuillas could make his ideal bread. In his view, the grain, the flour, the bread were all connected and he wanted his hand in all of it. "Can you imagine a wine maker making wine without knowing his grapes?" he said. If he was going to be a *boulanger*, he was going to do it his way—not unlike the carpenter howling into the wind.

On that first morning in Cucugnan, I had gone for a run on the winding road that swept down from the village and then off onto a dirt path that snaked through the vineyards in the valley. The vines were old, weathered, and gnarled, though young shoots were sprouting out of those branches that had been pruned. It was cool, and the wind, as usual, was howling. The soil was rocky and dry, so the vines had to work that much harder to get any life from it, and perhaps that's what concentrated the smoky, earthy character of these Corbières wines. It also proved a difficult surface to run on, but I wasn't complaining. There wasn't anything like it—running through the ancient vines of France in the early morning light.

Feuillas was baking that day, but wasn't in a rush, so after my jog I took a shower and strolled into the wooden house that serves as an office, kitchen, and part-time baking school for visitors. He was around my age—in his mid-fifties—and looked, as I often do when I'm writing at home, like he had just rolled out of bed. His hair was askew and he was in his baker's whites, though he was wearing a black plaid shirt on top, to guard against the chill. He had just lit a wood fire in the hefty iron cook stove, where lunch would be made, and it was slowly heating up the room.

The day had started at a relaxed pace because he was just baking bread for the full-time residents of the village. In the summer, when seasonal residents and tourists arrived, he would ramp up production dramatically, which is why he encouraged me to visit in March. That first day I finally ate the bread he'd made from this mélange of ancient wheat, in the form of three small slices of toast

— Loaves made with Feuillas's ancient wheat

with a shot of espresso. The bread itself was several days old, because he and Valérie had just returned from a trip to Paris, but I paid it no mind. Since it had been made with *levain*, it wasn't yet stale. The crust was a little hard, but I appreciated it. At home, I eat bread as it progressively gets harder; if it was still edible, why waste it? Of course, you can make bread crumbs with old bread, or soak it in water and add it to new dough, or make bread pudding, but you can also rip it apart with your teeth and eat it, which is what I usually did. Feuillas appeared to feel the same way.

The interior of the bread was darker than I expected—not just creamy colored but edging toward a lightish brown—which surprised me because when we had visited the stone mill downstairs, he showed me how he sifted out the bran when he milled flour. "It's white bread, not whitened bread," he had said. Nothing was done to make it appear more than it was, which is true, but I also thought to myself, "He's taking out bran! The intestinal vitality!" When I brought this up, Feuillas mentioned that the flour *did* have all the germ and most of the aleurone layer—the outermost layer of the endosperm with the highest level of nutrients that usually gets discarded with the bran. This stone ground and bolted flour would have been familiar to any miller or baker who baked bread in antiquity. I looked into the bolting barrel coming out of the side of the stone mill, which was sheathed in silk cloth. As the flour flowed out of the stones, it passed into the barrel, which rotated at a moderate speed. This allowed the finer flour to pass through the cloth and fall into a wooden bin below. The coarse bran remained inside the barrel, emptying into a bucket at the end. The flour was fine, but yellowish in color, not white. I looked forlornly at the bran piling up—"animal feed," Feuillas called it—and I almost wanted to mix up bran muffins.

When I had eaten the toast that morning, I noticed the bread had a remarkable taste that clearly wasn't the same as white flour. The *levain* influenced the taste, though Feuillas mentioned something else when I brought up the unique flavor: the water. When I had downed a few glasses of tap water after my run, I noticed it had a remarkably clean and bright taste. It came from a deep spring, filtered by those stones I had jogged through in the vineyard, so perhaps the mineral content was coming through. The bread was more refined than what I usually made, but it was also delicious. And because of the flavor, it didn't need a lot of salt. Feuillas used only fourteen grams of salt per kilo of flour, or 30 percent less than what most recipes call for. When I returned home I began to experiment frequently with these stone ground and bolted flours, which sift out a portion of the bran. One, a bolted French Mediterranean flour from Anson Mills in South Carolina, which specializes in rare heritage grains, was remarkably similar to Feuillas's in taste.

Glenn Roberts, the company founder, told me the variety was passed down from French Huguenots who settled in the Carolinas and Virginia in the eighteenth century, so perhaps it was similar to what Feuillas was growing.

For lunch that day, Feuillas's elderly mother, Maryse, who was visiting from Provence, made *civet de lapin* (rabbit stew). She had marinated the meat in red wine for twenty-four hours, then simmered it the night before in still more wine. While we'd been talking and sipping coffee that morning, Maryse had continued to braise it on the wood-burning stove, filling the kitchen with an intoxicating aroma. *Civet de lapin* was a specialty of the South, Feuillas told me, and this version dated back to a handwritten family recipe book more than a century old.

That was the way it was every day: lunch was the main meal and the entire family sat down to eat it, polishing off a bottle or two of a local vintage along with a loaf of bread. I told Roland that during these meals, I felt welcomed like a friend—a friend in the global

Roland Feuillas serving me at family lunch

family of bakers. I knew if I had just shown up as a journalist to interview him, I would have missed the entire story.

After lunch that first day, we did bake bread, and I realized that for Feuillas the flour was anything but a blank canvas. It was the essence of flavor and, yes, very much like wine. So many times, when I'd ask him a question about why he did something, he would answer with the simple phrase, "Terre Madre," Mother Earth. "Do you know what this is? Terre Madre?" he said.

I nodded.

It was the reason for everything he did. Everything went back to the soil and ultimately to God. He was simply a facilitator along the way.

"So Roland, what's the name of this bread?" I asked one day about a loaf with honey, walnuts, and almonds.

"This is bread with honey, walnut, and almonds," he replied.

"Yes, I know," I replied, this time in French. "But what's the name?"

"Bread with honey, walnut, and almonds," he said again in English.

I look at him, puzzled.

"I don't name the bread," he said, stopping this time, looking at me. "The bread is not mine. This grain is not mine. This flour is not mine. It's Terre Madre. It's Jesus Christ—how can I name it?" It was the same when he slashed the loaf, with just a simple diamond pattern.

"I don't put a special cut into it. I don't, because it's not mine."

I realized that for him, Terre Madre or Jesus Christ was his way of saying that in the totality of bread making, he was part of a larger whole. He was like a pilgrim, this ancient wheat and the bread making his meditation. The Zen master Suzuki Roshi once said, "We should be interested in making bread which looks and tastes good. Actual practice is repeating over and over again until you find out how to become bread. There is no secret in our way. Just to practice Zazen and put ourselves into the oven is our way." The bread wasn't his to name because he didn't own it.

And the bread wasn't the conclusion of the process. As his customers from the village came into the store, he greeted them by name, shook their hands, and kissed them on each cheek. Bread had been reserved and set aside for his regulars. He chatted to catch up on the news for several minutes. If the customer had a baby, he'd shake the baby's hand, too, then invite the father around the counter so that the child, held aloft, could see the bread as it came out of the oven.

"Children love *levain* bread," he said, "because it has lactic acid and if it's done right it smells like milk—like mother's milk."

I'm not as romantic, or maybe just not as French, though I, too, have experienced a posse of kids scurrying into the kitchen, saying, "Sam, do you have any bread?" Maybe it is like milk, maybe it's just good bread, but it doesn't matter. It's what these hungry kids want.

After we finished baking one day, I asked if we could go look at Terre Madre—the fields where he grew his wheat. Although it was only March, I thought we might be able to see the winter wheat poking out of the soil. The almond trees were flowering with little white buds, and new green shoots were emerging from the grape vines, but little else of spring was evident. He had told me that the fields were only sixteen kilometers (ten miles) away, so I figured we would jump in the car and be there in twenty minutes. But once we started driving on the narrow winding roads, I soon grew doubtful. We circled up hills, then went down the other side; we went past farms, through tiny villages and dark forests. A half hour into the journey, my stomach was getting a bit queasy from the twists and turns, and I asked how much longer it would be.

"In total, it will be about one hour," he said.

"Wait, I thought you said it was sixteen kilometers."

"Yes, as the bird flies! But we are not birds."

So we continued on the twisting roads, the once picture-book villages like Cucugnan giving way to smaller and progressively more unkempt places as we ventured farther into the countryside. This region of southern France began to look less like a quaint postcard of stone houses and vineyards than like the scrappy hill country of Appalachia. We passed what looked like nearly abandoned farming villages, with a rusted tractor here and there, a dangling Coca-Cola sign and a few chickens scurrying about, but not much else. The land was too hilly, the fields too small, the farms too scarce to have anything like the critical mass to compete with farms in other regions of France, or with Spain, Turkey, or North Africa, for that matter.

Finally, we reached a clearing and pulled over. The wind was blowing fiercely when we got out, which was quite welcome after the slightly nauseating ride. We walked over to a wire fence surrounding a field and there it was: his ancient wheat. There wasn't much to look at, for the plants were only a couple of inches high. But Feuillas smiled. This was it—his land, with hardly anything else around. "The closest farmer is twenty kilometers away," he said. It was perfect, because he didn't want to be exposed to any agrochemicals that might drift over his wheat. I took a few pictures, then we got back in the car and drove a bit farther down a potted dirt road to another field. "Spelt," he said, pointing to the field on the right. Again, the land was almost bare. Tiny grass seedlings were poking out of the ground. Feuillas, who was still in his baker's whites and clogs, braced against the wind as he wrapped his coat around himself.

He looked content, but it was sad, too. The nearby village we had passed through seemed nearly deserted, as if the old stone buildings might collapse under their own weight. The fields just across from his own were filled with underbrush and young trees, with nary a farm animal or cultivated crop in sight. We looked over the landscape, slowly returning to nature. "My farmer friend back in the U.S. calls these 'dead farms,'" I said. Pennsylvania was filled with them, too small to be productive and too far from any city to attract weekenders or tourist trade. All they had going for them now was oil and gas production from fracking wells.

My first thought looking over this land was, "God, what potential." It seemed perfect for some young couple who wanted to grow organic produce and maybe sell it on the coast, a couple of hours away. The winter was mild, the sun intense, like northern California. A few greenhouses and the dry summer could keep ambitious young farmers busy for a long time. Yet no one, at least in this vicinity, was trying to do anything remotely close to that except for Feuillas, and he was only growing wheat. When I asked him whether the land was expensive, he just shrugged. "No one wants it," he said.

Such was the state of Terre Madre.

The dough from this ancient wheat was unusual: less glutinous, less elastic, and it appeared to stretch out forever. Feuillas handled the dough very gently, letting the mixer run for only a couple of minutes, then giving the dough a rest. "We say the young children are joining hands and in the middle is the *levain*, the salt, the air, and just the flour and water," he said. "Then we let the children rest so they can make stronger bonds, and then add more water. If you add all the water at once, the children can never make a strong bond." He carried out this mixing and resting a few times, taking the hydration level very high, but he was right. Even this extensible, stretchy dough was able to develop strength, which is what you need for the bread to rise in the heat of the oven. He held up a piece of dough to show me, stretching it to a thin window, so that we could see through it—the "window pane" test. It was clear this ancient wheat had the qualities a baker would want.

By the next morning, after an all-night rise in the chilly retarder, we took the dough out to proceed with baking. It looked a bit like soup, with a few bubbles on the top. I was skeptical, wondering how we would manage to turn this gloppy mass into anything resembling a loaf of bread. Feuillas showed me how, and in the process gave me a new bread-making technique.

He dumped out the bin on a well-floured counter and patted it down gently with his palms. He then took a thin piece of wood—

Roland Feuillas shaping loaves with a single cut

what's known as a baguette flipper—and straightened out the sides of the dough so it made a rectangle. With the dough in this rough shape, he lifted one side with his hands and forearms and simply folded the dough in half over on top of itself. On this smooth surface, he sprinkled flour to make five distinct lines across the top of the dough. Then he picked up the piece of wood again and made five indentations by pressing down on the lines of flour with the edge of the board, returning again with the wood to cut through the dough. If he had used a bench scraper, or knife, he would have cut through the dough immediately. By using the blunt edge of the wood, he formed a sealed seam before the loaves were cut. (I found that a chopstick or the handle of a wooden spoon achieves a similar effect when I tried the technique at home.) And there it was. One fold and then five cuts to make five loaves. Finally, he lifted up the five pieces of dough and set them in a linen *couche*—a piece of fabric folded like an accordion with a loaf between each of the folds. He set this in a wooden cabinet for the second rise.

"It's the simplest method," he said. "It's also one of the oldest, and it's very fast."

When the loaves had risen sufficiently, we slashed a simple pattern on the top and loaded them into the brick oven with a long wooden peel. Despite my skepticism about this loose dough, the bread did spring up. It also had marvelously large and varied holes in the crumb, because it had been shaped so minimally. As for the smell: well, people began to arrive just as the bread was exiting the oven.

That trip to Cucugnan came in 2012 at the end of my travels, and I knew I wouldn't be coming back to France soon. So after saying good-bye to Feuillas and his family, I returned to Paris. On my final night there, I splurged and took Denise, my friend and translator, to a little neighborhood bistro. We had a great time catching up, but I felt something was lacking in the meal. I mean everything was right, the food was delicious, I had a good Bordeaux with dinner and a friend to share it with, but I realized what was missing was the long wooden table filled with Feuillas's family and the smell of the meal cooking on the stove. We were eating good food here, but we weren't with the people who had made it.

The next day, my last in France, I got up, ate a quick breakfast at the hotel, and then went around the corner to a Paris Vélib' kiosk to get a bicycle. I went for a ride in the morning sun, parked the bike at another stand, and then hopped on the Métro. I wanted to revisit Boulangerie Arnaud Delmontel, where I had worked three years earlier, which was really the experience that set me on this path. I hadn't called Arnaud to see if he was around. I figured I would just take a chance and show up, since I had only a couple of hours to kill before I had to leave for Charles De Gaulle airport. I got off at Saint-Georges in the ninth arrondissement, and, remembering the neighborhood, walked the few blocks to the *boulangerie*.

The side-door entrance to the baking room was shut but I looked into the glass window and saw my old teacher, Thomas Chardon, working inside. When I rapped on the door he immediately recognized me. I gave him a warm hello, told him why I was back in France—all while he was removing some baguettes from the oven. We chatted for a bit and then he went back to work. It was the same routine, every morning, and he seemed completely in his element.

I asked if Monsieur Delmontel was around, and Thomas pointed upstairs. I went up the spiral staircase to the office and Delmontel looked up, surprised, and stopped what he was doing. As we talked, he told me he had a good laugh when he found out I had won the best baguette contest in Washington. But then he said, "No, I am proud, because you came here, you really wanted to learn, and you did learn." It didn't matter that I wasn't a professional; it didn't matter that I was doing all this because I simply wanted to; it didn't matter that I wasn't going to run a bakery. I had tried to bake a true loaf of bread and I had done it, and that was enough. It was just the kind of recognition you get from someone who appreciates the craft in its own right. We had a coffee and a couple of his croissants, and that was it. I said good-bye, bounced down the street to another Vélib' bike station, and rode back to my hotel. The sun was shining, the air was warm, and I was heading back home. It was the perfect coda for the trip, actually the perfect coda to the entire journey that had begun one cold February morning three years earlier. Yet I wasn't quite done. Because Feuillas had spurred some ideas to consider closer to home.

N ow, I wasn't Roland Feuillas. I had tried to grow wheat in my community garden plot and failed miserably. So I knew that if I was really going to bake with local wheat, as he was doing, I'd have to find a source other than my garden. Luckily, I didn't have to look farther than the FreshFarm Market in Dupont Circle in Washington, where Heinz Thomet, a Swiss-born organic farmer, was selling grains at his farm stand.

On Cobb Neck in southern Maryland, about an hour south of Washington, he had begun growing cereal crops as "green manure." Organic farmers often add grasses or legumes into their crop rotations, plowing them into the soil to build biomass and fertility. But since he was growing them, he figured he could also harvest the kernels, getting at least some revenue for the effort. Grains were also attractive because he didn't need much labor. Finding workers on Cobb Neck who would plant, weed, and pick his vegetables was a continual headache, which is perhaps why he often worked

Heinz Thomet on his tractor

ungodly hours. Vegetable farming was also backbreaking work, though on one of the days I visited, two young workers had a flat-bed contraption that ameliorated any back bending at all. They were lying facedown on a four-wheeled trolley, about a foot off the ground, with a little cushion to support their foreheads. As they rolled along through a row of spinach, they picked out weeds with their hand hoes and flung them aside.

Seeing this work, it was obvious why this produce was not cheap. Perhaps it was also the reason grains looked promising, since they could be harvested with a tractor. As Heinz ramped up this effort, I kept abreast of his work and planned on visiting his farm during the fall season when he would be sowing wheat, barley, and rye.

"Well, we need about three weeks of dry weather before I can get onto the ground," he said, when I called him one day in October.

"I know, but just give me a heads-up before you do it."

"Well, there's not a lot to see. It's not like it's a Brueghel painting or anything. I'm on a tractor."

"I know," I said. "But I still want to see it."

One warm day in late October, when planting was finally auspicious, I visited Next Step Produce. The small farm is beyond the suburban sprawl of Washington and it's not particularly evident that such a bucolic spot—Brueghel painting or not—would sit a quarter mile or so off the main highway. The farm had several fields, all sloping down toward the forest and marshland that is part of the Chesapeake Bay watershed. When I arrived, Heinz's wife, Gabrielle Lajoie—who is French Canadian and started out as an employee on the farm—came out of the house and said hello. His three young girls were climbing on the tractor, and before long, Heinz, in his well-worn work clothes, scraggly beard, and bushy hair, which looked a bit like broccoli rabe, showed up. He was tall and solidly built, perhaps the most husky vegan I've met. After shaking my hand, Heinz took me to see the operation.

The business was more complicated than just growing wheat, because the kernels had to be cleaned. Heinz had bought a range of blowers, shakers, and sieves to remove damaged grains, weeds, rocks, and dirt that might find their way into the bags destined for market. It's hard to appreciate what's involved when you buy those bags of pristine farro that are now so popular, until you compare freshly harvested grain with the final result. It was quite remarkable what this equipment, much of it new to his farm, could achieve in removing detritus. When he first started growing grain a few years back, Heinz gave me some rye but it wasn't pure. Weedy legume seeds were mixed in with it, too, so I spent what seemed like an hour sorting the tiny, black, round peas from the greenish rye grains before I just gave up. I couldn't clearly identify the other seed but figured it couldn't be all that bad—so I just ground it all into flour and made rye bread. Now, he had advanced, and had all the specialized equipment to address such impurities, and a walk-in refrigerator, too, to prevent bugs from infesting the stored bags of grain. The setup was impressive, especially for the scale of the small farm.

Aside from his reputation among farmers for being an extremely hard worker and tough boss, Heinz also let no opportunity for idle labor to pass, so, as we were talking, he pulled out a bag with a small amount of seed and asked if I might count the number of seeds it contained. Apparently, this was necessary to gauge the number of seeds in an ounce, and ultimately in an entire seed bag, so that he could figure out how many bags he needed to sow his fields that day.

"Of course," I said, rather naively. So, sitting at a small table in the barn, I used a knife to gently push wheat kernels into piles of ten, then added ten together to make one hundred, and so on. At one point, Gabrielle came out to the barn and smiled. "Oh, I see Heinz has you counting seeds." After about a half hour, I had counted more than three thousand seeds. Heinz then ripped open the appropriate number of seed bags, emptied them into the seeder attached to the tractor, and off we went to the fields.

It was a good day for sowing wheat but he was right: there wasn't a lot to see, other than the tractor riding back and forth over the soil depositing seed in furrows. It took a couple of hours to complete the job. One of his daughters came along for the ride and sat in his lap on the tractor, then eventually jumped down and wandered over to a patch of grass where she watched her father ride back and forth over the fields. She picked a wildflower. I joined her in the warm afternoon sun and watched Heinz, too.

. . . . .

When he began this pursuit, one problem that he ran into quickly was finding wheat varieties suited to southern Maryland. Hardly any wheat was being grown in this part of the country, so it wasn't as if he could turn to neighboring farmers for advice. He scoured the Internet looking for seed stock, and talked to other farmers in different regions of the country about what might work in the mid-Atlantic. But all of this was largely an experiment, since wheat growing on the Eastern Seaboard is relatively rare. Even now, with the locavore movement in full swing, it's still confined to small pockets.

To find the epicenter of the nation's wheat production east of the Allegheny Mountains, the clock needs to be turned back to the mid-nineteenth century. At that time, the Shenandoah Valley, that fertile finger of land in Virginia about three hours west of Heinz's farm, had served as the granary for the Confederacy during the Civil War. The valley is still fertile, but you won't find much wheat there today. By the close of the nineteenth century, wheat production had shifted a thousand miles west, to Kansas, Texas, and Nebraska. The softer, lower-protein wheats once grown in the East fell out of favor, supplanted by the hard red wheats of the plains states that became the standard for bread making. It became conventional wisdom that bread wheat could not be grown on the Eastern Seaboard.

Heinz, though, was curious, and wanted to give wheat a try, so he experimented with a few modern varieties, as well as Turkey Red. I passed him some wheat seed that Eli Rogosa had given me up in Massachusetts, which came from biodynamic farmers in Germany. I thought that it might be suited to his farm because Heinz used biodynamic farming methods, too. Since there were only about one hundred seeds in the packet, he would have to grow them out and then plant them again the following year, increasing the amount of seed annually before he had enough to sell.

Heinz grew winter wheats—those varieties planted in the fall for harvest the next summer. He also planted spring wheats, but took the unusual step of sowing them in the fall because in the mid-Atlantic they could survive the mild winters and might mature more quickly. "It was something we used to do in Switzerland," he said. It seemed as if Heinz would do anything to get a wheat crop.

All the varieties he planted originated in the Great Plains, where the climate was dryer and cooler than Maryland. He didn't have much choice, however, because all the wheat breeding programs until very recently were centered on the nation's breadbasket, with a smattering in other regions. Stephen Jones, a professor at Washington State University, is one of the few wheat breeders developing local varieties. "I remember when I began looking into local breeds about ten or fifteen years ago, I got a comment on a grant application, 'There is no interest in local wheat and there won't be,'" he told me. This was not unusual; the work was unprecedented.

Heather Darby, another agronomist at the University of Vermont, was aware that some farmers were growing wheat in Vermont and around 2006 began testing varieties that might be appropriate for the region. Nearly all were from the Dakotas, Minnesota, Saskatchewan, and Quebec, though she did find an heirloom variety that had thrived in Vermont a century ago, known as Champlain. It proved highly productive, though not all heritage wheats ranked as high. "Just because they're old doesn't mean they'll do well," Darby said. With another agronomist in Maine, she found more varieties; then, with Jones's guidance, she began to breed wheat suited to northern New England. When I asked Darby when was the last time a wheat variety had been bred in Vermont, she said: "1870."

While it was novel, maybe even foolhardy, to grow wheat in the East, it clearly wasn't impossible. And it wasn't just farmers in Vermont who were doing so, but others in western Massachusetts.

Bakers such as Hungry Ghost Bread in Northampton, Massachusetts, were enthusiastically using the flour. In the town of Skowhegan, Maine, I toured the Somerset Grist Mill, which opened in 2012 in a former jail and sold stone ground flour under the Maine Grains label. In Asheville, North Carolina, I visited Carolina Ground, a multipronged affair run by a former baker, Jennifer Lapidus, which brought together farmers, a new stone mill, and a coterie of local bakers. Through Thom Leonard, the baker who had first championed Turkey Red wheat in Kansas, I learned that the same variety being grown in North Carolina was quite good. In northern California, Community Grains had launched a local grains effort with the help of Craig Ponsford, a superlative baker in San Rafael who sent me on my way with a five-pound bag of their whole wheat flour. In Portland, Oregon, bakers were using Shepard's Grain flour, which came from a grain farmers' co-op in the central part of the state. In New York, chefs and bakers were buying 65,000 pounds of local flour a month through the Greenmarket farmers' markets. And then there was Anson Mills, in South Carolina, championing heritage grains grown by farmers around the country.

But even with all this activity—and there were many more efforts, from Arizona to Washington State—local grains were just beginning to break out on the food scene. The movement made a lot of sense for artisan bakers, who had been troubled by the spikes in global food prices in 2007. They wanted a direct connection with farmers, not one mediated by the gyrating grain markets, commodity index funds, and Big Food. But the knowledge of what might be accomplished, especially in the East, was largely a blank slate, because it had been so long since wheat of any consequence had been grown here.

Now, Heinz was getting in on the action, too, but unlike those in Maine, Vermont, or North Carolina, there wasn't a strong network, or rather, any network, to tap into in the mid-Atlantic. Two highly regarded restaurants, Nora's Restaurant in Washington and Woodbury Kitchen in Baltimore, were buying his rye and wheat, but aside from these customers I knew of only one other baker making bread with his wheat—me. At Heinz's stand at the farmers' market, the grain was pricey, $4 for a one-pound bag—and that was just for the grain. So Heinz had to trade on the qualities of this wheat: that it was local, and organic. Would that be enough to close the deal? People were just discovering whole grains and various types of flour, such as spelt, buckwheat, and rye, thanks to the efforts of bakers and writers who were pushing the envelope— people like Heidi Swanson, with her cookbooks and Web site, Maria Speck with her ancient grains cookbook, and Kim Boyce, who had explored whole grain pastries in yet another book, and, of course, Peter Reinhart. But none of this was as easy as slicing an heirloom tomato and popping it into your mouth.

As for the price, I could make two decent-size whole wheat loaves from Heinz's grain for around $2 a loaf, which was still cheaper than any bread I could buy. By comparison, organic white or whole wheat flour from the supermarket would bring the cost of a homemade loaf to less than $1. For me, that difference was hardly a deal breaker. This was a rationale I used with much of the specialty grains and flour I bought, whether the Turkey Red from Heartland, the French Mediterranean flour from Anson Mills, or Heinz's wheat: the biggest savings, by far, came from baking at home. Adding the occasional specialty flour to the mix might cost more, but it would not erase these savings. In any case, rock-bottom, price-busting bread was the least of my motivations. After sticking with store-bought flour for a decade or more, I found that this array of grains and flours opened up new paths for experimentation.

Around the time I went off on this local grain jag, I had to take a work trip to San Francisco, so I dropped in on Chad Robertson at Tartine. We started talking about local grains, which he had experimented with from a farm in northern California. While he liked the flour, he also found it expensive, and wasn't sure it would work in the context of his bakery. Still, he wasn't writing it off. "When Alice Waters switched to grass-fed beef at Chez Panisse, we thought she was crazy because there was only a farmer or two doing it," he said. "But you know what? Everyone now has grass-fed beef on the menu. So who knows? Maybe that will happen with local grains, too."

Before his forays into wheat, Heinz had sold only barley, oats, and rye. I made terrific bread with the rye, but I wondered how good the wheat would be—whether it would be reminiscent, say, of what Roland Feuillas had achieved in southern France. So one day, late in 2012, I met Heinz at the farmers' market. He reached into a box and pulled out six one-pound bags of whole wheat kernels. Each looked slightly different, especially the white wheat, which was tan rather than brown. He was curious about whether they'd make good bread, and so was I.

I brought the grains home, put them in the freezer, where they would keep for a long time, and then left them. I wasn't eager to test the baking quality of the wheat because, as much as I loved the idea of local wheat, part of me feared it might make terrible bread. And then what would I tell Heinz? Plus, I had never tested flour before and wondered what an appropriate protocol would be. Should I mill the wheat and then sift out the bran? That way I might get a better idea of the protein strength unimpeded by the bran's tendency to break down gluten. The other option was to bake 100 percent whole wheat loaves, which are not among my favorite. But that way, I could at least assess the true flavor of the grain. Should I also mill the flour and then let it sit for a couple of weeks so it oxidized and increased in gluten strength? Or should I bake with it right away, as Weichardt did in Berlin? Rather than make a decision, I avoided the issue for about six weeks while the grains sat in the freezer. But Heinz kept asking me whether I had tried the wheat, so I knew I couldn't put him off any longer.

Finally, one weekend in February, I took the grains out of storage and lined them up on the kitchen counter. I brought out the countertop KoMo stone mill, which could mill a range of flours from fine to coarse. The stone mill was housed in wood, with a grain hopper on top, and a funnel protruding out of the front from which the flour flowed into a bowl. Milling added a whole new variable to my baking, since the quality of the bread would be determined not just by my baking skills or my sourdough starter, but by the vagaries of the wheat and how the flour was milled. I ended up passing the grains through the mill three times, coarsely at first and then adjusting the mill wheels closer with each succeeding pass. I also took my time, letting the flour cool after each run through the mill, so I wouldn't compromise any nutrients that degrade in heat. By the end of the process, some of the flour was quite fine, but it still had flecks of bran.

To test the flour, I decided to stick to a 100 percent whole wheat loaf—perhaps I could learn to love the assertive taste of this bread, after all. Using a starter I had mixed up with Heartland Mill's whole wheat flour, I began making my test doughs. To be clear, I was blending two types of flour in each loaf: about 20 percent Heartland whole wheat flour, which was in the sourdough starter, and the remaining 80 percent from each local variety. I marked the bowls of dough so I wouldn't confuse them and then began mixing by hand.

All four doughs came together quite nicely. Some were more extensible than others, while a baseline loaf made entirely with Heartland flour had the strongest gluten. I left the doughs to rise, folding them every thirty minutes or so, then shaped the final loaves quite gently, careful not to tear the skin or compress the loaf.

Then, after a second rise, I baked them. They sprang up in the oven, and because they were 100 percent whole wheat, they came out rather dark when they were done. I had cut a diamond shape over the top of the loaves and the pattern opened up, not as dramatically as with white flour, but still noticeably.

When I finally sliced into them a couple of hours later, I was pleasantly surprised. This wasn't dense, doorstop whole wheat. The crumb was light and pliable, which showed the gluten had developed sufficiently. When I e-mailed pictures of the test breads to Randy George at Red Hen in Vermont, he e-mailed back that one of the loaves, made with a hard red spring wheat, was so airy it looked like a croissant. I had thought that loaf was going to turn out to be a disaster because it had trouble holding its shape. While it flattened out into a disk before I put it into the oven, it puffed up

Whole wheat test loaf made with Faller wheat
from Heinz Thomet

in the heat into a bulbous round loaf. This wheat variety, Faller, was obviously a keeper. The test loaves all varied slightly, but the differences weren't very noticeable and they all had decent loft. My family ended up eating some of the bread, then I passed the samples on to Heinz.

My conclusion: bread wheat, and good-quality bread wheat, can be grown in the East. The flour might not be strong enough to withstand industrial mixing machines, but if handled gently, it made a very good loaf. The key was to use a generous amount of sourdough starter as well as water, to fold and stretch the dough to build strength, and to keep an eye on fermentation, since these whole grain loaves rose quickly.

I was quite excited about these tests so I also e-mailed Jeffrey Hamelman at King Arthur, who was testing locally grown Vermont wheat with Randy George. He was enthusiastic. "Your loaves all look good," he wrote back, "and we'll never know why there is such a variation, but that's no big deal."

Variation, after all, was something that bakers always faced before flour was blended, before baking parameters were standardized, before wheat was modernized, and before roller mills created highly refined flour. Locally grown stone milled flour might be inconsistent, and inappropriate for efficient uniformity. But it allowed for variability, and out of variability arises personality. To unlock the intrinsic qualities of the wheat, the baker had to adjust to whatever nature might offer. And it is that attention to detail, to learning, to repetition, all with a sense of humility, that in some way defines the craft—the humanity—of the baker.

So I began to think of this project with Heinz as far more than a way to bake "local bread." It was really about working with all nature has to offer—first, in the wheat varieties Heinz grew, on a specific piece of farmland in the mid-Atlantic. Then, in my sourdough, because of the diverse microbiota I nurtured within it; and finally in the bread itself, which reflected my own hands. It reminded me of what the French bakers had said to me: how could you make bread without knowing the wheat? It was such a simple question but it had been forgotten in the commoditization of flour and in the loss of craft.

But now, a busy few were finding a new way. It was hardly a romantic notion of "returning" to the past, for everything had changed: Heinz wasn't growing wheat that the colonists had brought with them from Europe. He was sowing wheat from the Great Plains and trying to make it work in a very different climate, with surprising success. Maybe this work was a distant echo of the very earliest grains, which were traded and shared and eventually made their way out of the Fertile Crescent. The seeds were planted in places where these grasses had never been grown before, becoming the landraces of the future, the source of future breads. Maybe these early farmers, these prototypical bakers, were experimenting, too, feeling something akin to the excitement I felt when I ate this bread from wheat sown in Heinz's fields.

The following year, Heinz had a new variety in the mix, which he took to calling "Sam's Wheat." It had originated with those German wheat kernels that Eli Rogosa passed on to me a couple of years earlier. Now, he had enough seed on hand to sell, and also a new stone mill from Germany in which he could grind flour. When I got the flour from Heinz, I made a small, dark *miche* that had a surprisingly high amount of acidity, perhaps owing to an overly long fermentation—or perhaps due to the grain itself. Eating the bread, I realized I could trace the wheat back to Rogosa, and from her to the farmers in Germany who had passed it on. Heinz was just the latest stop. While he insisted on calling it "Sam's Wheat," I finally told him, "Heinz, it's not mine! It's not my wheat!" Roland Feuillas had been right all along. I was just one link in this journey.

Pain Nature

(MODERATE)

Makes 4 loaves

⟿ Sourdough loaves made with
Anson Mills French Mediterranean flour

I had failed to bring back any flour from my trip to southern France, which was kind of a shame because it had such a marvelous taste. But while looking around, I came across a bolted white flour from Anson Mills in South Carolina that caught my attention. The mill's French Mediterranean white bread flour was "milled from 18th century white heirloom wheat emanating from Provence, in France." The variety was a family heirloom, originating with French Huguenots and passed down through generations. I was pleasantly surprised by this wheat, which is stone milled and then sifted to remove the bran, for it came very close to the flavor I had experienced at Feuillas's bakery in the south of France. The only cautionary remark: Anson's flour absorbs far less water than you might expect, probably owing to a lower level of protein. Observe that caveat and you will make a decent loaf of bread.

Anson's founder, Glenn Roberts, is fanatical about freshness and mills the flour just before he ships it to customers. He also maintains it in cold storage so that the flavor doesn't deteriorate and suggests his customers do the same. The flour is expensive, but if you want to splurge and experiment, it's worth it.

As for Feuillas's ancient wheat, I did manage to persuade my brother-in-law, who was returning from Paris, to visit a baker who had some on hand. Through a couple of e-mails, the baker generously agreed to sell a 2-kilo (4.4-pound) bag of this flour, which then went into Marc's carry-on luggage. He was a bit dubious about bringing a plastic bag filled with fine white powder into the United States, but here's a tip: declare it in customs. I've found the officials look at the entry card, say something like, "Flour, huh?" and then wave you on through.

This recipe closely follows the *pain de campagne*, so look there for more details on the hand kneading technique.

Tools
    Bowl
    Rectangular baking stone
    Rimmed baking sheet
    Plastic dough scraper
    Dowel or wooden spoon with a long handle or a chopstick
    Parchment paper
    Single-edged razor blade, *lame*, or knife
    Baking peel or cutting board, to move the loaves to the oven
    Cooling rack

Levain Ingredients
    100 grams Anson Mills French Mediterranean white bread
        flour
    65 grams water
    20 grams starter

Final Dough Ingredients
    150 grams *levain*
    400 grams water
    600 grams Anson Mills French Mediterranean white bread
        flour, plus more for the counter
    12 grams salt

Morning, First Day

Mix the ingredients for the *levain* and let it rise overnight until it
has domed and is bubbly. Use the *levain* after it has risen 8 to 10
hours, though the longer it sits, the more sour the flavor will be.

Evening, First Day

Mix the starter with 375 grams of the water. Add the flour and mix
until combined so that all the lumps are gone. Make an indentation
in the top of the dough, and add the salt and then about a tablespoon
of the remaining water and let the salt dissolve in this pool for 30
to 40 minutes.

Turn the dough in the bowl by folding the edges to the middle,
10 to 12 times, incorporating the salt as you go by pinching the
dough with your thumb and fingers. Then flip over the dough so
that the smooth side is up. Add the remaining water, as necessary.

After 30 minutes, repeat the folding action. Then repeat this
again after another 30 minutes, so that you've done three folding

actions after the initial mix. Then place the dough, covered, in the refrigerator for 12 to 24 hours.

Second Day

Preheat the oven to 460°F (240°C). Place a baking stone on the middle rack. Place a rimmed baking sheet on a shelf below the baking stone.

Take the dough out of the refrigerator. Lightly dust the counter with flour. Remove the dough from the bowl in one piece, dust it lightly with flour, and form it into a rough rectangular shape. Cut it in half with the dough scraper and place half of the dough back into the bowl and into the refrigerator.

Fold the dough in half so that the smooth, flour-covered side is now on top, and so that it makes a rectangular shape. Sprinkle a thick line of flour down the middle of the dough, so you will have two loaves when you cut through the line. Then, using a chopstick or the handle of a wooden spoon or blunt-edge piece of wood, press down on the floury line. Finish cutting with a dough scraper so that you have two loaves of bread.

Move the loaves to flour-dusted parchment paper, making sure they are separated, and cover with a light towel. After 60 minutes, check the dough by pressing on it gently with a finger. If it strongly springs back, let it rest for another 20 minutes and check again. The dough should gently spring back when you touch it and be ready for the oven after a total of 60 to 90 minutes.

Place the parchment paper with the loaves on a peel or cutting board. Slash them with one long cut down the middle of the loaf, about ¼ inch deep. Then move the loaves to the baking stone. Pour ⅓ cup of water into the pan at the bottom of the oven and bake the loaves for 20 minutes. Release the steam by opening the oven door quickly and then closing it again right away. Bake for another 10 minutes, then turn the oven down to 440°F (225°C) and continue baking until nicely dark for another 10 to 15 minutes, 40 to 45 minutes in total. Turn the oven off, prop open the door slightly, and let the loaves rest in the oven for another 5 to 7 minutes. The loaves should sound hollow when you knock them.

Repeat the baking process with the second piece of dough, making two more loaves.

Let the loaves rest on a cooling rack for at least 1 hour before cutting into them. Store the loaves in a towel or paper bag for one day, then in a plastic bag after that point. You can also freeze a loaf after it cools. When you are ready to eat the frozen loaf, let it defrost at room temperature and then crisp it up in a 400°F (205°C) oven for 5 minutes.

Epilogue

Early on in this journey, in December 2010, I took a trip to rainy Portland, Oregon, to meet Tim Healea, the owner of Little T American Baker. Healea had recently opened the bakery and lavished attention on the retail space—a kind of sleek, modernist affair, with counters and tables in natural wood, polished cement floors, and large picture windows looking out over the street in southeast Portland. The morning I arrived, the store hadn't yet opened, but the bakers were rushing about; the unmistakable odor of freshly baked bread wafted from behind the doors that separated the store from the kitchen. It was a smell I would come to expect over the course of the next two years in many other bakeries across the United States and Europe.

Soon, Healea came out of the back and said hello. Well built, with thick arms and a T-shirt to show them off, he was also soft-spoken, and maybe a little shy. But he was passionate about his bread, which was neatly arranged on wooden racks by a window. There was the "slab," the name for an airy and addictive focaccia (which was immediately devoured when I brought it home to my friends); a sandwich loaf that looked like a multigrain bread except that it also contained shredded carrots; a hearty whole spelt and flaxseed loaf; and a baguette, which was reputed to be the best in Portland. (I would say it's a tossup with Ken's Artisan Bakery, another superlative bakery across town.) Then there was his "house" bread, a round, airy sourdough with a remarkable crust that looked like a sheet of cracked ice in snowy flour.

I spent several mornings with the friendly crew, making these unfamiliar loaves. In the process, it became clear to me that Healea was among a new breed of American bakers. If the 1980s and '90s had been about Old World breads, the new century was taking American bread in a fresh direction. You wouldn't call Little T a *boulangerie* because, aside from its baguette and superlative croissant, you wouldn't find bread like this in Paris. Little T suggested what was possible going forward.

I saw aspects of this new direction in bread whenever I came across committed bakers. I saw it with Chad Robertson's whole grain loaves. And in the ryes that suddenly seemed to be appearing everywhere in New York. And Pichard's unusual long-fermentation baguette, and Zakowski's cracked Kamut bread. In Cucugnan, Feuillas was rediscovering relic wheats, and then there were other farmers who were trying to bring back wheat to regions where it had long been absent or were working to preserve ancient varieties. All those efforts meant that the end product—the grain, the flour— might offer new colors and textures for the bakers' palette and for us to eat. What I was witnessing was a blossoming of diversity and creativity.

Diverse wheat varieties have been viewed as an invaluable genetic resource to ensure future wheat harvests, which they certainly are. Yet very few wheat breeders have tried to breed grains that played off the inherent culinary differences in these grasses. In order to create a more productive resource, they bred inconsistency out of the wheat genome rather than celebrating the variation within it. This standardization met the expectations of bakers, millers, and, yes, bread eaters around the world about how white flour should perform and what bread should taste like. But the bakers I met on my journey—and the farmers, millers, and wheat breeders who worked with them—were searching for something else: heterogeneity in flours and whole grains, and variety in the breads they produced. Long-ignored grains, such as barley, rye, and ancient wheat, would help achieve this result, but the methods couldn't be ignored—the coarseness of the millstone, the sourdough culture, the fermentation regime, the touch of the hand on the dough—because all these variables create the taste of bread.

It's doubtful that global wheat breeders will change their focus, because their job is to ensure the most acceptable wheat product for the largest number of people. But this parallel movement to diversify the grain supply could have important ramifications, too, considering the advances that bakers are making in the palatability of whole grains. These small bakers, these renegade wheat breeders, these committed farmers and micro-millers, who are working with forgotten grains and trying to discover a new relationship with the "staff of life," will lead the way with bread, widening the possibilities not only for the committed few but for many others who follow. Some call this "real bread" and from many vantage points it is, especially when it comes to the taste of the bread and the work that goes into creating it.

I won't pretend that we're beyond the very start of this enterprise, and there will be a lot of surprises and failures along the way. But without that sense of adventure, without the possibility that this work entails, it probably wouldn't be worth it. After all, it was this relentless curiosity about bread that drove me forward, and I imagine is driving others as well, whether in a professional setting or at home.

When I began baking many years ago, I didn't set out to promote whole grain bread, champion artisan bakers, or eat local grains. I simply wanted good bread for my table. I was pursuing memories of the bread I ate as a child, and learning a craft. What I realize, though, is that I learned a lot by engaging with this most basic of staples. Baking opened up a new world to me, introduced me to bakers, and made me think about bread in an entirely new way, beyond the confines of my home and my own desires for a decent loaf. But even now, I'm careful about protecting the special role baking has played in my life.

As I was finishing this book, we took a summer family vacation to the coast of Rhode Island. One day, we found ourselves on a beach with few people. On cliffs that backed up to the sandy beach, ragged plant life and red clay had been exposed by the wind and rain. Looking around, I realized that this was the perfect place to bake bread, for everything was there—sand, clay, and seawater that could be used to mix mortar and build an earth oven. I had built an oven like this once before at the Kneading Conference—an annual gathering of baking enthusiasts in Maine—and I had studied Kiko Denzer's classic book on the subject, *Build Your Own Earth Oven*. So my wife, Ellen, and I, and our daughter, Nina, and our two friends, Mark and Susanna, and their son, Niko, got to work. We mixed the clay and sand, adding water to create a loose, muddy mortar. It wasn't too different from the sand castles we'd been building on the beach all week, though in this instance it helped that Mark had huge feet, and could churn the substance while jumping around. Once the mud was ready, we began building the oven, using a pizza stone that I brought along for the floor. After a couple of hours of work, we finished the dome and left it to set. A couple of days later, I returned and lit a fire inside, with driftwood I gathered on the beach. It became so hot I could barely approach the opening, but I kept feeding it to heat up the thick walls. Two hours later, Mark showed up with pizza dough and toppings.

We swept out the coals as best we could, using a stick and a kind of improvised seaweed mop. We had to work carefully to avoid getting any sand on the dough, but we managed it and then slid an eight-inch pie into the oven. Mark and I sat there, in the sand, facing the waves, the wind blowing gently, watching the pizza bake. Although it cooked unevenly, it was done in about five minutes and we dove in. The crust, where it had fully cooked, was dark and crispy, the cheese gooey. We made a couple more pizzas. Mark snapped open a couple of beers.

It surely wasn't the best pizza I've ever eaten. The ingredients were unremarkable, the dough had overfermented in the sun, and a bit of the crust was undercooked. But as we ate, we marveled at this most primitive of ovens we had built by hand on a beach on the Atlantic Coast. We hadn't mastered the fire, or the way the oven worked, or really how to make pizza in it. But it hinted at what was possible. We knew we could make something edible from this earth. And we knew we would have to return and try again.

Earth oven made with clay, sand, and seawater

Acknowledgments

This book is really part of a process that began with my first visits to bakeries as a child: the iconic images of bakers in front of their ovens are still etched in my memory. I was also guided by bakers who over the years opened up their baking rooms to me. I'd like to acknowledge Tim Healea, Mike Zakowski, Chad Robertson, Kathleen and Ed Weber, Richard Hart, Jeffrey Hamelman, Craig Ponsford, Roger Gural, and Susan Tenney. I'd also like to thank Alice Waters, who encouraged my bread baking at a pivotal moment, and Nancy Silverton and Jim Lahey, who also welcomed me into their bakeries.

Those I met in France were unfailingly helpful: Arnaud Delmontel, Roland Feuillas, Frédéric Pichard, Steven Kaplan, Alexandre Viron, and Jean-Philippe de Tonnac. A special thanks to Thomas Chardon, who showed me how to make not just one baguette, but hundreds. Many of these interviews would never have occurred without the tireless help of Denise Young, a former colleague and my Paris-based interpreter. Along the way, Laurent Bonneau generously agreed to provide some of Roland's flour to my Paris courier (my brother-in-law, Marc Morjé Howard). I want to give a hearty thanks to *Afar* magazine for sending me to Paris in the depths of the recession. Photographer Brian Doben shot that story, then generously shared his pictures with me for this book.

In Berlin, Heinz and Mucke Weichardt were extremely generous in opening their busy bakery to me. Karl Steffelbauer proved an invaluable guide to making rye breads. Berlin-based researcher and journalist Molly Hannon was also helpful in tracking down resources on German bread making.

Other bakers offered valuable advice and expertise. I'd like to acknowledge Thom Leonard, who answered many questions and offered resources on Turkey Red wheat; Jeffrey Hamelman, who was unfailingly helpful; Randy George, who was always available for a quick chat on baking with local wheat; and Richard Miscovich, who patiently answered my questions. Dave Miller, Martin Philip, and Harry Peemoeller also offered advice; so did many bakers on the Bread Bakers Guild of America e-mail list.

Wheat breeders and milling experts also offered their time. Andrew Ross, an associate professor at Oregon State University, advised me on many issues of bread baking and cereal science, generously referring me to scientific papers and even reviewing portions of this manuscript. Stephen Jones, a professor at Washington State University, also spent time with me and provided references to various studies. Richard Little and Devin Rose, at the University of Nebraska, were helpful in exploring questions regarding wheat breeding and milling, respectively. At Heartland Mill, Mark Nightengale was especially generous in explaining all facets of his business. Tod Bramble at King Arthur Flour was also helpful about milling, as was Glenn Roberts at Anson Mills.

Professor Michael Gänzle at the University of Alberta was especially patient, answering all my questions regarding sourdough microbiology and sharing numerous articles with me. Professor Marco Gobbetti and his colleague Raffaella Di Cagno at the University of Bari were equally generous about questions regarding sourdough and celiac disease. Ariane Lotti of the National Sustainable Agriculture Coalition in Washington took time out of her busy schedule to serve as interpreter in an interview with Professor Gobbetti. Dr. Hetty van den Broeck at Plant Research International, Wageningen, the Netherlands, also discussed her research and shared articles with me.

Charles C. Mann offered invaluable advice one night at the Monterey Bay Aquarium, informing my research on Neolithic farmers. And of course, the farmers who grow the grain were helpful on many fronts. I'd like to thank Mary-Howell and Klaas Martens, Heinz Thomet, Karlan Koehn, and Eli Rogosa.

This book would not have been possible without the thoughtful comments of my editor, Kathryn Court, who helped me hone my ideas and approach. Her assistant Lindsey Schwoeri ably marshaled the manuscript to completion. Copyeditors and proofreaders don't always get their due, but I'd like to thank Michael Burke, Jayne Lathrop, and Diane Turso, who combed through the entire manuscript, raised crucial questions, and did a superb job. Any remaining errors are, of course, my own. The rest of the Viking team—production editor Kate Griggs, interior designer Francesca Belanger, and jacket designer Nick Misani—were also a pleasure to work with. My long-time agent, Denise Shannon, has always managed to pull decent ideas out of me, often to my surprise. Thanks as well to Elissa Altman, who upon reading one of my blog posts on bread making told me during a break at a conference, "You have a book there."

My friends and colleagues at the Food & Environment Reporting Network—Tom Laskawy, Susan West, Paula Crossfield, and Naomi Starkman—were especially understanding of my book deadline, and I thank them for their flexibility. I'd also like to thank the many talented journalists I've worked with at FERN, who raised the bar for my own efforts.

Finally, a big thanks to the bread eaters, including my most trenchant critics: my daughter, Nina, and her friends; and my wife, Ellen, who patiently prodded me on, even as I worried that this project had under- or overfermented. Slicing off another piece of rye, she assured me it had not.

Glossary

Alveoli—The holes created in the crumb of the bread. The aim in many artisan breads is to create an uneven and random structure marked by nearly translucent strands of gluten.

Amylase—Enzymes that convert starch into smaller chains of sugar that can be easily digested by yeast. In the form of malted barley or fungal amylase, these enzymes are also added to flour to help with fermentation. Amylase is also present in saliva in the form of ptyalin—an evolutionary adaptation to the digestion of starch.

Autolyse—After flour, water, and an optional pre-ferment are gently combined in the initial period of mixing, the dough is left to rest, or literally, to "self-digest." After the rest period, the remaining ingredients are added and mixing can resume. The technique improves the extensibility of dough and was developed by the renowned French bread authority Raymond Calvel. Some bakers also include salt during the autolyse, though this can result in tighter gluten.

Backferment—An organic sourdough fermentation culture produced by the German company Sekowa, that is made with chickpea flour, honey, and organic wheat. The fermentation culture, sold as dried granules, favors the production of lactic acids in dough fermentation.

Barley (*Hordeum vulgare*)—One of the "founder" crops in the Fertile Crescent, used primarily for beer making and animal feed. Its origins date back to the foundations of agriculture, though it is barely consumed in bread these days.

Glossary

Bolting—The process of removing a portion of bran from stone milled flour, with either a fine mesh screen or fabric.

Bread wheat (*Triticum aestivum*)—A hexaploid, with six sets of chromosomes, which has no wild analog. It arose when cultivated emmer wheat interbred with wild goat grass (*Aegilops squarrosa*) around the southwestern shores of the Caspian Sea.

Celiac disease—An autoimmune disease brought on by the ingestion of gluten. It affects about 1 percent of all people. Discrete parts of gluten proteins trigger an immune reaction, causing the body to attack itself.

Couche—The French word for a linen cloth that supports loaves such as baguettes during their final rise.

Crumb—The interior of a loaf of bread.

Diastatic malt—Malt with active amylase enzymes that promote more vigorous fermentation and darker crust color. In nondiastatic malt, these enzymes are deactivated.

Einkorn wheat (*Triticum monococcum*)—A founder crop in the Fertile Crescent. Domesticated einkorn appears to have originated with a wild species that grows in southeast Turkey on Karaca Dağ mountain, but wild relatives grow over a large swath of western Asia. Einkorn is a diploid with two sets of chromosomes, the simplest genetic structure in wheat.

Elasticity—Refers to the ability of dough to spring back once it is stretched out. This quality reflects the presence of glutenin proteins.

Emmer wheat (*Triticum dicoccum*)—Another foundation wheat species which originated in the Fertile Crescent. Wild relatives are found in Israel, Jordan, Syria, Lebanon, and southeast Turkey. By the fifth century B.C., emmer was being grown in central Europe alongside einkorn. It has four sets of chromosomes, making it a tetraploid wheat. It is an ancient relative of durum (*Triticum durum*), or pasta wheat.

Epitope—A precise sequence of amino acids—the building blocks of proteins—that trigger an immune reaction in the human body.

Many epitopes have been located in gluten proteins that trigger celiac disease.

Exopolysaccharides—A type of nondigestible fiber that can be created by sourdough microbiota during grain fermentation. These fibers are considered a "prebiotic" because they feed microorganisms dwelling in the gut.

Extensibility—Refers to the ability of dough to stretch without breaking. The more stretchy the dough is, the more extensible, reflecting the presence of gliadin proteins.

Extraction rate—The percentage of the wheat kernel that remains after elements such as the germ or bran are removed (or extracted). White flour generally has an extraction rate of about 72 percent, meaning that 28 percent of the wheat kernel is removed for another use. Whole wheat flour has an extraction rate of 100 percent.

First rise—The first fermentation, after the dough is mixed but before the loaf is shaped. Also known as "bulk fermentation."

Free-threshing wheat—A genetic mutation in wheat that causes the naked grain to fall free of its hull when the grain is threshed. It is a sign of domestication, because wild wheats are hulled. But not all cultivated wheat is free-threshing. Einkorn and spelt are hulled wheats and must be pounded to release the grain, adding an additional step after threshing.

Gluten—The proteins that create the viscoelastic properties of bread, allowing dough to stretch out and maintain its shape. Gluten is made up of gliadin and glutenin proteins and accounts for about 80 percent of wheat's protein.

Grigne—The French term for the open cut in a loaf that appears after the dough is slashed and baked.

Hard red spring wheat—Wheat that is sown in the spring for harvest in the summer of the same year. It is generally sown in the northern plains.

Hard red winter wheat—Wheat that is sown in the fall and harvested the following summer. It is suited for the southern plains states. It has a moderate level of protein and is favored in artisan breads. The bran is also tinted reddish brown, as opposed to the creamy-colored bran of white wheat.

Hybrid wheat—Two distinct varieties of wheat that have been cross-bred to create a new variety. Wheat is self-pollinating, which means that interbreeding occurs only infrequently in nature. In modern hybrid wheat, varieties are mated and then their progeny are inter-bred for several generations, before a new variety is released. Bread wheat itself is a hybrid, the result of a natural crossing of emmer wheat and goat grass. Hybrid breeding techniques are also distinct from genetic modification, which involves inserting genes of another species. Currently, no genetically modified wheat has been approved for sale.

Hydration—The percentage of water in dough in relation to flour, measured by weight. A hydration rate of 70 percent, for example, means 700 grams of water for each kilo of flour.

Kamut—A trademarked variety of Khorasan wheat (*Triticum turgidum* subspecies *turanicum*), Kamut is a tetraploid wheat (like emmer and durum wheat) whose kernels are about twice as large as hard red wheat. An American airman sent Khorasan wheat, which originated in Egypt, to his family in Montana after World War II. The wheat variety languished until the 1980s, when it was introduced to the natural foods marketplace.

Lactic acid bacteria—Populations of bacteria that live in sourdough cultures, helping dough to ferment and creating a range of both lactic and acetic acids that strongly influence the flavor, texture, and keeping quality of bread.

Lame—A long-handled tool designed to hold a double-edged razor blade used to score, or slash, loaves.

Landrace wheat—A diverse population of wheat selected and cultivated by farmers, adapted to a local climate and bioregion. Most landrace wheats have become relics as modern wheat varieties, bred by specialized crop breeders, have become dominant.

Maillard reaction—The reaction that occurs when a mix of protein, starch, and water is heated above 250°F (120°C). It contributes to the browning of the bread crust and creates its unique flavor.

Oxidation—Oxidation strengthens gluten bonds in dough and bleaches out white flour's cream-colored pigments. Oxidation can be achieved by aging freshly milled flour for at least two weeks, or more quickly by adding chemical oxidizing agents such as potassium bromate, potassium iodate, benzoyl peroxide, calcium peroxide, or ascorbic acid (vitamin C). Potassium bromate is a known carcinogen that is banned in Europe, Canada, and Japan and must be labeled in the United States. Azodicarbonamide, a bleaching and oxidizing agent, is generally recognized as safe in the United States, though it is banned in Europe because of evidence that it can induce asthma.

Peel—A long-handled flat wooden spatula used to load or remove bread from the oven.

Pentosan—A gumlike sugar that can absorb ten times its weight in water. These gums are especially prevalent in rye, which is why rye dough requires far more water than wheat. Pentosan forms viscous gels that are responsible with starch for the crumb formation in rye bread.

Phytic acid—An acid found in the innermost layer of bran that blocks the body from absorbing beneficial minerals, such as iron, calcium, magnesium, and zinc. Phytic acid is neutralized by sourdough.

Pre-ferment—A portion of dough that is fermented and then added as an ingredient to the final mixture of dough. It is made with flour, water, and yeast, or with sourdough. A poolish is a type of pre-ferment made with yeast.

Proofing—The final rise of dough, after it is shaped. Also known as the "second rise."

Protein level—An imperfect measurement of a dough's gluten strength. High-protein spring wheats yield strong gluten, whereas low-protein cake flour has very weak gluten-forming qualities and makes light, crumbly cakes. That said, high protein does not always mean strong gluten. Ancient wheats such as einkorn are high in protein but don't have the qualities to create a strong gluten matrix.

Retarding—Slowing the fermentation of dough by refrigeration, either during the initial bulk rise or during the proofing stage.

Rye (*Secale cereale*)—Although rye dates back to the beginning of agriculture, it may have arisen as a weed amid other cultivated cereals. It is now primarily grown in eastern, northern, and central Europe. Rye is low in glutenin, which is why rye breads rely on a network of pentosans and starch to form their crumb. In white rye, the bran has been removed; whole rye (sometimes labeled "medium rye") consists of the entire kernel; dark rye is made up of the remaining kernel after white rye has been removed. But these labels are not always consistent and medium rye may not always be "whole rye" flour. To avoid these issues, I generally buy "whole rye," which is the equivalent of whole wheat flour, for it contains 100 percent of the grain.

Saccharomyces cerevisiae—A prevalent species of yeast that converts sugar into ethanol alcohol and carbon dioxide used as a fermentation agent in alcoholic beverages and bread since prehistoric times. Although wild varieties of this species exist, many specific varieties have been domesticated and cultured for wine, beer, and bread making.

Sourdough—A culture of wild yeast and lactic acid bacteria that ferments cereal grains. Also known as "sourdough starter," "natural leaven," and *levain*.

Spelt (*Triticum aestivum subspecies spelta*)—An ancient hulled subspecies of bread wheat favored in ancient Rome. It can have higher protein levels than bread wheat, but this is not true of all spelt varieties. Some varieties of spelt have also been interbred with modern bread wheats to improve baking qualities, as spelt often lacks elasticity.

Wheat kernel—The kernel is composed of the germ, endosperm, and bran. Wheat germ makes up 2 to 3 percent of the seed, containing lipids (oils), sugars, vitamins, amino acids, and minerals. The endosperm consists largely of starch (70 to 73 percent) and protein (10 to 14 percent). The endosperm includes the aleurone layer, which is rich in minerals, vitamin B, and other essential nutrients and which is removed in milling white flour. The bran or protective coating of the wheat seed accounts for 13 to 17 percent of the grain and is composed of protein, minerals, and fiber.

White wheat—A variety of hard wheat that has a recessive gene that changes the pigment of the bran from reddish brown to a creamy color, altering the flavor of whole grain bread so that it is less assertive. White flour milled from white wheat (in which the germ and bran are removed) is even lighter in color than white flour milled from hard red wheat. Most of the white wheat grown in the United States is exported to Asia, where it is used in the production of noodles.

Notes

Introduction

8 *one fifth of humanity's calories* International Maize and Wheat Improvement Center (CIMMYT) and International Center for Agricultural Research in the Dry Areas (ICARDA), "Wheat: Global Alliance for Improving Food Security and the Livelihoods of the Resource Poor in the Developing World," August 30, 2011.

11 *The ancient Romans* The latin *fornix* means arch, referring both to the arch of the oven ceiling and the vaulted arcades around the Colosseum in Rome where prostitutes plied their trade. The word may also reflect the association of the oven as life giving. Jeffrey Hamelman, *Bread: A Baker's Book of Techniques and Recipes* (Wiley, 2004), p. 21.

Chapter 1: Boulangerie Delmontel's Baguette

19 *The poorest slept* Steven Laurence Kaplan, *The Bakers of Paris and the Bread Question, 1700–1775* (Duke University Press, 1996), p. 71.

26 *By 1987, a cultural critic* Steven Laurence Kaplan, *Good Bread Is Back: A Contemporary History of French Bread, the Way It Is Made, and the People Who Make It* (Duke University Press, 2006), pp. 98 and 340.

29 *"There was no danger"* James MacGuire, "The Baguette," *The Art of Eating* 73/74 (2006).

30 *Home bakers experienced* Mark Bittman, "The Secret of Great Bread: Let Time Do the Work," *The New York Times*, November 8, 2006. For more variations on the recipe, see Jim Lahey, *My Bread: The Revolutionary No-Work, No-Knead Method* (W. W. Norton & Company, 2009).

31 *Before the 1920s* Jim Chevallier, *About the Baguette: Exploring the Origin of a French National Icon*, self-published e-book available on Amazon.com.

31 *they drove oxygen into the dough* Oxidation causes a breakdown of

lipids in flour, which includes vitamin E. The oxidation of carotenoids also compromises beta-carotene and other antioxidants.

31 *Ascorbic acid* Raymond Calvel, *The Taste of Bread* (Aspen Publishers, 2001). See the section "Excessive Oxidation and Its Consequences," pp. 30–37.

32 *bread consumption declined* Edward Behr, "Paris (or What Is French Food?); Part I, Posing the Question and The Classic Parisian Baguette," *The Art of Eating* 45 (Winter 1998), p. 10.

32 *one quarter of the nation* Eleanor Beardsley, "Outsourced Croissants Outrage Traditional French Bakers," National Public Radio, August 7, 2012.

43 *This process was crucial* There is evidence that wild yeasts contribute to endogenous fermentation, though the point has been debated. Others suggest that the primary yeast species in wine fermentation are domesticated species added by vintners. See LeGras et al., "Bread, Beer and Wine: *Saccharomyces Cerevisiae* Diversity Reflects Human History," *Molecular Ecology* 17 (2007).

43 *Pichard motioned* The hydration of this dough ranges from 78 to 82 percent, though Pichard stressed that it depends on the flour.

44 *before baker's yeast* The fresh baker's yeast is generally 0.2 to 0.4 percent of the flour weight.

44 *On the surface of the dough* Pichard revealed another aspect of his method, which was crucial to understanding why it worked. The white flour did not have any additives, not even enzymatic malt. Since flour alone contains less than 1 percent fermentable sugar, the enzymatic agent found in barley malt is often necessary to help the fermentation process along. Most white flours contain these added enzymes. So why then does Pichard avoid malted flour? Because in the "endogenous" fermentation, what few enzymes are present in the flour have plenty of time to work. If the dough hasn't fermented sufficiently, Pichard just lets it sit longer. If the flour contained malt, the result would be an excess of enzymatic activity over that period, meaning that too much starch would convert to sugar, causing the loaf to break down into a gummy mass. This is precisely what happened when I tried Pichard's technique at home, because my flour contained malt. I let the flour and water sit at room temperature for a full day, but when I added yeast and made the dough, it never properly developed and the baguette was gummy inside. The prognosis? The enzymes in the malt had broken down too much starch in the "endogenous" fermentation. If I was going to try his method again, it would have to be with unmalted flour.

46 *Compared with table salt* One gram of coarse sea salt contains 350 to 375 milligrams of sodium chloride, compared with 400 milligrams in kosher salt.

51 *Tim immediately liked the idea* Tim Carman, "Can Local Baguette Makers Compete With an Ace Home Baker? Our Debut Competition Raises Bread Discourse to a New Level," *Washington City Paper*, May 8, 2009. Available at www.washingtoncitypaper.com/articles/ 37173/can-local-baguette-makers-compete-with-an-ace-home -baker.

Chapter 2: Culturing Wild Leaven in My Kitchen

71 *More than one billion bacteria* Interview with Michael Gänzle, April 2, 2013.

72 *a minute amount of wild yeast* Jill A. Snowdon et al., "Microorganisms in Honey," *International Journal of Food Microbiology* 31.1 (1996): 1–26. See also Peter B. Olaitan et al., "Honey: A Reservoir for Microorganisms and an Inhibitory Agent for Microbes," *African Health Sciences* 7.3 (2007).

72 *arabinoxylan* Marco Gobbetti and Michael Gänzle, eds., *Handbook on Sourdough Biotechnology* (Springer, 2013), chap. 9, p. 235. See also Paula Figoni, *How Baking Works: Exploring the Fundamentals of Baking Science* (Wiley, 2007), p. 70.

73 *millet made the best sourdough* I actually tried to make the millet starter Pliny describes, but after two days of fermentation I saw little activity, so when I fed it a second time, I added malted barley. Not much happened, so on the third day, I added rye, honey, and millet. I continued this feeding regime until the sixth day, when I switched to rye entirely. After two weeks, it was very powerful and had a slightly sweet smell from the honey and it worked as well as my other starters that were then on vacation in my refrigerator, but it would be inaccurate to say it was a millet starter. Given its prevalence in archeological sites, I'm likely to give millet starter another try.

73 *millet wine has been found* Patrick E. McGovern, *Uncorking the Past: The Quest for Wine, Beer, and Other Alcoholic Beverages* (University of California Press, 2009), Kindle edition, Kindle location 1073.

74 *One recently investigated vector* Irene Stefanini et al., "Role of Social Wasps in Saccharomyces cerevisiae Ecology and Evolution," *Proceedings of the National Academy of Sciences* 109.33 (2012): 13398–403.

74 *ripe grapes with punctured* Robert Mortimer and Mario Polsinelli, "On the Origins of Wine Yeast," *Research in Microbiology* 150.3 (1999): 199–204.

75 *called the aleurone* The aleurone contains the only living cells of the grain and is the most nutrient-dense element, with more protein, vitamins, minerals, and fiber than any other part of the seed. Its antioxidants are such a powerful preservative for the seed kernel that they have been studied to extend the shelf life of food products; its phytosterols have been shown to lower cholesterol, reduce blood pressure, and offer a host of other health benefits. But it is removed in the milling of white flour.

75 *Saliva, which contains ptyalin* Ptyalin is also a powerful piece of evidence against the oft-stated "Paleo diet" thesis which says that humans have not adapted to eating cereal grains. We have, when it comes to starch digestion. Populations that historically ate a high amount of starchy foods, such as grains and cereals, show a predominance of genes that favor the production of amylase enzymes in the saliva and thus starch digestion. See George H. Perry et al., "Diet and the Evolution of Human Amylase Gene Copy Number Variation," *Nature Genetics* 39.10 (2007): 1256–60.

76 *the yeast begin a process* Emily Buehler, *Bread Science: The Chemistry and Craft of Making Bread* (Two Blue Books, 2006), pp. 34–38.

76 *651 variants* Jean Luc Legras et al., "Bread, Beer and Wine: Saccharomyces cerevisiae Diversity Reflects Human History," *Molecular Ecology* 16.10 (2007): 2091–102.

76 *Yeasts—a fungi—are actually ubiquitous* Interview with Chris Hittenger, assistant professor, University of Wisconsin, December 17, 2012.

76 *At least 23 yeast species* C. Meroth et al., "Monitoring the Bacterial Population Dynamics in Sourdough Fermentation Processes by Using PCR-Denaturing Gradient Gel Electrophoresis," Applied and Environmental Microbiology 69(1) (Jan. 2003): 475–82.

77 *But if wine came before* Interview with Sol Katz, August 3, 2011. Katz caused a stir on the microbrew circuit in the 1990s by helping concoct a contemporary version of Mesopotamian beer, based on the translation of a poem from 1800 B.C.

78 *Rice and honey mead* McGovern, *Uncorking the Past*, Kindle locations 1572–73, for China. The Göbekli Tepe site in Turkey, from 11,600 years ago, appears to have evidence of beer making as well. Oliver Dietrich et al., "The Role of Cult and Feasting in the Emergence of Neolithic Communities: New Evidence from Göbekli Tepe, Southeastern Turkey," *Antiquity* 86.333 (2012): 674–95.

79 *Debra Wink, a home baker* Wink's instructions on this method were provided in a two-part post on TheFreshLoaf.com.

Notes

80 *Scientists are just starting to tease out* Marcia Shu-Wei Su et al., "Intestinal Origin of Sourdough Lactobacillus reuteri Isolates as Revealed by Phylogenetic, Genetic, and Physiological Analysis," *Applied and Environmental Microbiology* 78.18 (2012): 6777–80.

80 *But lactobacilli are far more prevalent* Jens Walter, "Ecological Role of Lactobacilli in the Gastrointestinal Tract: Implications for Fundamental and Biomedical Research," *Applied and Environmental Microbiology* 74.16 (2008): 4985–96.

80 *Or they might arise* Gobbetti and Gänzle, eds., *Handbook on Sourdough Biotechnology*, chap. 5.

80 *Insects may also play a role* Willem H. Groenewald et al., "Identification of Lactic Acid Bacteria from Vinegar Flies Based on Phenotypic and Genotypic Characteristics," *American Journal of Enology and Viticulture* 57.4 (2006): 519–25.

80 *fruit flies lay their eggs* McGovern, *Uncorking the Past*, Kindle locations 277–79.

81 *acid-tolerant bacteria* Fabio Minervini et al., "Lactic Acid Bacterium and Yeast Microbiotas of 19 Sourdoughs Used for Traditional/Typical Italian Breads: Interactions Between Ingredients and Microbial Species Diversity," *Applied and Environmental Microbiology* 78.4 (2012): 1251–64.

82 *German Detmolder rye sourdough* See Jeffrey Hamelman, *Bread: A Baker's Book of Techniques and Recipes* (Wiley, 2012), p. 200.

83 *That is why scientists have found* I. Scheirlinck et al., "Molecular Source Tracking of Predominant Lactic Acid Bacteria in Traditional Belgian Sourdoughs and Their Production Environments," *Journal of Applied Microbiology* 106(4) (Apr. 2009): 1081–92.

83 *So far, fifty-five species* Gobbetti and Gänzle, eds., *Handbook on Sourdough Biotechnology*, chap. 5, p. 114.

83 *nineteen Italian sourdough cultures* Minervini et al., "Lactic Acid Bacterium and Yeast Microbiotas of 19 Sourdoughs."

83 *cultures can even change* Fabio Minervini et al., "Influence of Artisan Bakery- or Laboratory-Propagated Sourdoughs on the Diversity of Lactic Acid Bacterium and Yeast Microbiotas," *Applied and Environmental Microbiology* 78.15 (2012): 5328–40.

86 *It has higher levels of sugar* E. J. Pyler and L. A. Gorton, *Baking Science and Technology,* 4th ed. (Sosland Publishing Co., 2008), p. 169.

Chapter 3: California and the Country Loaf

103 *American artisan bakers generally seek out* French flours tend to have lower levels of protein, but they perform similarly to American ar-

279

tisan bread flours with one main difference: they require less water. As a general rule of thumb, you can reduce the water by 4 percentage points for French flours versus American all-purpose flours. So if a recipe calls for 700 grams of water for 1 kilo of flour, I'd start by adding 660 grams of water to the French flour to see how it performs.

109 *Robertson appeared on the cover* Daniel Wing and Alan Scott, *The Bread Builders* (Chelsea Green, 1999).

111 *Nathan Yanko, a distance runner* Yanko has since moved on, opening the bakery M.H. Bread & Butter in San Anselmo, north of San Francisco.

Chapter 4: Re-creating a Diverse Grain Pantry

127 *In the refrigerator, I store* Refrigeration isn't necessary if you're going to use the flour within a few months, but heat and humidity can lead to spoilage. Even if the flour continues to perform well over several months, when stored at room temperature, its nutritional properties gradually degrade as a result of oxidation. Refrigeration slows this process. See Andres F. Doblado-Maldonado et al., "Key Issues and Challenges in Whole Wheat Flour Milling and Storage," *Journal of Cereal Science* 56.2 (2012): 119–26.

131 *primary source of food* Aaron Bobrow-Strain, *White Bread: A Social History of the Store-Bought Loaf* (Beacon, 2012), p. 4.

132 *a New World starch, the potato* Charles C. Mann, *1493: Uncovering the New World Columbus Created* (Alfred A. Knopf, 2011), p. 208.

132 *Portuguese* broa de milho See a description of this bread on the blog "Azelia's Kitchen," www.azeliaskitchen.net/broa-northern-portugal/.

132 *famines occurred* See Mann, *1493*, p. 209. Also see Bernard Dupaigne, *The History of Bread* (Harry N. Abrams, 1999), p. 38.

133 *in Russia, four million to seven million* Richard Manning, *Against the Grain: How Agriculture Has Hijacked Civilization* (Macmillan, 2004), p. 69.

134 *the grain was spelt* Patrick Faas, *Around the Roman Table: Food and Feasting in Ancient Rome* (University of Chicago Press, 2005), p. 176.

137 *the origin of marble rye* Stanley Ginsberg and Norman Berg, *Inside the Jewish Bakery* (Camino Books, 2011), p. 57.

137 *Hippocrates* Pliny the Elder, *The Natural History*, Book 18, chaps. 15, 26.

137 *barley sustained soldiers* Ibid., Book 18, chap. 14. See also health benefits of barley at the Whole Grains Council: http://wholegrainscouncil.org/whole-grains-101/health-benefits-of-barley.

138 *a prison riot* Kaplan, *Bakers of Paris and the Bread Question*, pp. 34–36.

Notes

139 *With every 100 grams of wheat bran* See tables for "crude wheat bran" and "white wheat flour" in *USDA National Nutrient Database for Standard Reference, Release 26.* Bran represents around 12 to 17 percent of the kernel.

139 *Bakers could now rely* The full and fascinating story of white bread can be found in Bobrow-Strain, *White Bread.*

141 *Grasslands cover* The 40 percent figure excludes Greenland and Antarctica. See J. M. Suttie, S. J. Reynolds, and C. Batello, eds., *Grasslands of the World*, Plant Production and Protection Series No. 34 (Food and Agriculture Organization of the United Nations, 2005).

141 *Wild wheat and barley* Michael Balter, "Seeking Agriculture's Ancient Roots," *Science* 316.5833 (2007): 1830–35.

141 *The oldest evidence* J. Mercader, "Mozambican Grass Seed Consumption During the Middle Stone Age," *Science* 326.1680 (2009).

142 *This mutant trait* George Willcox, "The Roots of Cultivation in Southwestern Asia," *Science* 341.6141 (2013): 39–40. See figure 3.

142 *evolved before hulled spelt* For a discussion of spelt's separate evolution from free-threshing wheat, see Francesco Salamini et al., "Genetics and Geography of Wild Cereal Domestication in the Near East," *Nature Reviews Genetics* 3.6 (2002): 429–41.

142 *This is apparent in the domestication of wheat* George Willcox's Web site has an illuminating map of these remains. See http://g.willcox.pagesperso-orange.fr.

143 *Domestication accelerated only* Balter, "Seeking Agriculture's Ancient Roots."

143 *This process occurred at multiple locations* Willcox, "Roots of Cultivation in Southwestern Asia."

144 *11,000-year-old Syrian site* George Willcox and Danielle Stordeur, "Large-Scale Cereal Processing Before Domestication During the Tenth Millennium Cal BC in Northern Syria," *Antiquity* 86.331 (2012): 99–114. The site is now covered by the waters of the Tishrine dam.

145 *As Klaus Schmidt, the archeologist* Charles C. Mann, "The Birth of Religion," *National Geographic*, June 2011. See also Ken-ichi Tanno and George Willcox, "How Fast Was Wild Wheat Domesticated?," *Science* 311.5769 (2006): 1886.

146 *Along with einkorn, emmer* Daniel Zohary and Maria Hopf, *Domestication of Plants in the Old World*, 3rd ed. (Oxford University Press, 2000). Zohary and Hopf discuss the origins of all the founder grains.

147 *95 percent of all wheat* CIMMYT, "Global Strategy for the Ex Situ Conservation with Enhanced Access to Wheat, Rye and Triticale Genetic Resources," September 2007.

148 *crossbred with other nonspelt* T. Schober et al., "Gluten Proteins from Spelt (Triticum Aestivum Ssp. Spelta) Cultivars: A Rheological and Size-Exclusion High-Performance Liquid Chromatography Study," *Journal of Cereal Science* 44.2 (2006): 161–73.

148 *if a major portion of the wheat crop* John H. Perkins, *Geopolitics and the Green Revolution: Wheat, Genes, and the Cold War* (Oxford University Press, 1997), p. v.

Chapter 5: Turkey Red: Heritage Grains and the Roots of the Breadbasket

155 *Rewind to 1912* E. G. Heyne, "Earl G. Clark, Kansas Farmer and Wheat Breeder," *Kansas Academy of Sciences* 59.4 (Winter 1956).

157 *a field of Turkey Red wheat* While often described as Ukrainian in origin, the seed originated in Crimea and did not reach Ukraine until 1860. A Mennonite immigrant to the United States, Bernard Warkentin, reportedly imported 25,000 bushels of the seed and planted them in several hundred test plots near his home. Alan L. Olmstead and Paul W. Rhode, "The Red Queen and the Hard Reds: Productivity Growth in American Wheat, 1800–1940," *The Journal of Economic History* 62.04 (2002): 929–66. See also Report of the Kansas State Board of Agriculture 39.15566: 218.

157 *farmers settling the Great Plains* William Cronin, *Nature's Metropolis: Chicago and the Great West* (W. W. Norton, 1991). See chap. 3 for a brilliant history of grain trade during this era.

158 *He and his wife, Jane* Alan L. Olmstead and Paul W. Rhode, *Creating Abundance: Biological Innovation and American Agricultural Development* (Cambridge University Press, 2008), pp. 26–27.

159 *when Turkey Red was near its peak* Ibid., chap. 2.

164 *high-extraction flour is common in Europe* In Europe, there are grades of flour that denote how much mineral content they contain, which is a proxy for bran (for minerals reside in the bran) and also the extraction rate. To figure the mineral content, a sample of flour is incinerated. The remaining ash, made up of minerals, is then measured. In France, these flours can be found as type 80 (0.80 percent ash, corresponding to an 82 to 85 percent extraction rate) or type 110 (1.1 percent ash, or roughly 85 to 90 percent extraction). In Germany, a flour classified as type 1150 (1.15 percent ash, or a roughly 90 percent extraction) is also between white and whole wheat flour. In the United States, whole wheat flour may be roller milled; that is, separated and then mixed back together to approximate the ratio in the original kernel. Using stone ground flour will likely ensure that

you're getting the entire kernel—that is, a 100 percent extraction—in a milled product, rather than one that is reconstituted. To get close to bolted wheat, you can mix two-thirds white flour with one-third whole wheat flour.

168 *A wake-up call* Melinda Smale et al., "Dimensions of Diversity in CIMMYT Bread Wheat from 1965 to 2000" (CIMMYT, 2001).

168 *Aside from corn leaf blight* Jochen C. Reif et al., "Wheat Genetic Diversity Trends During Domestication and Breeding," *Theoretical and Applied Genetics* 110.5 (2005): 859–64.

169 *pool of genetic resources* National Research Council, *Genetic Vulnerability of Major Crops* (National Academies Press, 1972).

169 *semidwarf wheat varieties* Susan Dworkin, *The Viking in the Wheat Field* (Walker and Co., 2009). See chap. 2. For yield figures, see Rodomiro Ortiz et al., "Climate Change: Can Wheat Beat the Heat?," *Agriculture, Ecosystems & Environment* 126.1 (2008): 46–58.

170 *less suited to dry land areas* Smale et al., "Dimensions of Diversity."

170 *"a narrowing of genetic diversity"* M. L. Warburton et al., "Bringing Wild Relatives Back into the Family: Recovering Genetic Diversity in CIMMYT Improved Wheat Germplasm," *Euphytica* 149.3 (2006): 289–301.

170 *"replaced the landraces"* Ibid.

171 *97 percent of all spring wheat* Smale et al., Dimensions of Diversity.

171 *By 1993, the National Academy* National Research Council, *Managing Global Genetic Resources: Agricultural Crop Issues and Policies* (National Academies Press, 1993).

171 *In developing countries such as India* Ortiz et al., "Climate Change."

172 *conventional breeding techniques* The specific technique they use is marker-assisted breeding, which uses molecular genetics to identify plants with specific traits bred conventionally. This is distinct from genetic engineering techniques used to create a genetically modified organism.

172 *more diversity than before the Green Revolution* See Warburton et al., "Bringing Wild Relatives Back into the Family," and Smale et al., "Dimensions of Diversity." Also see Jorge Dubcovsky and Jan Dvorak, "Genome Plasticity a Key Factor in the Success of Polyploid Wheat Under Domestication," *Science* 316.5833 (2007): 1862–66; Maarten van Ginkel and Francis Ogbonnaya, "Novel Genetic Diversity from Synthetic Wheats in Breeding Cultivars for Changing Production Conditions," *Field Crops Research* 104.1 (2007): 86–94.

172 *more than 168,000 different* CIMMYT, "Genetic Resources at CIMMYT," private communication from CIMMYT press officer, 2013.

172 *The practice by farmers* Perhaps the most eloquent defense of in situ breeding has been made by Gary Paul Nabhan, *Where Our Food Comes From: Retracing Nikolay Vavilov's Quest to End Famine* (Island Press, 2008).

173 *"More and more land"* Hakan Özkan et al., "Geographic Distribution and Domestication of Wild Emmer Wheat (Triticum dicoccoides)," *Genetic Resources and Crop Evolution* 58.1 (2011): 11–53.

173 *In 2013, wheat researchers* Kansas State University, "Resistance Gene Found Against Ug99 Wheat Stem Rust Pathogen," June 27, 2013, www.k-state.edu/media/newsreleases/jun13/sr3562713.html. See also Sambasivam Periyannan et al., "The Gene Sr33, an Ortholog of Barley Mla Genes, Encodes Resistance to Wheat Stem Rust Race Ug99," *Science* 341.6147 (2013): 786–88.

173 *these grasses have been ignored* In a CIMMYT paper spelling out the need for robust wheat collections, the state of landrace and wild wheat cultivars was described as "poor." The paper stated that these collections should be given priority. See CIMMYT, "Global Strategy for the Ex Situ Conservation with Enhanced Access to Wheat, Rye and Triticale Genetic Resources," September 2007.

173 *recently been defined* Anna Sapone et al., "Spectrum of Gluten-Related Disorders: Consensus on New Nomenclature and Classification," *BMC Medicine* 10.1 (2012): 13.

174 *Norwegian researchers in 2005* Øyvind Molberg et al., "Mapping of Gluten T-cell Epitopes in the Bread Wheat Ancestors: Implications for Celiac Disease," *Gastroenterology* 128.2 (2005): 393–401.

175 *"This suggests that modern wheat breeding"* Hetty C. van den Broeck et al., "Presence of Celiac Disease Epitopes in Modern and Old Hexaploid Wheat Varieties: Wheat Breeding May Have Contributed to Increased Prevalence of Celiac Disease," *Theoretical and Applied Genetics* 121.8 (2010): 1527–39.

175 *gliadin proteins transferred* Molberg et al., "Mapping of Gluten T-cell Epitopes in the Bread Wheat Ancestors."

175 *While some studies have found that einkorn* On einkorn toxicity to celiac patients, see Carmen Gianfrani et al., "Immunogenicity of Monococcum Wheat in Celiac Patients," *The American Journal of Clinical Nutrition* 96.6 (2012): 1339–45. For a wider discussion, see the editorial by Eric V. Marietta and Joseph A. Murray, "Testing the Safety of Alternative Wheat Species and Cultivars for Consumption by Celiac Patients," *The American Journal of Clinical Nutrition* 96.6 (2012): 1247–48.

176 *These modified grains* Javier Gil-Humanes et al., "Effective Shutdown in the Expression of Celiac Disease–Related Wheat Gliadin T-cell

Epitopes by RNA Interference," *Proceedings of the National Academy of Sciences* 107.39: 17023–28.

186 *It is not even clear how much whole grain* The definition of whole grains remains a "guidance statement" from the FDA, without impact if a manufacturer chooses to ignore it. It was written in February 2006. The statement says: "Cereal grains that consist of the intact, ground, cracked or flaked caryopsis, whose principal anatomical components—the starchy endosperm, germ and bran—are present in the same relative proportions as they exist in the intact caryopsis—should be considered a whole grain food."

Chapter 6: A Rye Journey to Berlin

197 *freshly ground whole grains were the richest nutritionally* Andres F. Doblado-Maldonado et al., "Key Issues and Challenges in Whole Wheat Flour Milling and Storage," *Journal of Cereal Science* 56.2 (2012): 119–26.

202 *known as* altrus Ginsberg and Berg, *Inside the Jewish Bakery*, p. 59.

208 *Peter Reinhart* Peter Reinhart, *Peter Reinhart's Whole Grain Baking: New Techniques, Extraordinary Flavor* (Ten Speed Press, 2007), pp. 39–45. For greater detail on the biochemistry, see Gobbetti and Gänzle, eds., *Handbook on Sourdough Biotechnology*, chap. 8, "Sourdough: A Tool to Improve Bread Structure." The "starch attack" incidentally is less of an issue in wheat, because amylase is largely deactivated by heat before wheat starch gelatinizes. But it still can occur, especially if the flour has an excess of amylase during fermentation.

209 *Cereal scientists suggest* Milling the bran to a finer consistency frees up enzymes, ferulic acid, glutathione, and phytates, all of which impede gluten bonds. See Doblado-Maldonado, et al., "Key Issues and Challenges in Whole Wheat Flour Milling and Storage." See also Martijn W. J. Noort et al., "The Effect of Particle Size of Wheat Bran Fractions on Bread Quality—Evidence for Fibre-Protein Interactions," *Journal of Cereal Science* 52.1 (2010): 59–64.

210 *the benefits of whole grain fiber* Joanne L. Slavin et al., "Plausible Mechanisms for the Protectiveness of Whole Grains," *The American Journal of Clinical Nutrition* 70.3 (1999): 459s–63s.

210 *Coarsely ground grains magnify* Kenneth W. Heaton et al., "Particle Size of Wheat, Maize, and Oat Test Meals: Effects on Plasma Glucose and Insulin Responses and on the Rate of Starch Digestion in Vitro," *The American Journal of Clinical Nutrition* 47.4 (1988): 675–82. See also David S. Ludwig et al., "Dietary Fiber, Weight Gain, and

Cardiovascular Disease Risk Factors in Young Adults," *JAMA: The Journal of the American Medical Association* 282.16 (1999): 1539–46.

210 *white sourdough bread raises* Anita Mofidi Najjar et al., "The Acute Impact of Ingestion of Breads of Varying Composition on Blood Glucose, Insulin and Incretins Following First and Second Meals," *British Journal of Nutrition* 101.3 (2009): 391.

210 *These fibers are known as "prebiotics"* Interview with Michael Gänzle on exopolysaccharides. For the benefits of prebiotics, see Leo Stevenson et al., "Wheat Bran: Its Composition and Benefits to Health, a European Perspective," *International Journal of Food Sciences and Nutrition* 63.8 (2012): 1001–13.

211 *short-chain fatty acids* Slavin et al., "Plausible Mechanisms for the Protectiveness of Whole Grains."

211 *One study published in the spring of 2013* Jens Walter et al., "Holobiont Nutrition: Considering the Role of the Gastrointestinal Microbiota in the Health Benefits of Whole Grains," *Gut Microbes* 4.4 (2013): 340–46. A 2012 study in Europe of more than 470,000 people over eleven years did find an association between fiber consumption and lower cancer risk. See Neil Murphy et al., "Dietary Fibre Intake and Risks of Cancers of the Colon and Rectum in the European Prospective Investigation into Cancer and Nutrition (EPIC)," *PloS one* 7.6 (2012): e39361. A large U.S. study did not find a correlation between fiber intake and lower cancer risk but it did find one with whole grains. See Arthur Schatzkin et al., "Dietary Fiber and Whole-Grain Consumption in Relation to Colorectal Cancer in the NIH-AARP Diet and Health Study," *The American Journal of Clinical Nutrition* 85.5 (2007): 1353–60.

212 *showed no adverse reaction* See Raffaella Di Cagno et al., "Proteolysis by Sourdough Lactic Acid Bacteria: Effects on Wheat Flour Protein Fractions and Gliadin Peptides Involved in Human Cereal Intolerance," *Applied and Environmental Microbiology* 68.2 (2002): 623–33. See also Raffaella Di Cagno et al., "Sourdough Bread Made from Wheat and Nontoxic Flours and Started with Selected Lactobacilli Is Tolerated in Celiac Sprue Patients," *Applied and Environmental Microbiology* 70.2 (2004): 1088–96.

213 *fast fermentations common in industrial breads* Carlo G. Rizzello et al., "Highly Efficient Gluten Degradation by Lactobacilli and Fungal Proteases During Food Processing: New Perspectives for Celiac Disease," *Applied and Environmental Microbiology* 73.14 (2007): 4499–507.

213 *sourdough fermentation can maintain* Gobbetti and Gänzler, *Handbook*

on Sourdough Biotechnology, chap. 9, "Nutritional Aspects of Cereal Fermentation with Lactic Acid Bacteria and Yeast."

213 *Certain strains of lactic acid* Vittorio Capozzi et al., "Biotechnological Production of Vitamin B$_2$–Enriched Bread and Pasta," *Journal of Agricultural and Food Chemistry* 59.14 (2011): 8013–20.

214 *sourdough breaks down phytic acid* Stevenson et al., "Wheat Bran."

214 *Mineral deficiencies* Modern wheat breeding may have also exacerbated mineral deficiency in wheat. See F. J. Zhao et al., "Variation in Mineral Micronutrient Concentrations in Grain of Wheat Lines of Diverse Origin," *Journal of Cereal Science* 49.2 (2009): 290–95. See also David F. Garvin, Ross M. Welch, and John W. Finley, "Historical Shifts in the Seed Mineral Micronutrient Concentration of US Hard Red Winter Wheat Germplasm," *Journal of the Science of Food and Agriculture* 86.13 (2006): 2213–20.

214 *A few nutrients* Doblado-Maldonado et al., "Key Issues and Challenges in Whole Wheat Flour Milling and Storage."

Chapter 7: Local Bread in Cucugnan and Cobb Neck

225 *village of Cucugnan* Cucugnan is pronounced Coo-coo-nyon.

245 *"I remember when"* Interview with Stephen Jones, March 29, 2011.

245 *Heather Darby, another agronomist* Interview with Heather Darby, April 12, 2012.

Epilogue

261 *I had studied Kiko Denzer's classic book* Kiko Denzer, *Build Your Own Earth Oven: A Low-Cost Wood-Fired Mud Oven, Simple Sourdough Bread, Perfect Loaves* (Hand Print Press, 2007).

Bibliographic Note

When I began baking bread, there were not nearly as many books available as there are today, but I still return to those that were helpful, including Daniel Leader's *Bread Alone*, Nancy Silverton's *Breads from the La Brea Bakery*, Joe Ortiz's *The Village Baker*, and Carol Field's *The Italian Baker*. Since then, there has been an explosion of bread-baking books and resources online—so much so that a beginner might not know where to begin.

If you are new to bread baking, I'd pick up Jim Lahey's *My Bread*, which grew out of the extremely popular piece Mark Bittman wrote in *The New York Times* about Lahey's no-knead method. I wish I had had this book when I started baking. I would put another no-knead series in the same category—the *Bread in Five Minutes a Day* books by Jeff Hertzberg and Zoë Francis. My only quibble with Francis and Hertzberg is that they relied on copious amounts of yeast in their first book; in their most recent version, they advise that you can cut down the yeast and still get good results. What I most like about the no-knead method is that it will get the most nervous and insecure person baking bread, with a lot of success.

Flatbreads are especially worthy of exploration by the beginning baker, which I didn't realize for many years after baking with yeast and sourdough. This category of breads is generally underappreciated even though they can be made quickly and with such satisfying results. I'd recommend two books that offer a wide span of recipes: Anissa Helou's *Savory Baking from the Mediterranean* (which goes beyond flatbreads) and Jeffrey Alford and Naomi Duguid's *Flatbreads & Flavors* (which mixes flatbread recipes with other foods).

Once you've mastered these approaches, you might want to develop your skills a bit further. I've thoroughly enjoyed Ken Forkish's *Flour Water Salt Yeast*, which is a kind of Baking 201 to the 101-level no-knead books. Another good book that straddles the beginner and intermediate levels is Peter Reinhart's classic, *The Bread Baker's Apprentice*, which was one of the first books that explored a baguette similar to the one I encountered in Paris.

As your interest and knowledge grow, you'll soon be moving on to sourdough loaves. Although her method for culturing a sourdough starter is more complicated than it needs to be, Nancy Silverton's recipes in *Breads from the La Brea Bakery* stand the test of time (her chocolate cherry bread is memorable). I'd also include Maggie Glezer's valuable book, *Artisan Baking*, which uncovered recipes by many of those who created the bread revolution in the United States in the 1990s. If you really want to drill down into sourdough, Chad Robertson offers a thorough, thirty-seven-page recipe in *Tartine Bread*. Many home bakers, including me, were enthusiastic about this book, and their breads often came out looking like the quintessential Tartine loaf.

The United Kingdom has a number of notable bakers with equally interesting books: I'd include Dan Lepard's *The Art of Handmade Bread*, which among other things first gave me the idea of making a starter with beer. It's also worth following his column in *The Guardian* newspaper, which is available online. Andrew Whitley's *Bread Matters* offers many interesting whole grain and rye recipes and also delves into what has gone wrong with industrialized bread. Finally, I'd include the books of Richard Bertinet, a French baker living in Britain. The DVD included in his book

Dough was a key to my early success at kneading very wet and sticky doughs. All three bakers, incidentally, offer baking classes in the United Kingdom, as does Roland Feuillas in the south of France.

As bakers have started exploring whole grain breads, a number of notable books have appeared. Peter Reinhart's *Whole Grain Breads* includes a thorough exploration of the way these grains differ—and what you might do to make better loaves with them. While not a bread-baking book, Kim Boyce's *Good to the Grain* was a path-breaking book for cakes, pastries, and quick breads made with various whole grain flours. As I write this, Chad Robertson has just released *Tartine 3*, which focuses on whole grain breads and pastries, including breads made with oatmeal and various grain mashes, hearty and dense ryes, and whole grain cookies and crackers.

If you're looking for a good bagel or challah, try Stanley Ginsberg and Norman Berg's *Inside the Jewish Bakery*, which includes recipes and an illuminating, if brief, history of Jewish baking.

Now that you've got a thorough understanding of baking, you will probably want to read a bit more about baking methods and where they came from. Elizabeth David's *English Bread and Yeast Cookery* is a classic that reaches back to the earliest days of British milling practices and might offer a good companion to George Eliot's novel *The Mill on the Floss*. (David discusses British home bakers who baked breads in overturned ceramic flower pots surrounded by coals—a precursor of the pot method championed by Jim Lahey.) Another all-encompassing baking book is Jeffrey Hamelman's *Bread*, which is a valuable resource for baking methods. He has a facile way of explaining concepts and techniques, making this the first book I reach for when I have a question about bread making. It also contains the largest collection of rye recipes I've come across in an English-language baking book. He and his team of bakers also teach classes at King Arthur Flour in Norwich, Vermont.

For those interested in baking with wood fire, you can make an oven in a day following the instructions in Kiko Denzer's *Build Your Own Earth Oven*. For a deeper dive, including brick oven building and baking, Richard Miscovich's *From the Wood-Fired Oven* is essential and a good companion to the classic *The Bread Builders*, by Daniel Wing and Alan Scott.

Beyond books, I've relied on many Web sites by talented home bakers the world over. I'll just mention a couple that would be suitable for all levels of bakers. The first is The Fresh Loaf, where home bakers post their questions, recipes, and results. The group has grown over several years, with bakers from Scandinavia to Italy to Australia to the United States posting pictures and sharing tips. But you need to spend some time on the site to find the truly superlative home bakers, whose explanations are often as good as any baking book. The Wild Yeast blog is another great resource by professionally trained home baker Susan Tenney. Her recipes and photographs are excellent, and she offers links to home bakers around the world with her Yeast Spotting feature (usually weekly). I also have recipes and tips on my blog at ChewsWise.com and also feature pictures of my breads on my Twitter feed @fromartz.

Finally, I would be remiss if I did not mention the resources of the Bread Bakers Guild of America, though it is more focused on professionals than home bakers. The recipes by artisan bakers featured in the monthly newsletter are worth the price of membership and the Bread Bakers Guild e-mail list is a highly valuable source of information and tips. Plus, if you take BBGA classes, you can rub shoulders with professionals and learn as I did.

Index

Index

Index

Index

Index

Index

Index

Index

Printed in the United States
by Baker & Taylor Publisher Services